Betrayal, Trust, and Forgiveness

A Guide to Emotional Healing and Self-Renewal

REVISED

BETH HEDVA, PH.D.

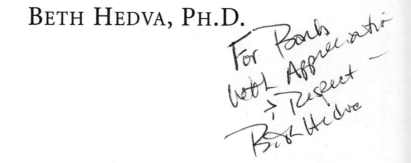

*For Barb
With Appreciation
& Respect —
Beth Hedva*

CELESTIALARTS
Berkeley • Toronto

CELESTIALARTS
P.O. Box 7123
Berkeley, California 94707
www.tenspeed.com

Distributed in Australia by Simon & Schuster Australia, in Canada by Ten Speed Press Canada, in New Zealand by Southern Publishers Group, in South Africa by Real Books, in Southeast Asia by Berkeley Books, and in the United Kingdom and Europe by Airlift Book Company.

Cover design: Catherine Jacobes
Book design: Larissa Pickens

"Children Learn What They Live" copyright © 1972, 1975, 1992 by Dorothy Law Nolte. Reprinted with kind permission of the author.

"The Vocabulary of Feelings" from *Improving Therapeutic Communication: A Guide for Developing Effective Techniques* by D. Corydon Hammond, Dean H. Hepworth, and Veon G. Smith, copyright © 1977 by Jossey-Bass Inc., Publishers. Reprinted with kind permission of the publisher.

Originally published as *Journey from Betrayal to Trust: A Universal Rite of Passage* (Celestial Arts, 1992, ISBN 0-89087-660-6).

Library of Congress Cataloging-in-Publication Data
Hedva, Beth.
    Betrayal, trust, and forgiveness : a guide to emotional healing and self-renewal / Beth Hedva.
        p. cm.
    Rev. ed. of: Journey from betrayal to trust. 1992.
    Includes bibliographical references and index.
    ISBN 1-58761-096-5
    1. Trust—Problems, exercises, etc. 2. Betrayal—Psychological aspects.   I. Hedva, Beth. Journey from betrayal to trust. II. Title.
    BF575.T7 H43 2001
    158.2—dc21
                                    2001002678

Printed in the U.S.A.
First printing, 2001

1 2 3 4 5 6 7 8 9 10—05 04 03 02 01

Acknowledgments

Heartfelt appreciation to my favorite betrayer, Matthew Jon Prest.

I would also like to thank the sixty or so people who have given me their written permission to share with you their betrayal-to-trust stories.

Many thanks go to my agent, Peter Beren. And to David Hinds, Victoria Randall, Brie Mazurek, Tom Southern, and all others at Celestial Arts and Ten Speed Press.

Special thanks to Carolyn Cavalier Rosenberg for our regular walks and talks. To Harold Finkleman for expanding upon my dreams. Much appreciation to Ana Doris Guillen and Penel Thronson, and many thanks to my old and new community of friends in the San Francisco Bay Area and in Calgary, Alberta, Canada—colleagues, teachers, and guides on my own journey from betrayal to trust and forgiveness.

Credit goes to Susan Kelly for artwork.

Much gratitude to Zan Evans Prest for the use of her extensive library and also to my writer friends and colleagues, Harold Finkleman, Alexis Masters, Nesta Rovina, Dr. Victoria Felton-Collins, Sharon Rose Lehrer, Krishna Singh Khalsa, Demetra George, and Dr. Barry Martin. Special thanks to Barry for feedback and technical advice on Chapter 8. Thank you for your encouragement, critical feedback, and support. Thank you, also, Katherine Kittides and Shea Garridan.

I would also like to acknowledge my parents, Harold Chaim Milinsky and Tova Snyder Milinsky, and our ancestors. And I extend special recognition to my grandfather, Wolf Snyder, and his ancestral tribe, the Levi. To the keepers of the Temple in ancient days, I offer this work upon the altar of my heart in the inner temple of the soul. Thank you.

In the soil of shattered dreams
inessentials decompose
soul seed sprouts . . .
life

—Beth Hedva

To the Mystery that Heals and Renews.

Contents

Foreword

Betrayal is strong medicine, a real catalyst, the ultimate homeopathy. Things get worse before they get better. It's a medicine for our time. We're in the time of Kali Yuga, the last phase of the cycle, the time before darkness turns to light again. It's a paradoxical time, when suffering accelerates personal development. We have to pay attention. We have to stop when it hurts. We have to turn inward when bitter medicine catalyzes change. We've all been there, sitting up late with ourselves and wishing it was time for breakfast. Forget development. When betrayal hits, it does not read as an opportunity for change.

The last few years have brought us an infusion of psychological and Spiritual technology. Not a moment too soon. The number of choices that we face in an ordinary day would have driven us crazy twenty years ago. All those options and their consequences. All those desires and disappointments. All those opportunities for betrayal. Emotional life has never been as rugged. If change can be catalyzed by emotion, the rate of change should be astronomical.

Betrayal, Trust, and Forgiveness focuses the work of psychology and sacred tradition on a charged emotional issue. For once, intuition is properly placed as a useful source of help, rather than being categorized as a tool for psychic prediction. Intuition is the way of telling the difference between projections fueled by pain, and the genuine insights that direct a new course of action.

This is a good book for the hours before daylight, when the medicine is working, and we know we have to change. We sound ourselves out and think things through, and try to make sense of all that has happened. In retrospect, such moments serve us well. We look backward in time with the marvelous clarity of hindsight, and remember them as peak moments of life, when we dipped deeply into ourselves. With the marvelous clarity of hindsight vision, we remember our greatest moments as the times in which we changed.

Helen Palmer
Author of *The Enneagram* and Director of the Center for the
Investigation and Training of Intuition

Preface

My interest in betrayal sprang from my own inner work with my shadow—my unconscious feelings—and started by examining my harsh judgments and criticisms of other people. As I began to explore the intensity of my feelings, I suddenly realized, "Oh my God! At the core of all this righteousness, underneath it all, I feel betrayed!"

As always happens when we start working on ourselves, the inner process is reflected in the outer world. Over the next five years I noticed that my clients' stories were betrayal stories, as were the stories of my friends and colleagues. Even features on the nightly news were tragic reports of deceit, treachery, and trauma. Everywhere, the pain of unresolved betrayal wounds called out to be recognized. I observed how we struggle with infidelities, childhood neglect, sexual abuse, emotional abuse, and physical battering by our mothers, fathers, and lovers. Accompanying unexpected job layoffs, stock-market crashes, wars, earthquakes, fires, and floods, I heard the same painful plea, "Why is this happening to me?" These devastating events evoke righteous resentment, suspicion, fear—all symptoms of our feelings of betrayal.

I wanted to find out more about this experience of betrayal. After researching whatever I could find in psychology, I began to investigate not only personal betrayal stories, but stories from literature, including cross-cultural myths, fairy tales, and legends. I began to see that betrayal was, indeed, a universal theme. There were many sacred myths concerning betrayal, like the Indian tale of Arjuna, whose betrayal of his family led to the fulfillment of his spiritual path; or the myth of Psyche, whose betrayal of her promise to Eros sent her on a journey through the underworld, after which she emerged, eventually to be deified and joined with Eros throughout eternity. Even the story of Jesus, who was betrayed by Judas, tells us that crucifixion and death are stepping-stones to resurrection.

Betrayal by our intimates initiates experiences of separation, alienation, and emotional distance. However, as in cross-cultural rites of passage, betrayal can also be a time of sacred separation that leads to resurrection or rebirth. By applying the principles of the ancient mystery schools of initiatory rites of passage, this book reframes the experience of betrayal as a spiritual event in one's life. Ancient mystery schools teach initiates how to recognize and pass through the five phases of initiation: *separation, purification, symbolic death, new knowledge,* and *rebirth.*

The experience of *separation* is a spiritual crisis that is symbolic of our perceived separation from God/Goddess—the universal, creative Source that is our true spiritual center. *Purification* evokes fear of loss, so one may become aware of false attachments, old patterns, or identities that have outlived their purpose. Initiates are trained to pass through a *symbolic death* of the ego, triggered by the experience of loss, which gives us *new knowledge* of our true identity, our creative Self. This new knowledge serves as a catalyst for more spiritual growth, which leads to a *rebirth* and a new sense of self. I use a capital "S" in "Self" to distinguish the universal creative Self within consciousness from our socially conditioned ego-self (lowercase "s") that comprises our ordinary sense of identity.

Purification, which traditionally includes ritual ordeals and tests of strength, courage, and mastery, is part of every initiatory rite of passage. This initiation from betrayal to trust has five distinct and treacherous emotional ordeals:

1. Righteous resentment, which leads to obsession about the betrayer. This fuels the desire for vengeance or vindication.
2. Bitter resignation springing from denial of the positive and seeing only the negative in one's betrayer. This leads to projection of the shadow— that is, the dark, unconscious side of one's own self.
3. Attribution of the betrayer's negative traits to all others deemed like one's betrayer. This generalization fuels cynicism, prejudice, and bigotry.
4. Betrayal of one's ideals, essential values, or vital dreams. Denial of one's essential Self, as expressed through denial of one's personal values and visions, leads to self-betrayal.
5. Denial of one's existential right to be, one's right to live one's dreams. This leads to fear, control, and manipulation—creating rules to protect against future betrayals.

You will find practical tools to help you master these five emotional ordeals of the traditional betrayal response. You will learn how to use inner resources to free yourself from your obsession about your betrayer. You can be free from bitter resignation and resentment, free from the baffling attraction to people who betray or wound you and perpetuate the painful betrayal pattern. And you can be free from the self-punishing guilt, remorse, and self-reproach that underlie self-betrayal. This book will give you step-by-step instruction on how to turn inward rather than simply act out, to transform the five emotional ordeals of purification—resentment, denial of the positive, cynicism, self-betrayal, and paranoia—into five spiritual teachings:

1. To find and express your truth and develop good communication skills.
2. To develop compassion for yourself and your betrayer through releasing righteousness by recognizing both positive and negative traits within yourself.
3. To use intuition to understand the highest good and special teaching or soul purpose that is hidden in your betrayal experience.
4. To commit to the fulfillment of your soul's dream by taking a stand in life.
5. To be free to be who you are and fulfill your vital dream, and to allow others the same freedom through learning to trust the process.

Each chapter is designed to help you heal yourself, rebuild self-trust, and free yourself from the pain of the past so you may embrace the future, ready to take risks, and to truly trust yourself. Exercises and personal practices accompany each chapter to help you develop your intuitive skills and spiritual resources. This, along with examples of people who have suffered the pain of betrayal and found their way to Self-trust, will train you to use natural expanded states of consciousness to communicate directly with your higher Self. You will learn to use your intuition to remember who you really are: a spiritual being having a deeply personal, human experience.

You will discover how, ultimately, betrayals are *for-giving* you an opportunity to come to know yourself much better . . . and having discovered your "True Self" you *give-forth* your greater Self to the world. You will also learn how to respond to others as you continue to grow. In the fulfillment of your vital dream, in which you live by and follow your inner truths, you may be accused of being a betrayer—and, at times, you *will* be a betrayer. You will betray "the old way" and others' expectations of you. As you gain confidence in your Self, you will forgive yourself and others for being in different phases of the journey from betrayal to trust and forgiveness. This book will teach you to accept your new role in your community and it will encourage you to act in new ways—Self-inspired ways. Finally, you will learn how to apply personal betrayal-to-trust learnings to collective concerns, to act as an agent for the spiritual evolution of social consciousness and global healing.

Beth Hedva, Ph.D.
Calgary, Alberta, Canada
January 1, 2001

Chapter 1

Journey from Betrayal to Trust

A Universal Rite of Passage

Karen and Joe bought a house after living together for five years. Some time during the first six months after their move into the new home, Karen got the feeling that Joe was seeing another woman. Joe denied it. Yet Karen just couldn't shake the nagging feeling that there was someone else in the picture. Karen even felt she knew who it was. After about a year of what Joe called "continuous interrogations," they went into therapy together. Karen's "unfounded" jealousy and insecurity became the topic of discussion during their six months of therapy. In time, the interrogations stopped and the therapy ended. One evening, about a year later, when Karen and Joe were sharing a quiet intimate evening together, Joe said to Karen, "You know how you used to think I was having an affair with Shelly? Well, you were right! I was."

Betrayal is shattering. Yet deception, broken promises, unkept agreements, disappointments, and unfulfilled expectations in every arena of life are fertile ground for personal growth and an increased capacity for trust. This trust is not trust in your betrayer or anyone outside yourself. This is a profound sense of trust in your Self, your inner Source of wisdom, healing, and love—a higher power within the psyche that brings each of us to and through every experience in life, including betrayal.

Because betrayal is archetypal, that is, universal in nature, one taps into a collective force that has tremendous power. It feels bigger than you, and seems to have a life of its own. This greater power has enough potential energy to transform you completely, if you know how to work with it. With archetypes, one's personal stories are actually reflections of profound universal forces. As we experience our personal stories in terms of universal spiritual teachings, we connect more consciously with the greater transformative power within our experience. Let me give you an example by telling you one of my favorite betrayal-to-trust stories. This is the story about the Frog Prince; but, unlike the popular Disney-like version, it is not a magical kiss that transforms the frog.

In the older, Grimm Brothers'[1] version, the story opens with the king's youngest and most beautiful daughter weeping and wailing, lamenting the loss of her golden ball that has tumbled down into the depths of a well so deep that its bottom cannot even be seen. A frog, who happens to be by the well, offers to retrieve the ball if, and only if, the princess will agree to take the frog as her companion, to love him, to play with him, to let him eat with her at her royal table, and to sleep with him in her royal bed.

"Anything!" the princess cries. "Anything you wish!" But once the princess gets her golden ball back, she realizes what a mistake she has made. Without even a word of thanks, she leaves the frog in the forest by the well. "After all," she thinks to herself as she turns on her heels and heads toward the palace, "a frog is no companion for a princess." It takes the frog till the next day to hop to the palace and gain admittance. The princess then tells her father, the king, the story about the golden ball, the well, and the promise. And the king declares, "That which is promised must be performed! Now you must share your plate with this frog and take him into your bedchambers with you just as you promised."

When alone with the frog in her royal bedchamber, the princess shudders and shrieks at the thought of sleeping with that horrible frog in her nice, clean bed, let alone kissing those cold, wet, slimy, green frog lips. When the frog threatens to call the king in to make the princess keep her promise, she is beside herself with rage. She picks up the frog and hurls him against the wall! As he falls to the floor, all at once the frog turns into a naked knight, a noble prince with beautiful, kind eyes. Once he is returned to his original human form, the prince explains to the princess that he was turned into a cold-blooded frog by an evil witch, and only the princess could break the spell. At long last, the spell is broken and they can go to his father's kingdom together.

The Frog Prince story continues beyond the transfiguration of a frog to a prince. The Grimm Brothers' story ends with the prince's servant, faithful Henry, arriving at the palace with a magnificent carriage drawn by eight majestic white horses. Henry has come to transport the bride and groom home. As they are traveling the prince hears a strange creaking noise, and, concerned that one of the wheels of the carriage is breaking, draws the sound to the attention of his faithful servant. However, Henry replies,

> The wheel does not break,
> 'Tis the band around my heart
> That, to lessen its ache,
> When I grieved for your sake,
> I bound round my heart.[2]

With the prince restored, betrothed, and returning to his father's kingdom, faithful Henry's heart is so full of joy that it breaks all the bands clean away.

Fairy tales are like dreams. They are filled with archetypal symbols. Every symbol reveals a key to some part of the psyche. The seemingly absurd and grotesque image of a frog being smashed against the wall represents the secret power of betrayal to transform consciousness, from frog consciousness to nobility. Notice how one's noble true Self, the prince, has beautiful, kind eyes. How is it that betrayal can generate beauty and kindness? This is indeed a mystery. The princess's betrayal of her promise to the frog and her rebellion against her father's command are somehow part of the magic that releases the power of the wicked witch's spell over the Frog Prince. The stakes are great for both the princess and the frog. The princess could suffer her father's condemnation, ever to remain a little girl; the frog may never come to know his true form as a man; and, unbeknownst to the prince, his faithful servant's heart may never be free.

Each one of us has a frog, a princess, and a faithful Henry within us (though we may tend to play one of these roles more frequently). In fairy tales, wicked witches and evil queens are symbolic of betrayal wounds inflicted by the mother, just as kings, sorcerers, and wizards represent the father. Many of us are under the spell of a wicked witch or cruel king and feel overpowered by a giant or ghost from our past. This was certainly true of Karen and Joe. When I saw them for an appointment, Karen said she grew up with an authoritarian, alcoholic father. Joe's authoritative denial of his affair with Shelly the year before and then during their six months of therapy opened an old wound. Like the frog, who retrieved the princess's golden ball from the depths of the well, Joe's betrayal of Karen sent her to her emotional depths. And, at the age of forty-seven, she emerged from the betrayal experience with the golden awareness that she can trust the authority of her intuition instead of giving her power away to the kings in her life—her former therapist and Joe, in this case.

Joe was also caught up in a curse from the past. He described himself as the oldest and only boy in his family of immigrant refugees from World War II. As a child he was obliged to take care of his perfectionistic, demanding mother and younger siblings, while his father worked long hours to support the family. Joe, who turned fifty when their house was in escrow, said he felt overloaded with responsibilities and financial obligations after he and Karen bought the house together. Our discussion revealed that his affair with Shelly somehow made him feel carefree, like the prince before he was turned into a frog by the witch.

Today's spells and curses are cast in a variety of ways. Suffering through physical and verbal abuse or neglect, sexual or emotional incest, or any of the wide range of dysfunctional family patterns associated with alcoholism and drug abuse all evoke the experience of parental betrayal within a child's psyche. Uncontrollable events like a war or national disaster, a death in the family, divorce, illness, accidents, sudden changes in residence, and even seemingly innocuous events can also fuel the betrayal fires within one's experience.

Yet adult reactions to childhood wounds and re-wounding by our intimates are only half the story. Faithful Henry's role in the Frog Prince's transformation reminds us also that there is a faithful companion who follows us through life, though we are unaware of him. As we unify with our true Self, this faithful companion becomes known to us and helps us "return to the father's kingdom"—symbolizing the spiritual nature of this psychological journey from betrayal to trust. The rewards of psychospiritual transformation are well worth the price. Faithful Henry's example shows us that our hearts can be truly free.

Betrayal is a sacred event that has the power to transport us into a deeper spiritual truth that brings joy to the heart.

Like the prince who was turned into a frog and forced to leave his father's kingdom, or the princess who is alone at the well, lamenting the loss of her golden ball, betrayal is attended by feelings of isolation, alienation, rejection, and loneliness. Some of the tests and trials in the Frog Prince story echo the challenges of betrayal that Joe and Karen felt as well: the princess was required to live with a frog—eat with it, sleep with it, keep it as a companion. And the prince who lost his human form through no fault of his own, suffers rejection at the well and is flung against the wall for being a frog. However, as a result of knowing each other, both princess and frog change radically—into a bride in her full authority and a beautiful, naked knight. Joe and Karen were also transformed as they learned more about themselves and each other. Understanding and integrating the mystery of betrayal is an essential part of the story.

Fairy tales like the Frog Prince story follow an archetypal pattern of growth and change found in ancient and indigenous cross-cultural rites of initiation. Initiatory rites of passage may show us how to find our way through the pain, separation, alienation, and shock of betrayal—to feel fully alive again. We start by looking at the experience of betrayal as a sacred event in our lives that has the power to initiate a personal spiritual awakening. Like initiates through the ages, we can train ourselves to recognize and respond to five distinct stages of initiation:

1. Separation
2. Purification
3. Symbolic Death
4. New Knowledge
5. Rebirth

Betrayal always initiates experiences of separation, isolation, or rejection. Alone at the well, the princess meets her initiator and is transformed from the innocent, beautiful, youngest daughter of the king into a woman of royalty with the authority to make her own decisions. At first, the princess mourns the loss of her golden ball that has fallen into a well so deep that she cannot see the bottom. This well symbolizes the core of her being, while the golden ball represents her brilliance—that is, Self-awareness. Before she gets her ball back, the princess is still the innocent, beautiful youngest daughter. In her naiveté, she willingly promises to give the frog anything in return for retrieving her ball. After the ball surfaces from the depths of the sacred well, the princess is changed. She becomes Self-aware. She can now stand up to her father, the king, and take a prince for a companion instead of a frog.

Once our consciousness reaches these depths, we are transformed. When our golden ball of consciousness is returned to us—even if it is returned by a frog—we are irrevocably altered. The emotional ordeals of the betrayal-to-trust initiation reveal your true Self. Within your heart, at the very core of your being, is a truth you can trust. It was the princess's *coeurage* (*coeur* is French for "heart") that allowed her to defy her father and take on the role of divine initiator in her relationship to the Frog Prince. The violent shock of rejection delivered by the princess to the frog when she threw him against the wall was the initiatory ordeal that provoked the frog's transformation into a prince.

Some of us get smashed against walls, and some of us touch what feel like bottomless depths. These are examples of the emotional ordeals that attend the rites of purification. Betrayer and betrayed serve a deeper mystery that purifies them both, just as the frog and the princess were intrinsic to each other's transformation of consciousness.

Through the relationship between the initiator and initiated, the betrayer and betrayed, consciousness is purified, transfigured, and altered. This profound change in consciousness is represented by the death phase of initiation. Though the death is symbolic, its impact on consciousness is irrevocable and complete. The frog did not die when he hit the wall. Yet the impact of hitting the wall destroyed the frog form and revealed a prince with beautiful, kind eyes.

The delivery of a spiritual teaching that brings meaning to the test or ordeal characterizes the new-knowledge phase of initiation. The appearance of faithful Henry at the end of the tale indicates the presence of someone who can help the princess and prince integrate the spiritual teaching. In traditional societies, the elders help the initiate understand the meaning or purpose of the initiatory ordeals, and they explain the value and use of one's newly found gifts. For example, menstruating girls are initiated into the blood mysteries and are taught the meaning of the life cycle by the older women in the clan. In advanced initiation rites, knowledge is primarily received intuitively from inner sources.

Faithful Henry, whose heart breaks free of its restricting bands, depicts the secret teaching that brings new knowledge, and illuminates the mystery of the betrayal-to-trust initiation. Heart knowledge is intuitive knowledge. The mystery that allows you to break through the defenses of your past requires that you recognize that those old ways of being, which you developed to cope with your earlier betrayal wounds, are like the constricting bands that kept Henry's heart from breaking. Our defenses keep our hearts from breaking, but they restrict us and prevent our growth and expansion into the joy of Self-deliverance. Henry reminds us that we will be delivered, that we will return to the father's kingdom. In this journey, the truth within our heart guides the way home to our Source.

Frequently, the death-rebirth cycle of initiation demands that the initiate demonstrate his or her newly found gifts and knowledge, or die. After she regains her golden ball and returns to the palace, the princess demonstrates her own authority when she challenges her father. She is no longer a child who must be told what to do. She takes a stand contrary to her father's expectations, showing that death-rebirth transitions teach the initiate to release any past prohibitions or personal inhibitions that might block one from accessing and implementing one's new talents.

Rebirth, the final phase of initiation, defines the process of return. Rebirth brings the individual back to life and back to one's community to fulfill a new role within that community. In puberty rites, girls become women, and boys become men. In the Frog Prince story, the prince returns to his father's kingdom, not as a prince or as a frog, but as a groom betrothed to a mature, self-confident woman. In traditional societies, not only does the individual gain personal fulfillment from their new, adult roles, but the whole community benefits from the added contributions of the individual. His or her life becomes a demonstration of the spiritual teaching received during initiation, and the community is strengthened by the individual's new level of involvement in communal life.

Separation: Answering the Call to Initiation

When we are betrayed, we feel devastated and bewildered, isolated and alienated from the one we love. Betrayal is always a shock. The grief and pain associated with betrayal amplifies existential emptiness, loneliness, meaninglessness, and futility. For the uninitiated, this soul death is the end of the journey. But the shock can also be the beginning of something new, a glimpse into a greater truth. For Karen, the shock of truth cleared away two and a half years of confusion and self-condemnation.

Sometimes the separation phase of initiation is marked by the initiate's rejection of the precepts of the status quo. One chooses to separate; like novitiates who isolate themselves in a monastery and take the vows of priest or nun, one enters a voluntary isolation from the community. Other cultures impose isolation, as in Australian aborigines' puberty rites for boys, in which the boys are removed from their homes and taken away from their mothers, sisters, and younger friends by the men of the tribe. After this dramatic event, the boys are taken to sacred ground far away from their childhood surroundings, where they are held in seclusion. This element is also reflected in the Frog Prince story. The prince was unwillingly separated from his father's kingdom when a wicked witch turned him into a frog. Separated from the comforts of the home, the prince and princess meet at the well, a symbol of sacred ground in European pagan cultures. Whether by circumstance or choice, separation is a sacred event imbued with supernatural powers.

After you suffer the shock of betrayal, choose to consciously separate yourself from your ordinary, patterned routines. Create sacred space in your life to help you examine the mystery of your betrayal experience. You are being invited to leave your ordinary life behind, and to embark upon an extraordinary personal journey of Self-transformation.

Purification: Facing the Emotional Ordeals of Betrayal

The purification phase of initiation brings negative thoughts, dysfunctional habit patterns, and toxic feelings to the surface, so they may be recognized and released. In traditional societies, rites of purification include ritual ordeals, tests, and trials that are designed to shock the initiate out of a state of complacency and move into a sacred and expanded state of consciousness. Like the shock of bull-roarers, masked demons, and separation from everything familiar and known experienced by the aborigine boys, exposure to startling and incomprehensible events begins the purification phase of initiation. You know you are in this stage if you feel like you are overwhelmed by and unprepared for the events that have occurred. You most likely feel like you are beset by emotional ordeals that test your composure and try your patience.

Ultimately, purification tests you to find your way through these ordeals by confronting and releasing old roles, false identities, attachments, and fears. During purification we may glimpse our true Self—our wisdom, courage, strength, or talent—that has been overshadowed by social conventions, fear, and other barriers. We then can confront who and what has prevented us from being true to ourselves.

While researching the topic of betrayal, I found it interesting that the words *betrayal, traitor,* and *tradition* all come from the same Latin root word *tradere.* The literal translation of *tradere* is "to hand over," "to deliver," or "to place in the hands of."[3] When we hand ourselves over to the anger, pain, and grief of betrayal, we are placed in the hands of a traditional response. We become traitors to the light within. We die a thousand deaths when we rationalize essential spiritual questions with the limited data provided by our social traditions, personal history, and cultural upbringing. Unenlightened actions or purely emotional reactions perpetuate the pain. To act from our feelings of betrayal kills relationships, trust, and faith, and destroys a deeper sense of meaning or purpose in life.

The question "Why is this happening to me?" or the more personalized version, "How could you do this to me?" fuels the existential dilemma. Though the rational mind first explains the injustice by blaming the betrayer, the irrational mind soon blames the self. "There must be something wrong with me that I am rejected by this one I trusted and loved." These feelings escalate when we look for reasons or causes to explain and justify the rejection we've suffered. This kicks off a series of deadly emotional reactions. In his book *Loose Ends,* James Hillman has identified five treacherous emotional reactions associated with betrayal.[4] I call these the five Emotional Ordeals, tests and trials of the betrayal-to-trust initiation of the soul.

9

Emotional Ordeal #1: Resentment

Righteous resentment. Obsession with the betrayer. Desire for revenge.

First, we wish to hurt our betrayer. We want them to hurt at least as much as we hurt. Righteous resentment and the obsessive desire for revenge define this emotional ordeal. Instead of confronting our betrayer, Hillman says we tend to let the wound fester, and we fume about the injustice of it. The test comes when we face our desire to hurt another and choose a different course of action.

Watch for thoughts like "How could he (or she) do this to me?" "It's just not fair," or "I don't deserve to be treated like this!" These types of thoughts fuel the desire for vengeance or vindication. As hard as it is to shift your attention away from your betrayer, this is the time to focus on *you,* your values, your needs, your truth. Instead of spending time and energy obsessing about your betrayer, devote that time and energy to yourself and your growth process.

Emotional Ordeal #2: Denial

Denial of the positive and seeing only negative traits in the betrayer. Bitterness, resignation, and projection of the shadow.

If we fail the first emotional test and give in to obsessing about the hurt and injustice, the next emotional ordeal increases in intensity. We now begin to see only negative qualities. Where once our betrayer was the apple of our eye, our idealized hero or heroine turns into a vicious villain. Our former loved one acts in ways we would supposedly never act. We deny that there is any good in them that might redeem them in our eyes.

This rejection of one's betrayer frequently reflects disowned or rejected aspects of oneself. The element within one's personality that is unconscious, socially unacceptable, or deemed to be inappropriate is called the *shadow. Watch for thoughts like "I always knew she (or he) was self-centered and inconsiderate."* This type of thinking may be a projection of your shadow. It is always easier to see someone else's blind spots, while our own remain unconscious, hidden from view in the shadow. Projecting our shadow onto our betrayer, we bitterly resign ourselves to the belief that he or she deserves our punishment. The test is to release the rationalizing and punishing mind, which splits life into good or bad. The soul is challenged to perceive both good and bad, darkness and light, vulnerabilities and strengths in oneself and in one's betrayer. Recognizing your own unconscious motives by coming to terms with your shadow builds compassion for yourself and others.

Emotional Ordeal #3: Cynicism

Cynical generalization. Projection of negative traits onto all others like the betrayer.

Generalizing, or attributing characteristics of the shadow to all others deemed by us to be like our betrayer, leads to the third emotional ordeal, cynicism. Cynicism distorts perception and corrupts our values. *Watch for thoughts like "That's just like a man" or "You know how women are."* Projecting your betrayer's negative traits onto groups leads to stereotyping and prejudice.

Healing stereotyped thinking, which is necessary to passing this emotional ordeal, has the added benefit of healing society. Healing personal betrayal wounds that have progressed into cynicism requires that we confront our generalizations, including those that take the form of sexism, racism, prejudice, and bigotry. The soul is challenged to look within and intuitively recognize one's relationship to the collective. The test is to stop generalizing. Instead, seek to understand your unique gifts and contributions—that is, what you offer to others. Ultimately, you should realize that every individual and group is part of the whole and as such, each has a part to play in the spiritual evolution of humanity.

Emotional Ordeal #4: Self-Betrayal

Self-betrayal. Self-rejection. Abandonment of personal ideals, principles, and dreams.

Cynicism injures one's faith in oneself. The real pain of cynicism comes not so much from the projection of the shadow as from the erosion of Self-trust. We ask ourselves, "How could I have been so blind, so stupid?" By the fourth ordeal, we too are included in the equation of untrustworthy people. Because we can not trust ourselves, we betray our most cherished dreams and desires. Notice if you have given into the abandonment of your ideals, essential values, or vital dreams. *Watch for thoughts like "I'll never love again," "Love hurts too much," or "I just don't have what it takes."* Self-betrayal is the denial of your essential Self as it is expressed through your personal values, gifts, and resources. Spiraling into the abyss of self-betrayal, you feel cut off from yourself, out of touch with who you are, and what matters most to you. You stop listening to yourself and acting on your own behalf.

Self-betrayal, and the pain of loneliness that it brings, is at the core of most betrayal experiences. This fourth test must be faced alone. Existentially, we are alone, and there is something positively unique about each one of us that also separates us from each other. Discovery of your unique gifts, talents, and resources inspires a sense of purpose in life. Spiritual purpose is the soul challenge of this test.

Emotional Ordeal #5: Paranoia

Suspicion of future betrayals. Fear, control, and manipulation. Contracts and agreements.

If one does not find a way beyond self-betrayal, one collapses into the fifth emotional ordeal. The world is perceived as a hostile place in which one is left to fend for oneself. Like when the Frog Prince made the princess agree to take him as a companion before he was willing to retrieve her golden ball from the well, when the betrayed person gets caught in this fifth emotional ordeal, he or she resorts to control and manipulation. Both conscious and unconscious rules and regulations guide one's interactions with others. Always afraid of being hurt again, one tries to extract contracts and agreements from others before engaging with them, in an attempt to protect against future betrayals. This is as far from trust as one can possibly get.

Notice if you are living by self-imposed rules, or if you find that you are afraid to take risks. *Watch for thoughts like "I'll go out with him (or her)—but if he (or she) shows up late or doesn't treat me right even once, that's it, it's over."* As we learn to distinguish our fears from the sounds of our true inner voice, we are tested to discover the deeper truth—that we are each free, spiritually, free to be ourselves.

Many of us take this traditional route through resentment, denial of the positive, cynicism, and self-betrayal to descend into a paranoid world of fear, control, and manipulation. We are plunged into the despairing darkness of this initiation. We never pass through the ordeals. In our righteousness, we assume the role of the Angel of Death, God's chosen one, who avenges injustice. We fool ourselves into believing that we are the initiator chosen to teach our betrayers "the lessons they deserve." The five ordeals of betrayal become traps—emotional snares that impede our growth and block our experience of wholeness.

Symbolic Death: Dealing with Fear and Loss

Symbolic death follows purification. This stage of initiation is designed to help the initiate let go of false identities and old ways of being that are no longer appropriate or no longer serve the soul's greatest good. One must confront and release any personal inhibitions or status quo prohibitions that impede our progress. It is instructive to recognize that our righteous resentment and desire for revenge, our denial of the positive in our betrayer, our cynical rationalizations and generalizations about others, and our depressing self-betrayal resemble the stages of mourning defined by Dr. Elisabeth Kübler-Ross in her landmark book *On Death and Dying.*[5] No matter how much terminally ill individuals deny that they are dying, get angry that they are dying, rationalize or bargain with God to live, grieve, cry, or otherwise carry on, death is an imminent reality for them. The power of death is greater than the power of their defenses. Acceptance of this greater force is the fifth and final stage of the death and dying process that Kübler-Ross describes.

Death of a dream is just as poignant as death of the body. Both lead to a profound sense of loss. Each of Kübler-Ross's stages of mourning—denial, anger, rationalization, depression, and acceptance—are akin to the instinctive reactions one might see in animals when their survival is threatened. Movement psychologist and sixth-degree black belt martial artist Stuart Heller, Ph.D., says that we are biologically wired to respond to change with an adrenal stress response—an instinctive fear reaction. In the animal world are four natural fear reactions—*faint, fight, flight,* and *freeze.* Like the possum who *faints* and looks dead to a predator, humans go unconscious by denying, forgetting, or feeling confused. Heller suggests that passive-aggressive denial quickly progresses to displays of anger, as is evident when someone becomes enraged when their denial mechanisms are challenged. This anger or attack response is akin to the aggressive *fight* reaction of a wolverine. Like a flock of birds who take to the sky to dodge a predator, *flight,* as filtered through human consciousness, expresses itself as avoidance of the loss through rationalization, as when our mind runs away with an idea to avoid reality. The deer in the headlights who stands still when threatened has a *freeze* reaction, and in humans this shows up as sadness, crying, and depression, as when one feels stuck, heavy, or immobilized by emotions. Heller suggests that in martial arts, the spiritual warrior chooses to act instead of react from anger, fear, or grief. The spiritual warrior is trained to confront reality as it is, and accept death of the ego as a part of the spiritual journey of life. We can learn to recognize these reactions in ourselves and so begin to master our fear of loss.

The natural fear reactions that Heller describes translate into the defense mechanisms and processes Kübler-Ross's outlines in her five stages of mourning. We can learn to recognize these reactions in ourselves and so begin to master our fear of loss.

1. **Denial:** This defense takes the form of minimizing the effect of the betrayal, avoidance of the impact, or withdrawal from one's betrayer. *Watch for thoughts like "It happened twenty years ago, it doesn't matter now." "It's my imagination. I'm making this up. I'm confused."*

2. **Anger:** This defense takes many forms, including resentment, impatience, frustration, blaming and shaming, and resignation. *Watch for thoughts like "How could you . . . ," "You always . . . ," or "You never . . ."*

3. **Rationalization:** This defense takes the form of righteous intellectualization, explanation, and justification of your emotional reactions. *Watch for thoughts like "It's not what you did, it's how you did it," "You could have . . . ," "You should have . . . ," "If only I'd . . . ," or "I should have. . . ."*

4. **Depression:** This defense hits when the above three defenses fail to make you feel better. Feelings of grief, sadness, and deep loss are strong. *Watch for thoughts like "I'm so tired of this . . ." or "When will this end?"*

5. **Acceptance:** Acceptance emerges as you confront life exactly as it is without adding anything to it or taking anything away from it. No matter what you say, think, or do, the betrayal happened just the way it did. At last there is no need to struggle anymore. Feelings of relief, release, peace, and resolution prevail. *Watch for thoughts like "I feel grateful that . . . ," "What a gift that . . . ," or "I'm so relieved that. . . ."*

Initiates of early mystery schools in both the East and the West were taught to master their fear of death and accompanying emotional reactions. Initiatory mystery schools understood the power of death to transform. They taught disciples that death and the emotional stages of mourning occurred whether the death was physical or symbolic. Betrayal leads to a symbolic death, and through symbolic death, innocence and naiveté die. But trust and innocence are not the same. Prior to betrayal, the innocent experiences no risk. Hillman says that trust cannot be fully realized without betrayal. Only after betrayal, when one knows the risks and trusts anyway, is true trust established. Rather than trust in the betrayer, or trust in the contracts and agreements we make to protect ourselves from future betrayals, the modern initiate learns to trust something deeper, something more essential. Betrayal presents the test: to come to trust in the life process, which prompts the modern initiate to discover the inner Self and that mystery that renews, heals, and transforms one's experience. By making contact with their inner resources; namely, their innate wisdom, power, and courage, initiates were trained to use their intuitive and psychic senses to help them see, hear, or feel their way through the dark shadowlands of death of the ego and loss of self.

Cross-cultural anthropologist Angeles Arrien reminds us of an ancient teaching that is true today. There is only one fear, and that is the fear of a loss of self. In the greater mysteries, this loss of ego-self is a spiritual crisis that is symbolic of our experience of separation from God/Goddess, our infinite creative Source—a fear of loss of Self. Arrien says that fear of loss expresses itself cross-culturally through two seemingly opposite forms in our interpersonal relationships—fear of rejection or abandonment, and fear of engulfment or enmeshment. In either case, one can temporarily lose one's sense of self to the fear of loss.

In your initiation, you too, move toward the acceptance of a remarkable mystery. The spiritual Self is never lost—yet it must be found. The purpose of symbolic death is to help you accept that there is an inner Source, a higher power within the psyche that brings you to and through every experience in life, including your experience of betrayal. This infinite, omniscient intelligence already knows what you need in order to heal. This is the one who will help you move beyond and through the grief of loss associated with each experience of betrayal. Using intuition, we pass beyond the death phase of initiation and start to receive new knowledge. This is the truth that sets us free—free to live fully instead of continually dying.

New Knowledge: Learning to TRUST Your Intuition

New knowledge is marked by gaining insight into a spiritual teaching that helps the initiate understand what they have been through and why they had to go through it the way they did. It teaches them that there is meaning or purpose to the initiatory ordeals. Whether we are betrayed on purpose or by accident, each betrayal experience initiates the movement from the loss of a dream, through the five stages of mourning, to giving birth to the truth. Trust is the act of faith that inspires us to live in truth. When we get past the pain of betrayal, we learn to risk in spite of opposition, counterinfluences, or discouragement. In other words, we learn to trust.

Trust grows from listening to a deeper truth within—a message from the soul of one's being. As James Hillman said, "It may well be that betrayal has no other positive outcome but forgiveness, and that the experience of forgiveness is possible only if one has been betrayed. Such forgiveness is a forgiving which is not a forgetting, but the remembrance of wrong transformed within a wider context."[6]

Remember your betrayal experience with the eyes of your soul. Though the uninitiated self, with its conditions, expectations, and demands, is lost, an infinite creative Source emerges within the psyche as the inner guide and teacher. The acronym TRUST can guide today's seeker beyond death's door into the fourth stage of initiation—the reception of new knowledge that gives value and meaning to the initiatory ordeals. This is the wider context that transforms betrayal into forgiveness.

TRUST: The Teaching of New Knowledge

T — **Turn Inward for Truth**
Turn inward to discover your deepest truth.
To thine own Self be true.

R — **Relax, Release, Receive**
Relax your body and mind and release fear,
then receive intuitive guidance.

U — **Use Intuition to Understand**
Use the tools you have, both inner and outer resources
to gain greater awareness.

S — **Speak, Share, Stand Up**
Speak the truth. Share your dreams. Take a stand.

T — **Try Again and TRUST**
Trust the process that continues to
return to your Source within.

We learn to trust not in our betrayers, but in the truth of the Self. This creative, inner Self guides us and protects us. The Self inspires us to make meaning out of life and directs us to align with a deeper purpose in all our relationships, including our relationships with our betrayers.

I find it fascinating that the words *trust* and *truth* come from the same root word. In fact, the words *trust, true, truce, troth,* and *betroth* are all related etymologically to the Old English word *treow.*[7] *Treow* stands for the concepts of fidelity, faith, and loyalty. Fidelity, faith, and loyalty to the Self is the sacred vow of the initiate. Truth is the sacred troth between the higher Self and your ordinary evolving self. As we betroth our truth, the bond of trust grows into an experience of personal integrity. Truth brings a truce to our painful inner battles and emotional struggles and eases our external conflicts with others.

The word *treow* literally means "tree." I like to think of betrayal as the fruit from the Tree of Knowledge of Good and Evil. We've spent centuries digesting our ancestral bite from the apple. Trust is fruit from the Tree of Life. It is time for us to take the next bite. Use the image of a tree in your meditations as a template for developing Self-trust. Imagine that your roots penetrate deep into the dark, rich ground of being, while your branches stretch upward and reach toward the sun, the light of consciousness. The deeper your roots, the more stable your growth. You weather the seasons—scorching hot sun, bitter winds of change, stormy rains, cold winters—with an innate trust in spring, the season when life within you sprouts afresh and new. Observe how you blossom and bloom. Notice how the branches of your knowledge grow full with the fruits of experience. Each fruit is harvested and shared and brings nourishment to yourself and others. Within the fruit of your experience is a seed of truth ready to be planted and harvested in its own cycle and season.

Aristotle says that intuitive reason allows us to know truth without the need for proof, as is required by scientific reason. We can trust our intuition to guide us to truth. As Karen demonstrated earlier, we have the ability to know truth for ourselves, from our inner Source, and when we surrender to the truth, it brings a truce to the mind at war with itself. Each time we turn inward and contact our inner Source, trust builds. We are renewed by being reborn into Self-awareness.

Intuitively, we each know what we need in order to grow, heal, and flourish. The Source within the psyche, which intuitively knows what we need and completely accepts the truth of those needs, is a reflection of the omniscience and unconditional love associated with the archetype of Divine Mother. We are nurtured by contact with the Mother of our soul. Like an infant suckling at the mother's breast, we draw our nourishment from the Source of truth within. Intuition also provides protective guidance from the Source of healing within the psyche. Protective guidance and direction are expressions of an omnipotent force in consciousness, the archetype of the Divine Father. Inner direction empowers us and prompts us to act on our truth in order to get our needs fulfilled. Direction and guidance come in the form of inner hunches as well as outer synchronicities. In time, we remember the sacred troth—we are not alone. We have inner resources, archetypal divine parents, to support us and guide us to outer resources that fulfill our needs.

Like Joe and Karen, many of my clients suffered from childhood wounds and earlier betrayals. In our sessions, I assist them in making intuitive contact with infinite inner resources like the archetypes of Divine Mother or Divine Father. This helps them to receive the love, nurturing, protection, or guidance they never received as children in their earlier relationships with their physical parents. Intuitively, with the help of this greater intelligence, they see that their betraying parent, lover, friend, or coworker acted out of unresolved pain, fear, or hurt, and as in the Frog Prince tale, the betrayer and the betrayal itself are instrumental in initiating soul growth and character development for the betrayed. The meaning ascribed to the betraying incident is very personal, though the betrayal is not. Our family and friends are bound to betray us just by the fact that they are human, not God.

Through contact with our Divine Parents within the psyche, we mature. In time, we grow beyond the divine parent-child relationship. Self-nurturance and self-direction become expressions of the Self. The Self is the archetypal representation of one's wholeness, a wholeness that we usually seek in or project onto our relationship with our spouse, lover, or partner. For example, colloquial expressions like "my significant other" or "my other half" allude to this projection of the Self onto one's partner or lover. As one matures, instead of looking for divine perfection in one's human companion, one seeks union with one's perfectly divine inner Self. Returning to our Beloved within, making love with the One who loves us so well, we are betrothed to our true companion. Our soul-mate relationship is really a union between the higher Self and the evolving self within the psyche. Higher Self is the one who will never abandon us, the one with whom we are truly One. The sacred marriage that the alchemists call the *hierogamos* is an inner marriage instead of an external affair.

The sacred troth is a vow to have faith in the process of life, which continually guides our return to our inner Source. All life's teachings allow us to renew our sacred marriage vows to the higher Self. Personal betrayal wounds of infidelity and jealousy frequently indicate a misplaced alliance projected onto one's lover, spouse, or partner—giving them godlike status. These false idols crash off their pedestals, and in the dust, we come to know the One within the psyche, in whom we can truly trust.

I love the fact that the word *intuition* comes from a Latin root word *tueri,* which literally means "to observe, guard, or protect."[8] Through self-observation, we come to know what we truly need. Intuition, not our psychological defenses, provides all the protection we require. Our intuitive resources guard us as we are guided to discover a deeper, more personally meaningful truth contained within our painful betrayal experiences. Hidden from the ordinary, rationalizing mind, which is caught in the traditional explanations of why the past causes one to be the way one is, nonrational intuitive resources extend beyond the limits of historical time and place to reveal that one is already whole. Returning to the metaphor that faithful Henry provides, the truth breaks the constricting bands of our psychological defenses and sets us free to trust and be true to our inner Self.

Truth is never punishing, shaming, or blaming. Punishment, as a construct for life, dies along with other fears, which block us from the truth. Punishment, whether self-punishment or the vindictive punishment of others, signals that we are caught in fear. Once we have quelled the punishing and judging mind, the silent voice of our impartial, observing Self can be heard. There is a difference between the judging, rational-irrational mind, which is full of beliefs and biases, and the nonrational mind, which intuitively knows truth without proof. To show you how you might distinguish between them, I'd like to tell you the tale of the Aged Mother.[9]

This story opens with the Aged Mother returning from the graveyard after attending the funeral of her last living friend. The Aged Mother is tired and weary as she rekindles the hearth fire in her empty cottage. Alone in the darkness, the Aged Mother sits before the crackling flames of the fire, musing on the life she has lived. Images and memories of her husband, two sons, friends, and family dance in the flames. One by one they all have died. Of all her losses, the death of her children is the hardest to bear. In her grief, she rages against God, blaming the Almighty for taking her sons from her when they were still children. Now there is no one to keep her company in her old age. She is all alone.

Soon she hears the church bells chiming. Thinking that she dozed through the night, the Aged Mother hurries off to the church. But when she gets there, a ghostly light filters out through the church windows. The Aged Mother opens the door, and she notices that every pew is filled. Rising from the Aged Mother's usual seat, a deceased aunt comes to greet her. All at once, the Aged Mother realizes that the hall is filled with all her dead relatives and friends long gone. "Look up, upon the altar," her aunt says to her, "and there you will find your sons."

The Aged Mother looks up and sees two strapping young men, one hung to death on the gallows and the other tortured upon the wheel. The Aged Mother falls to her knees and prays, giving thanks to God that her dear children did not live long enough to meet such cruel fates. Trembling and shaking, the Aged Mother makes her way home, grateful that God has dealt so kindly with both her and her sons. Three days later, the Aged Mother dies and rests in peace.

The lesson in this story suggests that to heal betrayal, we must move beyond the rational-irrational mind, which gives us easy answers based on our historical thoughts and feelings, unresolved security needs, low self-esteem, and other unhealed wounds of the past. The Aged Mother's righteous resentment about being alone in her old age pales against the wisdom, mercy, and power of a greater truth. The Aged Mother's clairvoyant visions, contact with spirit guides, and communication with her spiritual ancestors suggests that one may use a variety of psychic and intuitive resources to gain insight and understanding. Regardless of the form of introspection, one gains a new perspective on the past by reviewing one's experience in the clear light of intuition.

Moving from betrayal to trust is an advanced initiation. The spiritual teaching is supplied primarily by one's inner teacher during the new knowledge phase of initiation. The questions one asks oneself guide one's quest. Let your questions lead you to understand the greatest good contained in your betrayal experience. The message you receive from intuitive resources may contain a blend of personal elements, or collective, archetypal, and mythic elements. Intuitive truths are typically symbolic, instead of literal. Intuitive symbolic processes and your personal quest for meaning, value, or purpose guide your passage through betrayal to trust. A quest for meaning—to understand your soul purpose, teaching, or lesson—often provides new awareness, a truth that sets you free.

Use your intuition to awaken and acknowledge your inner teacher. Identify an intuitive tool or method to help you create contact with the Self. Commune with your inner Source of wisdom and healing. There are many ways to create contact. Watch your dreams and keep a dream journal. Notice synchronicities. Use augury: tarot, runes, I Ching, astrology, numerology, and channeling. Use meditation, creative visualization, guided imagery, affirmations, prayer, ritual, chanting, dancing, creative arts, creative writing, or journal keeping. Sometimes friends, support group meetings, teachers, or inspirational writings like poetry and other creative works echo the whispering voice of our inner teacher. Regardless of the form, the truth reveals a new perspective on the betrayal, one broad enough to encompass the paradox of feeling betrayed and feeling acceptance simultaneously.

Rebirth: Becoming the Creative Self

Listening to our intuition is a creative process and naturally leads to the final phase of initiation: rebirth. The creative birth process is the antithesis of the death process. During death and birth, archetypal forces are at work on the psyche, but in the death phase, we resist these forces. In the birth phase, we learn to relax, and let these forces guide us to our highest good, the birth of a new self. In the symbolic death stage of initiation, external events and circumstances beyond our control are killing us, forcing us to change. As we internalize these forces, we are empowered by them, and they deliver us to our greater Self. The gap between death and birth is an opening for the divine.

Rebirth is the phase in which you integrate the spiritual teaching as it relates to the fulfillment of your new role, and you reenter into your community. The process a pregnant woman goes through provides an excellent metaphor for the process of giving birth to one's creative Self. Self-realization plants the seed of a new possibility, a new way of being. It takes time for the seed to grow into its full form—a reminder that we need to be patient with our growth process and give ourselves the necessary time, energy, and self-care that will support our ultimate Self-fulfillment. Following the metaphor of birth, we find five stages of development: insemination, gestation, labor, transition, and delivery.

Step 1: Insemination—Realization
Insemination corresponds to that flash of insight or new awareness that shifts and expands our sense of who we are or what is possible. Become receptive to the possibility of something new being born. Use your intuitive tools to open and receive a spark of inspiration from a creative, infinite Source.

Step 2: Gestation—Observation
After we are impregnated with new knowledge, we must nurture and nourish the new perspective. It gestates within our being. Shift your attention to your observing, intuitive Self. Observe what nurtures and supports you and your process. Nourish your hunches by following intuitive cravings and observing results. Use inner and outer resources and continue to gain support for who you are as you grow in confidence in your new sense of self.

Step 3: Labor—Vacillation
You experience a paradigm clash between your new and old identities. Outmoded belief systems or old ways of being contradict your inner guidance and new vision. Consciousness contracts as we confront old expectations, patterns, and habits, and expands as we stay true to ourselves and live with integrity. You vacillate between your old and new ways, flip-flopping between the two. Continue to explore and live your truth. Relax. Release attachments to outcomes. Use all your resources, inner and outer, to

support growth. Watch for synchronicities that affirm your growth, and continue to contact and follow your inner guidance. Actively surrender "my will" to "Thy will" by trusting and acting on your higher Self's guidance.

Step 4: Transition—Creative Tension

It is not unusual to feel tremendous tension, self-doubt in and discomfort with how others respond to the "new you." You may even temporarily loose faith in yourself and feel as though you have slipped back into old patterns. The contradiction between outmoded belief systems and one's new awareness continues to increase in intensity as you alternate between self-doubt and Self-trust during the transition phase.

When you feel as though you haven't grown at all, and you have been just fooling yourself, know that you are in the thick of transition. This is a very delicate time where you might abort your mission by sinking into believing the negative thoughts and feelings—a quick path back to symbolic death. The possibility of slipping into self-betrayal is strong. Have no fear though, as symbolic death always leads to new knowledge eventually—you will come through. Self-betrayal will guide you to understand that your betrayal is for-giving you an opportunity to unite with your true Self, and to eventually give-forth this Self to the world. When extreme self-doubt and synchronistic signs of support and guidance are juxtaposed, forgive yourself for being a frail, evolving, human being. Use the tension of transformation as a sign to push forward in the direction of your values, ideals, and dreams. Remember to TRUST.

Step 5: Delivery—Integration

You become aware of how much you have changed. You notice how you are no longer doing things the old way anymore. You feel at ease and have a sense of release and relief. Congratulations! Create a ritual to acknowledge your growth and celebrate your new life. This is the final phase of rebirth in which one's return, reentry, and integration into the community brings with it satisfaction in one's new role within society, because this new role includes utilizing one's newly found powers and gifts that benefit the self and others. Integration of the initiation teachings within the context of community—one's family, circle of friends, or even in the workplace—is the reward that leads to a richer, fuller, and more meaningful life. You know you are at this stage when you reflect on all you've been through and feel a sense of appreciation for yourself, and all that you have become. You feel alive and excited about life.

ACT instead of React:
Getting from Soul Tests to Spiritual Teachings

Each death initiation teaches the initiate to accept that she or he has the power to turn inward and contact an inner Source of healing. We do this by taking the risk to turn inward and contact our creative Source of power within. In recontacting the Self, we find the One in whom we truly can trust. Our ability to continue to ACT—*accept, create,* and *trust*—over and over in all our relationships marks passage through the betrayal-to-trust initiation of the soul. The emotional ordeals of betrayal become five soul tests that provide us with five spiritual teachings.

Soul Test #1: Resentment, Obsession, Vengeance

Spiritual Teaching: Turn inward for truth. Discover and express your deeper truth. Learn to develop and use good communication skills when you share your truth with others.

Inner healing followed by new action is the basis of recovery, dignity, and freedom. We are delivered through the betrayal gateway into trust by the practice of living in new, nontraditional, non-betraying ways. When we interact with our betrayers from Self-trust, we transform our relationships. The experience of betrayal turns into a series of teachings that continue to inspire us to remember who we are—creators.

With practice, one learns to ACT in a nontraditional way in response to each of the five emotional ordeals, the tests and trials of betrayal as they surface in day-to-day life. As intuition guides one's personal journey in both the inner and outer worlds, each emotional ordeal of betrayal is transformed into a sacred soul teaching that guides and supports one's spiritual practice. The desire for vengeance, projection of the shadow, cynical generalizations, self-betrayal, and the need for control and manipulation become tests of creativity and Self-trust.

When one is confronted with a betrayal experience, it becomes a synchronistic event, an intuitive message from an infinite Source of intelligence guiding us to turn inward. Instead of vengeance, we use the pain as a signal to consult our inner Self and seek a deeper truth. The desire for revenge then becomes a cue to discover and communicate the truth. First, we recognize that rejection or abandonment by our betrayer stimulates the fear of a loss of Self. As we mourn our temporary separation from the divine, we remember to use inner and outer resources to recognize and release fear reactions. Then we can receive intuitive insight, which reveals a deeper truth. As we tell our truth to another, we can learn to make "I" statements and to use reflective and active listening techniques and other communication skills instead of blaming, shaming, and punishing our betrayer. For example, depending on how it is said, a statement like "I need space for now" can mark a time of sacred separation to connect with the Self, instead of a wounding act intended to reject and hurt your betrayer.

Soul Test #2: Denial, Shadow Projection, Bitter Resignation

Spiritual Teaching: Relax, release, receive. Develop compassion for yourself and others. Learn to relax your fear reactions. Release self-righteousness by recognizing both positive and negative traits within yourself. Continue to receive inner direction.

In taking space, the commitment is to own the shadow in yourself rather than project it onto your betrayer. The first step is to release your attachment to being right. This is accomplished through relaxing the body and the mind. The body holds tension, so breathing exercises and physical exercise like yoga, tai chi, racquetball, dancing, or hiking help the body relax. Relaxing the mind means letting go of emotional reactions like anger, hurt, and grief. "Release attachment to outcomes" is a helpful mantra to relax the mind. Many people across cultures employ meditation, self-hypnosis, song, dance, prayer, or ritual to relax the mind. Remember to use both inner and outer resources to help you in your process. The use of self-help books and audio tapes; talks with friends, therapists, or intuitive consultants; or participation in support group meetings can also help you release emotional reactions.

After releasing and relaxing, we become receptive to deeper truth. Intuitively, we can know the truth. One thing that is universally true is that each of us contains both positive and negative qualities. Instead of obsessing about your betrayer's negative traits, turn inward and observe how and when you betrayed yourself in the relationship. Recognize the unconscious motive, vulnerability, or underlying destructive pattern within your own psyche that allowed you to betray yourself. Or explore your past experience with one of your betrayer's worst negative traits and observe if you have ever felt or acted that way. The betrayal-to-trust initiation challenges one to acknowledge and accept one's own darkness and light—one's strengths and vulnerabilities. This builds self-acceptance, tolerance, and compassion for yourself and others.

Soul Test #3: Cynicism, Generalization, Stereotyping

Spiritual Teaching: Use intuition to understand. Seek to understand the highest good, deeper meaning, and special gift or soul purpose that is unique to you and that furthers your personal and spiritual growth. Learn to develop your intuition, using both inner and outer resources, to gain greater awareness.

Instead of projecting your personal betrayal wounds onto the collective by generalizing the negative, learn to use your intuition to gain personal insight and understanding. Remember that truth is not a value judgment, as in right and wrong or good and bad. Intuitive truth is guided by your personal quest for meaning and it rekindles Self-awareness.

Start by simply observing yourself instead of judging others. Self-awareness leads to the rediscovery of one's innate gifts and unique talents. This inspires self-worth and a sense of purpose in life and leads to the discovery of another profound universal truth. Just as you have a gift to give the world, every other individual and each group in our society has a unique gift to give to the collective. Cynically attributing the negative traits to all others challenges the soul to resolve prejudice, bigotry, and racism—to, in effect, join the human race. Unconscious projection of our personal betrayal wounds onto groups tests our collective ability to resolve the complex issues of our world today.

Soul Test #4: Self-Betrayal, Self-Rejection, Self-Abandonment

Spiritual Teaching: Speak, share, stand up. Commit to the fulfillment of your soul's dream. Learn to take a stand in life, speak your truth, and share your dreams.

We are born to express ourselves and give our gifts to the world. The fourth test, self-betrayal, challenges our commitment to fulfill our vital dream, vision, or purpose in life. Etymologically, the word *commit* comes from the same root as *mission*. Indeed, we each have a soul mission, a vital dream envisioned by the Self. Its fulfillment requires that we make use of our unique gifts and talents to activate our potential.

Rather than betray the Self, speak what you know and take a stand in life. The stand you take is congruent with your essential values and visions. Life becomes a spiritual practice as one lives one's truth within the context of the community. Your words and deeds illustrate integrity, wholeness, and a union between self and Self. Ideally, each person in society "follows their bliss," as Joseph Campbell put it. When one embodies one's deepest values and visions, one's personal healing begins to extend beyond oneself. As we creatively contribute our unique gifts, talents, and resources to the community, we collectively transform our society.

At first, one's new actions in the world might be upsetting to others. Our friends, family, or coworkers may even accuse *us* of being betrayers. And, in fact, we are! We betray our friends and family who like us the old way. We betray the vapid social and cultural mores of our time to bring a new sense of life to our world. We consciously betray the assumption that life is meaningless and that there is something wrong with us. We choose to be free. We unite with our greater Self and trust in the One within who guides our spiritual practice. Right action based on inner guidance becomes our way of life, both the process and the path.

Soul Test #5: Paranoid Fear, Control, and Manipulation
Spiritual Teaching: Try again and TRUST. Remember that you are free to be yourself and to fulfill your vital dream. Learn to allow others the same freedom. ACT, and TRUST the process that takes you on your soul's journey from betrayal to trust and forgiveness.

Ultimately, the impulse to react to betrayal with fear, control, and manipulation is a test of freedom. If you are free to fulfill your vital dream and mission in life as guided by your inner Source, so is every other human being. On this journey from betrayal to trust, we are all on a spiritual path. Yet we may be walking along the path at different paces. When your friends, lovers, family, or associates react to you with anger, or try to deny the truth of your experience by arguing with you and offering convincing rationalizations, tears, or threats, recognize that they have just entered the symbolic death phase of their own initiation.

Do not personalize their death reaction. Remember they are dying symbolically, and that they are on their own soul's journey toward rebirth. Trust the process that takes each of us from death to life. Rather than die with them by denying their process, or trying to control and manipulate them with angry arguments or rationalizations of your own, ACT and TRUST. *Accept* each of you for who and where you are in the journey from betrayal to trust. *Create* by trying to find a new way to deal with your feelings of betrayal. *Trust* the process. *Turn inward* instead of trying to control and manipulate your friend into understanding life from your point of view. Consider the feedback that they give you. There may be a grain of truth in what they say. What new insight does it give you about yourself? Discover whatever it is that is personally valuable in that grain of truth; allow it to grow into a pearl of wisdom in the belly of your experience. Know your own truth. *Release* the rest. Continue to *use* your inner and outer resources to gain deeper insight and understanding. Then, from this new understanding, express yourself again. *Speak* what you know and don't be afraid to turn inward and *try again.*

In our own small ways, we each play sacred roles as initiators and betrayers. We provoke each other to die and be reborn. Each rebirth brings new knowledge into the world. Healing personal betrayal wounds trains us to become agents for the spiritual evolution of social consciousness. As living, breathing models of TRUST, we discover that we are free to be true to ourselves instead of using fear, control, and manipulation to survive. We each have the right to be a divine expression of life. As we follow inner direction with integrity, we are able to fulfill our roles in the drama of the divine. We become the eyes, ears, hands, and feet of the Creator. First, we learn to cooperate with our inner companion. Next, we model this cooperation in our interactions with our outer companions. Together, we become cocreators determined to use our inner and outer resources to collectively transform our society and bring new life to our world.

We face many challenges in our world today. Social and environmental crises lead us to believe that our world is threatened and that we are doomed. Yet the betrayals of society, and even of our planet, are reflections of even greater soul challenges. Each wound is a distinct gateway that opens us to another initiation of the soul. All wounds are catalysts for personal spiritual awakening and the evolution of social consciousness. As we resolve our personal betrayal wounds, we become humane emissaries, and like the Frog Prince and the princess, we are able to act with integrity in our world in a new, beautiful, kind way. Collectively, we have all the inner and outer resources we need—creative intelligence, technical skill and ability, financial resources, human resources—to respond to the natural and man-made disasters that threaten to betray the continuance of life as we know it on our planet.

We are being trained by an infinite intelligence to trust the forces of evolution that are at work in our world. Working through betrayal is part of the divine design. The story of the Frog Prince provides us with an interesting image. The frog is an animal that took an evolutionary leap from being a sea creature to becoming a land creature. Journeying from betrayal to trust is an equally radical shift in states of consciousness. The same forces that molded life on this planet are molding the human psyche. Like the frog who mastered life on both land and in the water, we must master both betrayal and trust if we are not only to survive, but evolve.

We are learning to trust whatever mystery it is that created the universe, stars, galaxies, planets, and life. Betrayal is part of the mystery. Betrayal is a natural process that has the potential to open one's heart and awaken expanded states of consciousness: a deeper sense of knowing, a sense of purpose in life, and a sense of wholeness—a oneness with all creation. As we apply the ancient mystery teachings of initiation to our everyday life, we begin to use personal, social, and planetary betrayal wounds as a creative stimulus for personal, social, and planetary spiritual evolution of consciousness.

Self-Assessment Questionnaire

Read each of the statements below. Check off as many boxes as apply to you right now. Be sure to fill in boxes in each category to best describe your present experience.

1. Separation
- ☐ I feel isolated and/or alienated.
- ☐ I feel rejected and/or abandoned.
- ☐ I feel so alone. Nobody really understands me and what I've been through.
- ☐ I want to just hide.
- ☐ I'm not ready to _____ *(e.g., date again, marry again, etc.)*.

2. Purification
- ☐ I feel shocked, betrayed, unprepared, and beset by emotional ordeals.
- ☐ I don't deserve to be treated this way.
- ☐ It's just not fair!
- ☐ It hurts so much—whenever I think about it, it makes me sick.
- ☐ I am suspicious of _____ *(e.g., men, younger women, etc.)*.

3. Symbolic Death
- ☐ I feel plunged into the depths of so many feelings *(e.g., anger, grief, loneliness, emptiness, etc.)*.
- ☐ I can't believe this is happening to me.
- ☐ It's not what they did, it's how they did it that really gets me.
- ☐ I should have expected this. I should have known.
- ☐ I'm so tired of all this—when will it all end?

4. New Knowledge

- ☐ I feel inspired. I am learning so much!
- ☐ I'm stronger than I thought I was.
- ☐ I've grown so much from this whole thing.
- ☐ I see things so differently now.
- ☐ I understand _____ *(e.g., that I was in so much denial, that I needed something this dramatic to help me learn, etc.).*
- ☐ I forgive _____ *(e.g., myself, my betrayer, etc.).*

5. Rebirth

- ☐ I feel alive and excited about life.
- ☐ I really listen to myself now, I pay attention to my intuition.
- ☐ I want to share what I've learned with others, so they don't have to go through what I went through.
- ☐ I still doubt myself sometimes, but I know that, one way or another, things will work out.
- ☐ I feel so free.

Count up the number of boxes checked in each section and record your totals below:

Separation	0	1	2	3	4	5
Purification	0	1	2	3	4	5
Symbolic Death	0	1	2	3	4	5
New Knowledge	0	1	2	3	4	5
Rebirth	0	1	2	3	4	5

Your highest score shows you which stage of initiation you are in. Read the Stages of Initiation on pages 32 and 33 to determine what your scores mean.

STAGES OF INITIATION

Based on your highest score on the Betrayal-to-Trust Self-Assessment Questionnaire, circle the stage or stages of initiation that are the most significant to you right now or best describe your present experience.

Italics represent the deeper soul challenge that you presently face.

1. Separation
This signals that you are in the first stage of initiation. In cross-cultural rites of passage this is a time of sacred separation, in which entry into the sacred is provoked through rejection of, or forced isolation from, one's known world and the status quo of the community.

Now is the time to enter into the mystery of betrayal and to discover the deeper questions that will lead you to wholeness and Self-renewal.

2. Purification
In cross-cultural rites, exposure to startling and incomprehensible events begins the purification phase of initiation. The purification phase always presents initiatory ordeals, which are tests and trials of the soul. These ordeals prepare one for symbolic death while simultaneously revealing one's inner strengths or new talents. Betrayal evokes five distinct emotional ordeals: resentment, denial of the positive, cynicism, self-betrayal, and paranoia.

Discovery of newly found courage, strength, or talent marks successful passage through the purification phase. New skills transform the five tests to sacred soul teachings: communication of the truth, compassion, intuition development, personal commitment, and spiritual freedom. You will need these skills to continue on your journey.

3. Symbolic Death
Old strategies no longer work; and the new way is not yet clear. Clinging to old ways will kill you. The more you cling, the more pain and grief you experience—until you let go. The only way out is through.

Death brings you to a state of deep acceptance—of both yourself and the events in your life that led you to where you are right now. Death teaches you to discover and accept your self completely, including your personal limits and special gifts or talents.

4. New Knowledge

In traditional societies, the elders serve to help the initiate understand the meaning or purpose of the initiatory ordeals, and they explain the value and use of one's newly found gifts. In advanced initiation rites, knowledge is intuitively received from inner sources. Betrayal is an advanced initiation.

You are required to develop your intuition in order to receive insight into a personal spiritual teaching that gives meaning to your initiatory ordeals. Your inner vision or soul's vital dream returns to you a sense of purpose in life and gives you a new sense of identity.

5. Rebirth

This is the final phase of initiation, and it defines the process of spiritual renewal and return. Rebirth brings the individual back to life and back to one's community to fulfill a new role within that community. In traditional societies, during rebirth, one's new role brings personal fulfillment, and the community as a whole benefits from the added contributions of the individual.

Integration of the spiritual teaching you received relates to the new role you are to fulfill within your community—your workplace, circle of friends, family, church, temple, or community group. You are free to be true to yourself and to find the fulfillment of your soul's dream.

Recognize Symbolic Death

The behaviors listed below reflect the symbolic death stage of initiation. Read through the categories and behaviors and check off those that are relevant to you. Determine whether you are experiencing a symbolic death and, if so, where you are in this process.

Denial

Escapism through addictive outlets
- ☐ Alcohol
- ☐ Drugs
- ☐ Food
- ☐ Spending
- ☐ Work
- ☐ Sex
- ☐ Gambling
- ☐ Television
- ☐ Other

Avoidance
- ☐ Associating with nonsupportive individuals
- ☐ Occupying yourself with your affairs
- ☐ Keeping too busy to self-reflect
- ☐ Evading confrontation
- ☐ Placating or making nice
- ☐ Isolating yourself from sources that can help you heal

Anger

Acting out
- ☐ Temper tantrums
- ☐ Physical and/or verbal abuse
- ☐ Destruction of property
- ☐ Emotional blackmail
- ☐ Control and manipulation
- ☐ Threats and ultimatums
- ☐ Withdrawal

Vengeful behaviors
- ☐ Gossip
- ☐ Cruelty
- ☐ Punishing words and deeds

Rationalization
- ☐ Justifying your angry behavior
- ☐ Arrogance, condescension, and self-righteousness
- ☐ Shaming and blaming others
- ☐ Bargaining
- ☐ Suspicion and snooping

Victim attitudes
- ☐ Shaming and blaming yourself
- ☐ Pitying yourself
- ☐ Believing yourself to be inferior or unworthy
- ☐ Believing yourself to be a failure

Depression
- ☐ Crying jags
- ☐ Oversleeping
- ☐ Low energy
- ☐ Lack of appetite or eating too much
- ☐ Lack of motivation
- ☐ Feeling helpless and hopeless

Pass Through Symbolic Death

Depending on the phase of your journey from betrayal to trust and forgiveness, you may be struggling with the experience of symbolic death—caught in denial, anger, rationalization, or depression. Remember that, though we do not choose when we "die," we can choose how we deal with the experience. There are gestures that we can perform and environments that we can create to support moving through symbolic death to awaken deeper acceptance and eventual renewal and rebirth. Cultivate patience for the process. Give yourself time to heal. Demonstrate respect for and faith in your own and others' journeys from betrayal to trust.

Identify what makes you mad. Explore your anger through introspection:
- ☐ Write about it in your journal.
- ☐ Ask for a dream to give you insight before you go to bed.
- ☐ Observe how comfortable or uncomfortable you are with anger.
- ☐ Observe which emotions surface as you move through your anger.
- ☐ Keep the energy moving and notice where it leads you.

Examine how your body reacts when you feel angry:
- ☐ Do you hold tension in any particular place (neck, shoulders, diaphragm, etc.)?
- ☐ What happens to your breathing?
- ☐ What happens to your appetite?
- ☐ How do your internal organs (stomach, intestines, etc.) and body systems (nervous, digestive, immune, etc.) respond to this stress?

Find creative outlets for your energy:
- ☐ Draw your feelings with big bold crayons on large sheets of paper.
- ☐ Dance to loud music.
- ☐ Recycle glass and relish the sound of the glass smashing and crashing.
- ☐ Role-play a wild beast—get down on all fours and growl, claw, or pounce.
- ☐ Do the project you've been putting off—cleaning your closet, clearing out the garage, or mowing the lawn; make things the way you want.

Create a safe place to express your feelings:
- ☐ Talk to a friend, therapist, or healing guide.
- ☐ Pound some pillows.
- ☐ Scream into a pillow.

Release the emotional energy that is held in your body:
- ☐ Do breathing exercises.
- ☐ Take a martial arts class: judo, aikido, tai chi, karate, tai kuando, chi gung, wrestling, etc.
- ☐ Take up dance, yoga, movement, or hiking in nature.
- ☐ Get some exercise: Play racquet ball, tennis, handball; go running, jogging, or swimming.
- ☐ Take a self-defense class.
- ☐ Get a massage, or do bodywork, rolfing, bio-energetics, Rosen work, or therapeutic touch.

Be gentle with yourself:
- ☐ Don't yell or curse at yourself.
- ☐ Don't call yourself bad names.
- ☐ Don't judge yourself.
- ☐ Be kind to yourself.
- ☐ If you are unhappy with how you handled something this time, imagine how you would do things differently next time.
- ☐ Remind yourself that you are growing and that you do not have to know all the answers.

Accept loss as part of the journey from betrayal to trust:
- ☐ Expect to be on an emotional roller coaster for a while—don't fight it.
- ☐ Observe yourself as you move through the natural denial-anger-rationalization-depression-acceptance process.
- ☐ Recognize and accept disappointment.
- ☐ Communicate directly to others about your fears, disappointments, and needs when possible and appropriate.
- ☐ Listen to others' fears, disappointments, and needs when possible and appropriate.
- ☐ Acknowledge your fears and needs.
- ☐ Accept your current reality for what it is—and what it is not.
- ☐ Appreciate yourself, wherever you may be in your journey from betrayal to trust and forgiveness.
- ☐ Assimilate the process by taking the time you need to heal; be patient with your process.
- ☐ Allow your feelings to change, move, deepen, and surface.

BETRAYAL, TRUST, AND FORGIVENESS

Explore the Emotional Ordeals of Betrayal

In your own words, define each of the five emotional ordeals and give examples from your own life. Write about it in your journal or in the space below:

1. Righteous Resentment and Desire for Vengeance
   Your definition:

   Your example:

2. Denial that Leads to Projection of the Shadow
   Your definition:

   Your example:

3. Cynicism, Generalization, and Prejudice
   Your definition:

   Your example:

4. Self-Betrayal and Abandonment of the Self
   Your definition:

   Your example:

5. Paranoia that Leads to Fear, Control, and Manipulation
   Your definition:

   Your example:

Discover and Express the Truth

Turn Inward for Truth

Feelings of resentment, obsession, or vengeance indicate that there is a crisis in communication. This soul test challenges you to turn inward to discover and express a deeper truth. To thine own Self be true. Seek to understand yourself first, and your betrayer second. Learn to develop and use good communication skills when you share your truth with others.

When you are ready to communicate to your betrayer-initiator, practice using "I" statements instead of "you" statements.

To deepen your inner work, ask yourself:

1. What are my doubts about the other person?

2. What are my judgments or criticisms of their behavior or actions toward me?

3. What hurts me the most?

4. Why does this hurt so much? What is my interpretation of their behavior?

5. What have I withheld saying to them?

6. What would happen if I said that? What are my fears?

Know and Own the Shadow in Yourself

Relax, Release, Receive

Denial of the positive in your betrayer leads to shadow projection and bitter resignation. This soul test challenges you to discover and own the shadow in yourself. Develop compassion for yourself and others. Learn to relax fear reactions. Strive to release self-righteousness by recognizing both positive and negative traits within yourself. Continue to receive inner direction.

Relax your body and mind. Use breathing techniques or physical exercise, or talk to a friend to release tension. Practice releasing attachment to outcomes. Be gentle with yourself. Learn to perceive both positive and negative qualities in both your betrayer and yourself.

To discover and own your shadow, use your righteous resentment as a guide. Make a list of the negative traits of your betrayer. Circle the one trait that bothers you the most. Now ask yourself:

7. What is my past experience with this trait?

8. Have I ever acted (or wanted to act) like that?

9. What motivated me when I acted in that manner?

10. What bothers, upsets, or scares me most about acting that way?

11. What sets this fear pattern into motion?

12. Am I ready to be free of this pattern?

Be Aware of Your Special Soul Challenges

Use Intuition to Understand

Cynicism leads to generalization and stereotyping. This soul test challenges you to understand the highest good, deeper meaning, and special gift or soul purpose that is unique to you and furthers your personal spiritual growth. Develop your intuition to gain greater awareness.

Use inner and outer resources to recognize, accept, and release your personal and cultural preconceptions, prejudices, and patterns. Draw on intuitive tools—tarot, astrology, runes, I Ching, prayer, and friends and family. Keep your observing Self present.

To gain insight into the personal message, unique soul challenge, teaching, meaning, or deeper purpose hidden in your betrayal experience, recall your shadow work in Exercise 1-F. After you have reviewed your personal history and identified the patterns of behavior that constitute your fear reaction, ask yourself:

13. What in me has perpetuated this pattern?

14. What did my soul have in mind for me by bringing me this situation?

15. What is the highest teaching my soul wanted me to learn from this?

16. What is the best possible outcome for me in my life as I integrate this teaching?

17. Is there any additional guidance for me at this time that will assist me further?

Rediscover and Recommit to Your Dream

Speak, Share, Stand Up

Self-betrayal, self-rejection, and self-abandonment are the result of your denial of your dreams, values, or vital vision. This soul test challenges you to rediscover and recommit to your dreams. Learn to take a stand in life, speak your truth, and share your insights, awareness, and dreams.

Use creative visualization and affirmation to empower your vital vision. Commit to cooperating with your creative Source. Make this your primary relationship. Use self-reflection, contemplation, prayer, and meditation to open communication.

Develop your relationship with yourself as your primary relationship. Treat yourself the way you wish to be treated. Use this ideal relationship as a model for your interactions with others. Practice becoming a cocreator with your inner Source. Ask yourself:

18. Based on the best possible outcome, what are my ideals, dreams, and visions?

19. What am I like in my most ideal Self in relationship to my betrayer?

20. When did I stop being that way in our relationship? What trigger disempowered me?

21. What can I do to help me grow stronger, to support me in living out my ideals?

22. Can I do that now with my betrayer? Why or why not?

Train Yourself to TRUST

Try Again and TRUST

Paranoid fear, control, and manipulation arise in direct proportion to your denial of your existential freedom to be. This soul test teaches you to trust the process of life that returns you to your true spiritual source within. Remember that you are spiritually free. Allow others the same freedom. Learn to ACT, and TRUST the process that takes you on your soul's journey from betrayal to trust and forgiveness.

Fear reactions, such as anxiety, worry, anger, or hurt, are natural when we act in new and unfamiliar ways. Observe your emotional reactions and use them as an intuitive signal to return within for further guidance. Coming to trust yourself is both the process and the goal of this universal rite of passage.

When you are faced with tension or feedback that causes you to pause, try to turn inward first, rather than react. Ask yourself:

23. What blocks me from being "me" when I am with my betrayer?

24. What would happen if I were my true self? What is my worst fear or paranoia?

25. Has this fear ever been realized in this lifetime or past lifetimes?

26. What was the pattern or repeating theme?

27. What was the soul lesson or teaching?

Chapter 2

Betrayal of the Mother

Gateway to Self-Trust and Self-Knowledge

Wound: If you suffer from a mother wound, your self-esteem has been injured. You lack a sense of self in which you can trust.

Truth: Each one of us knows intuitively what we need, what nourishes us. We also know what doesn't feel loving or supportive.

Healing: Feed your inner knowing by nurturing yourself. Discover your Source of knowing, the One within in whom you can trust.

Betrayal of the mother is not personal. Throughout the natural kingdom, in the life of every animal there comes a time when the mother abandons her biological role. For some creatures this happens before birth. For example, we've all found sacks of spider eggs in abandoned webs in the corners of the house. In some cases, the separation is quite hostile. Remember the mother cat who one day hisses, scratches, and bites at her kittens if they continue to try to nurse. Some mothers only breed. Some mothers breed, feed, and wean their young. Still, every baby bird is pushed from the nest to discover the strength of its own wings.

The ancient Egyptians held that the human being contains all life-forms within the field of human consciousness. Mineral consciousness, plant consciousness, animal consciousness, plus the seed of something else—Self-consciousness—are all part of our physical and metaphysical being.

Different people experience the mother wound at different ages. Some felt rejected by their mothers in utero. Like the spider, they were rejected before birth. For example, they may have had the impression that they were born the wrong sex, or they grew up thinking that they were a diaphragm baby or a menopause baby. They felt like they were a mistake. Some people I have spoken with knew at birth that their biological mother would be unable to support, nourish, and nurture them. Still others associated their mother wounds with developmental stages like weaning, birth of a sibling, or toilet training. Social pressures due to a divorce or death in the family as well as peer pressure during adolescence can also stimulate awareness that Mother didn't know what was best. She may have been old-fashioned, outdated, or simply ignorant.

No matter what our age, if we personalize the archetype of betrayal of the mother, we suffer instead of grow. Mary is a good example. When I first met Mary, she was married to a fireman, worked full-time as a court reporter, and aspired to finish her bachelor's degree in acting. During our interviews, she often said she was desperately afraid of being rejected by those she loved and described herself as having abandonment issues. By the end of our first year of therapy, her marriage of nine years dissolved.

In time, we discovered that she was also afraid of being entrapped by those she loved. She continually tested the strength of her most intimate relationships. Mary always found a fatal flaw. She criticized her lovers harshly with abrupt, sometimes foul, and frequently punitive words or gestures. Her actions and words emotionally pushed people away and kept them at a safe distance if they became too close. Rejecting before being rejected gave Mary the false sense of being in control of whether others stayed or left. If a friend or lover stuck it out through these testy times, Mary felt remorse for acting like a jerk. She couldn't understand why someone would want to be with her. Negative thinking reinforced her low self-esteem. She felt unworthy of her friend's loyalty. She was insecure about and distrustful of her sporadic need for emotional distance. She began to think that she had a fear of intimacy.

She told me that her mother was frequently ill when she was growing up. Being the oldest, she felt obliged to take care of her mother and younger siblings. Raised to be a good Catholic, Mary learned to martyr herself and ignore her own needs when faced with someone who suffered more than she. She felt personally responsible for her mother's well-being and was decidedly uncomfortable with "evil" thoughts and feelings that contradicted the way she was raised.

I asked her, "How old were you when you realized that you could not expect your mother to be there for you?" In a hypnotic trance, Mary regressed all the way to her birth experience. She told me she remembered being presented to her mother in the hospital. Instead of being joyfully received, her mother's first uneasy glance turned to ice-cold terror as she held the crying infant. Mary's infant self felt rejected and emotionally abandoned. Throughout her childhood, glimmers of that initial terror continued to peek through her mother's eyes. Over time, Mary came to think of herself as some hideous, frightful monster. Something had to be dreadfully wrong with her that her mother could be so afraid of her. Mary realized her experience of emotional rejection and inadequacy was deeply rooted in her mother's initial discomfort and panic reactions when she was unable to quiet her newborn baby. Mary had personalized her mother's feelings of inadequacy.

A part of our psyche seeks an omniscient, all-nurturing being who will anticipate and take care of our every need. When this spiritual need is filtered through the limited perception of our psychological understanding, this immortal task is transferred to our biological mother. One's personal mother, however, is only mortal. She is a clumsy, flawed, human stand-in for the ineffable, omniscient spark of consciousness that exists in each of us. Our mothers are bound to betray us. It is natural. It is also painful and devastating. And, as we recover from the wound, it is empowering. Betrayal by our personal mother is part of the divine design. By going through this betrayal, we are led to rely upon something more eternal.

Without blame, Mary came to accept that her biological mother did not, and even could not, nurture her emotionally. I asked Mary to let her psyche provide someone who could nurture her, someone who would not be put off by her infant screams and cries. A great, white wolf appeared. Using guided imagery, we reviewed the birth scene in the presence of this spirit. The wolf spirit snarled in response to the smell of fear in the birth room. Taking her by the scruff of her neck, the great, white wolf snatched Mary away from her human mother.

The wolf carried Mary out of the hospital room, through a dark forest, into the depths of her lair. Like Romulus and Remus of myth and legend, Mary was suckled by this great Wolf Mother. Mary's Wolf Mother had much to teach her about balancing dependence and independence. Unlike her human family of origin, who castigated Mary for being selfish and demanded family loyalty at the expense of individual integrity, her Spirit Mother taught her how to be loyal to the clan and simultaneously retain her individuality. Loyalty to the wolf clan was a loyalty to a social network that shared distinct values: commitment to life, vitality, and playful companionship. Mary also learned the personal value of her independent nature. As a wolf child, she was taught to master her hunger by hunting for sustenance. Hunting was a solitary activity. As a lone wolf child, Mary developed skill, agility, and prowess.

Solitude is an essential soul need for Mary, an expression of her wolf nature. Mary's so-called sporadic need for space in her human relationships marks her need for loner activities and time to feed her hungry soul. In solitude she nourishes her creative skills and prowess as an actress. She hunts for inspiration in literature, poetry, music, and people-watching. Over the next two years, Mary learned to identify her inner experience of discomfort and panic as a signal to feed her soul. She also completed her bachelor's degree, left the security of her job as a court reporter, and began what grew into a very successful career in modeling as she continued to pursue her primary passion as an actress.

In her journey from betrayal to trust, Mary has learned self-acceptance and self-love. There is nothing wrong with her for taking time to be with herself. She has determined that she can trust her inner need for both social and solitary time. Now, Mary's struggle between her need for space and her need for love and connection is played out within her psyche more than in her interpersonal relationships. It is not surprising to find that the inner battle is subdued by respecting her innate wolf nature, though, like a wolf, she will attack if cornered or threatened. This attack instinct is trustworthy, too. Through continued inner work, it will lead Mary to a deeper truth, while helping her feel protected, strong, and able to take care of herself in the outer world.

Integration of one's soul teaching into daily life is the foundation of one's spiritual practice. Part of Mary's spiritual practice is to continue to create a lifestyle that nurtures her inner truth—a need for integrity that includes loner time and clan time. For Mary, this soul teaching challenges her to consciously create space, rather than unconsciously take or make space through petty arguments, faultfinding, and acting out in ways that harm or destroy her significant relationships. The tension between psychological dependence and independence is resolved through the practice of living her truth.

The fact that we are betrayed by our mother is not as significant as the awareness that we know that she is human and, therefore, she cannot always be there for us and will not fulfill our every need. Even as little children, we knew. Something within us knows. Discovery of your knowing Self is your umbilicus to Great Mother, an archetypal consciousness powerful enough to heal your personal mother wounds. We each have a Source of knowing within the psyche that communicates to us through our intuition and perceptions—seeing, hearing, feeling, and direct knowing. Communication is symbolic. Like Mary's Wolf Mother, each symbol is a gateway to self-knowledge and reflects a distinct soul lesson or teaching that has personal significance. Self-knowledge as expressed through the symbols of our psyche, or soul, gives us a new perspective on the natural events of our life.

Once, when I suggested to a group of workshop participants that we would make contact with an experience of our archetypal Divine Mother, a woman called out, "Oh, you mean in our imagination, a fantasy." It is important to distinguish between direct contact through expanded states of consciousness and fantasy. Fantasy is the projection of a *personal* image. Fantasy is based on your personal history and cultural, ethnic, and religious upbringing; as well as your composite conscious and unconscious thoughts and feelings as expressed through your wishes, desires, attitudes, and beliefs. After exploring the origins of a fantasy, the personal image dissolves. It loses power, just as Mary's image of being abandoned or rejected because she is a hideous monster or a bad girl loses some of its power when she explores the roots of her fear. The power exerted on her psyche by her family and personal history is significant, but limited. Once the personal nature of the image is exposed, its impact dissipates over time.

Archetypal images are impersonal in nature. Unlike personal material, archetypal themes are timeless. They surface synchronistically across cultures and are not limited by historical sequence and place. Though impersonal in nature, an archetypal image's impact on us is very personal and profound. When we explore the origin of our archetypal image, its power increases rather than diminishing or dissolving. We literally "go through and beyond the form" of the image. We grow more whole.

For example, the same week of Mary's Wolf Mother session, I had lunch with a psychic colleague of mine, Shea Garridan. Shea gave me the marvelous resource book *The Donning International Encyclopedic Psychic Dictionary* as a gift, and I began browsing through it. As synchronicity would have it, I was looking up a word in the *S* section and my eyes fell on an unexpected she-wolf entry, which read, "SHE-WOLF—a female who takes the form of a wolf in order to help children in distress; PSYCHIC transforms herself into a vibrational frequency for a passage of time long enough to travel the streets and assist children and parents that are in psychological need."[1]

Can you sense the power of Mary's image and how it increases with this added information? Archetypes are translated into images, symbols, or myths so we can have a personal relationship with a very impersonal aspect of existence. Great thinkers, from Plato to Einstein, agree that this dimension of reality is purposive, following a grand design beyond our imagining. Archetypal reality is, indeed, very real. Do not mistake it for mere fantasy.

Archetypal forces have the power to transform consciousness. We do not know how this mystery of transformation occurs, but it occurs, nonetheless. Carl Jung writes, "In any situation of panic, whether external or internal, the archetypes intervene and allow a man [or woman] to react in an instinctively adapted way, just as if he [or she] had always known the situation."[2]

With this in mind, we can begin to understand how Mary's great, white She-Wolf Mother acts to protect her. Mary instinctively knows when and how to take or create space or get involved. Mary is less afraid of being entrapped by the entanglements of her personal mother and dysfunctional family system. She can trust her instincts to protect her. The more we trust our instincts, the more we are able to take care of ourselves and our unique needs.

Trust your needs. They are divinely inspired to guide you to the Mother of your soul. There is a source of nurturance within the psyche. This is an infinite Source, one that expresses itself endlessly. The Great Mother fulfills your needs perfectly, as only a divine Source can. She can take any form you can imagine. She is limitless.

Here is another example. June, a legal secretary and artist, had the experience of feeling the soothing and comforting presence of this archetype when, in meditation, she visualized herself sitting in a particular chair. This chair was exquisite: magnificently carved in wood with a comfortable leather thong seat that supported June as she sat in the chair. Spontaneously, as June meditated on the experience of being seated, she opened to an expanded state of peace and calm. While sitting in her chair, June heard words of wisdom in her inner ear. Sage advice from her higher Self was directly available to her. June did not know that the ancient Egyptian hieroglyph for the goddess Isis, the Divine Mother of the Egyptian mythos, literally means "seat" or "throne." Pharaoh ruled Egypt from the divine lap of the Mother. June, too, was held in the lap of divine love, healing, and wisdom in her inner world.

This is the Source that helped her heal the pain of her incest memories. While seated in her wisdom chair, June reviewed the incest experience and replayed telling her personal mother about what happened. She got in touch with what the earlier self needed. Little June needed to be believed. She also needed the loving assistance of an adult who could help her understand this confusing experience.

As June became aware of this earlier unfulfilled need, little June became aware that there was someone else present with her and her mother. She looked around and saw this attractive, caring, adult woman sitting comfortably in a beautifully carved chair. Her name was also June. Little June crawled into adult June's lap, and they sat in the chair together and talked. Little June didn't understand what was going on. Why did her cousin touch her like that? Why did her mother say, "Don't say bad things about your cousin"? She was scared she'd get in trouble like her cousin said she would.

Adult June validated little June's feelings: Her cousin's touches felt "yuckie." In addition to addressing the above questions, adult June explained to her earlier self that as she grew older she would explore touching and being touched, and that sometimes it would feel yuckie and sometimes it would feel OK. It would even feel real nice. Little June started growing older, progressing from childhood into her early teens, late teens, early adulthood, and then into her twenties. Adult June was able to foretell the future and tell her earlier selves about her exquisite journey through sensuality and sexuality as a woman. She told the younger June how she would learn to love herself as a woman through sharing sexual and emotional intimacies with both men and women. Older, wiser June described how she would learn to recognize and refuse to subject herself to abuse and sexual violation, and that, eventually, when she was in her thirties, June would come to marry a man who loved her very much. She helped little June gain perspective on her journey and see how life would become more joyful and fulfilling.

Archetypal reality surfaces in both nonphysical and physical reality. For example, Kate had suffered tremendous physical trauma very early in life. When she was three months old, she weighed only four and a half pounds and was losing weight steadily. Kate could not digest her mother's milk because she had been born with celiac, a digestive tract ailment. Kate returned to the hospital and remained there for nine months. During this first year of her life, her mother was certain that Kate would die. She even stopped coming to the hospital for the last seven months of Kate's hospitalization.

In session, Kate returned to the memory of the absence of her mother, who had forsaken her as dead. She felt the pain of abandonment. Kate also remembered a nurse who gave her tender, motherly love, sang her lullabies, held her and rocked her, and cooed at her fervently. In trance, she gave a complete description of this nurse with dark hair. She checked out this memory with her mother. There was, indeed, such a nurse on the ward who had taken a particular interest in Kate's welfare.

Ultimately, we are learning to trust the feeling that we are loved and loveable, and that this intangible inner experience is valid. Unconditional love is real and available to us from within the psyche. Anything other than this quality of unconditional love is personal mother material projected onto the archetype of Divine Mother. The personal overlay distorts our perception. Learn to separate the two from each other. There is a Source of unconditional love in our universe. It is not a human being, though it may come through a human agent. If we haven't experienced this quality of love from our personal mother or other human stand-ins for the Divine Mother, we know it by our sense of longing for what we never had. In our heart of hearts, we all know what it feels like to be deeply cared for and loved. One's sense of longing for unconditional love leads the way to one's inner Source of nurturing.

Ken, another client of mine, followed this inner sense of longing in meditation in one of our sessions together. After focusing on the longing, I suggested that he relax into the sense of feeling the longing fulfilled and use his imagination to embellish the experience of feeling loved the way he always wanted. This experience of feeling loved filled Ken's heart. His breathing slowed into expansive, deep breaths and he reported that this feeling of being loved completely filled him up. Spontaneously, he described that he felt he was in the presence of a tremendous light—a radiant star. This star showered him with gentle, tender, caring love. He felt soothed and comforted—at peace with himself. Then Ken, who had a history of extramarital infidelities, realized that his relationship triangles were attempts to find this ideal, nurturing love. He realized how he tried to fill in the void and insecurity he felt with a person who would make him feel loved. Being touched and filled with love from the inside out had a profound impact on him, bringing healing to his insecurity feelings.

One way to make personal contact with the Great Mother is to use the power of Mother Nature. In meditation, imagine that you are in a glorious place outdoors, one that brings you a luscious sense of peace and joy. Allow one part of nature to absorb your attention completely. It can be anything—a lake, a tree, a leaf, a bird, a cloud—just let the central image emerge. Whatever surfaces as a focus is a symbol chosen by the deep psyche. Let this symbol epitomize your link to the archetype of Mother Nature. It has the power to nurture you and to help you contact the strength and energy of the archetype. Use your symbol as a gateway to greater consciousness.

Meditate on the sounds, sights, texture, tastes, and smells of nature. Immerse yourself in your symbol. Experience it completely. Draw a picture of it or find inspiring photos from magazines. Write down everything you know about it. The strength of the archetype is available to us when we begin to build a personal relationship to this impersonal greater force via our chosen symbol. Just like we project the archetypal Mother onto our personal mother, we can use the power of introjection (that is, when we internalize the energy) to experience the archetype Mother Nature directly. We do this by personalizing that part in nature. Identify it as your Mother, the Mother of your soul. One way to do this is to write a poem about Her based on your factual description.

For example, Jake, a man who works in the banking industry, came to one of my workshops. In his inner work he found himself by the ocean. After the meditation, when I asked him to describe the ocean, he wrote, "The ocean is vast, great, and deep. The ocean colors are blue and gray-green. It releases water to the air and sun, collecting water from land. It is a habitat to billions. It is the birthplace of life—the sustainer of life." Mother Nature led him to the archetype of the Mother, which is then personalized as the Mother of his soul. He took his factual description and wrote the following poem about the Mother of his soul:

> My Mother is the originator of life,
> Is life before life,
> Is life today.
> She is not alive, but She sustains all aliveness.
> She receives and releases,
> Oblivious to the lives She carries within Her,
> Yet caring for their essence.
> Moody, vast, creator, destroyer,
> Healer,
> Receiver and giver.
> Inside of me is some of Her,
> Blood
> Is just a kind of seawater.

Life changes when we remember who our real Mother is. Jake has permission to be the vast, deep being that he is. How could he be otherwise? He is his Mother's son. Unlike his personal mother, who smothered him with her expectations of how he should be, his Great Mother receives him and releases him to be himself. There is permission for us to be exactly who we are. Nature reflects our nature to us. In our human world, we are taught to betray ourselves and our deeper essence in favor of social standards and customs. Contact with our true parents nurtures the soul. Deep feelings of self-love, self-acceptance, and unconditional love permeate the experience of inner contact with the Mother of our soul.

The specific form of the symbol used by the archetype does not matter. Archetypal forces come through both animate and inanimate objects, real and imagined. The form is not important; the presence of divine love is. When in contact with this sense of being loved, we know what we need. We know, without a doubt, what nourishes and nurtures us. There are many ways to make contact with this expanded state of consciousness, a state of pure knowing. The sense of clarity and inner certainty is key. Lord Alfred Tennyson described it like this:

> When I have been all alone, I would go into this waking trance, by repeating my own name to myself silently till all at once, as it were, out of the intensity of the consciousness of the individuality, individuality itself seemed to dissolve and fade away into nothingness. And this is not a confused state, but the opposite, the very clearest and surest state, utterly beyond words, where death was an almost laughable impossibility . . . I am ashamed of my feeble description. Have I not said the state is utterly beyond words?

How do you make contact with the Great Mother of your spirit? Come to *know* yourself. Separate your personal mother from the archetype of the Great Mother. Separation is the first stage of initiation. Use the memory of a time when you became aware that your personal mother was not living up to her role as Great Mother, the infinite Source of nurturing, by remembering a time you experienced betrayal by your mother. Jung distinguishes four psychic functions: thinking, feeling, sensing, and intuiting. These are your inner resources. Do your inner work by exploring and observing the impact of your betrayal memory on each of the four functions. We purify our thinking, feeling, sensing, and intuiting functions through developing witness consciousness.

Notice how you experience your betrayal memory in your body. Sense it completely to purify your body memory. In your inner work, allow the memory to be as real as possible. Notice what happens to your breathing and heartbeat. Observe how your stomach feels. What about your neck, shoulders, head, hands, feet, or other body parts? After you focus your attention on the sensations in your body, witness how a variety of emotional reactions surface in your awareness. Emotional purification means knowing what you are feeling. How do you feel emotionally? Many of us were told that our feelings were unacceptable. Cultivate self-acceptance by feeling all your feelings, and bring healing to this form of self-betrayal that denies the truth of your experience. See Exercise 2-A on page 64 and the Vocabulary of Feelings on pages 66 and 67 to help you translate your inner experiences into words. You can learn to let your feelings wash over you like waves of experience that rise within you to cleanse and release charged memories. Remember, emotions are simply energy in motion. Keep them moving. Frequently, physical movement like dance, exercise, massage, or bodywork will help you purify emotions through the release of memories that are held as tension in your body.

To purify your thoughts, become aware of rationalizations, opinions, and beliefs. Rationalization is based on old thinking that reinforces the false image that you are in control of a situation that is beyond your control. You rationalize that you are either doing a lousy job of it—ego deflation—or a masterful job at manipulating circumstances or situations—ego inflation. For example, Jake had a false sense of omnipotence. He thought that he had the superhuman power to fix his parents' marriage. Mary also suffered from inflated thinking. She believed she could control her husband's thoughts and feelings by being good or bad, loving or rejecting.

Inflated and deflated thinking both express low self-esteem and distort the truth. The truth is, we are each responsible for our own inner experience. Holding the belief that someone can make you feel or think a certain way is an example of an unhealed, earlier betrayal experience in which you were victimized. Part of healing the fixation is accepting that we were not in control of certain events in our lives at the time of victimization. Holding the belief that we should have been in control, or were somehow responsible for the event, sustains the experience of victimization. Acceptance of the limits of our control is the essential teaching of the death phase of the initiation from betrayal to trust.

Purification naturally leads to the third stage of initiation, symbolic death. As you witness each inner experience, exactly as it is, without adding anything or censoring anything, expect to go through the stages of mourning, including denial, anger, rationalization, depression, and acceptance. If you find yourself fixating on feeling mad, bad, or sad, you are caught in the death part of the cycle of initiation. Keep moving toward acceptance, and remember that there is life after death.

Unbiased self-observation during the death phase will purify your intuitive function and open the gates of true inner knowing. New knowledge is the fourth phase of initiation, the gateway between death and birth. As you review your betrayal experiences, look upon your memory with new eyes. Remember more than just the surface level of the memory and become aware of what you knew, but forgot to notice.

Seek a new perspective. See with the eyes of your soul. Hear the subtleties in the sounds.

Open your intuitive perception. When you review thoughts and beliefs, track the sound of the voices associated with different thoughts. Is it your voice? Someone else's? Whose? Use your feelings and body sensations to help you return, in memory, to an earlier time, perhaps to the very first time you were impressed with this image of reality. Observe who is present with you. What do you remember? Let your memory expand. What do you see, hear, feel, or know? Where is your mother? How does she respond to your need? How does her response impact you?

For example, Kate had the thought, "You'll never make it," and then intuitively realized it was her mother's voice. "She'll never make it," she heard her mother telling the hospital personnel when she forsook her child as dead and decided to stop coming to the hospital. Use your feelings as a perceptual tool rather than as an emotional value judgment.

Let the archetype of an omniscient, unconditionally loving Mother support your process. From the safety of feeling loved and held by the dark-haired nurse, Kate was able to see and feel her mother's anguish with some emotional detachment. She perceived the agony of defeat and failure that her mother harbored from watching her firstborn child waste away before her eyes, screaming with hunger, instead of growing plump and healthy. Kate intuitively perceived that her mother felt personally rejected by Kate's physiological rejection of her mother's milk. Kate understood her history of neglect and physical abuse in a new light. Great compassion washed over her. By grace, Kate felt relieved of the burden of the pain of the past.

Review the scene of your betrayal memory. Notice what you see and hear when you open the gates of your intuitive perception. What do you know to be true? What do you need, wish for, or desire? Imagine who or what can fulfill your need. Understand and accept yourself and your needs, along with the circumstances or situation that did not allow your needs to be filled at the time.

In a conversation with my grandfather, Yiddish scholar and mystic Wolf Snyder, I learned that the Tree of Life is the kabbalistic representation of an atom of consciousness. One of the subatomic particles, represented by Binah, the second sephirah on the kabalistic Tree of Life, is associated with the Mother. Binah is the presence of understanding. The word *binah* is a derivative of the Hebrew verb *l'hitbonane,* which means "to look attentively, observe, consider, reflect, study."[3] Self-knowledge through self-observation can make such a profound difference in our personal lives. The more consistent we are in training our attention to observe, consider, reflect upon, and study ourselves, the more we know ourselves and our needs.

Florence Scovel Shinn says, "There is a *Divine Design* for each person. . . . It usually flashes across the consciousness as an unattainable ideal— 'something too good to be true.' In reality it is man's true destiny (or destination) flashed to him from the Infinite Intelligence which is *within himself*."[4] This infinite intelligence communicates with us through symbols, colors, sounds, words, and energy rushes—anything our bodies receive. Receptivity is one of the universal teachings associated with the archetypal feminine force of Great Mother. She teaches us to receive. First, we receive ourselves exactly as we are. This allows us to experience another one of her divine attributes, unconditional love. Receptivity is the reward that she gives us for learning self-acceptance. Once you have learned to receive yourself, you can receive all else that you need in order to live and flourish. Your deepest needs shall be fulfilled, but not necessarily in the way you expect, nor from whom you expect, nor at the time you expect.

One of the most challenging dimensions of this betrayal-to-trust initiation is coming to trust and accept the divine timing that determines when our needs get fulfilled. Some of our essential needs did not get fulfilled in childhood. This creates a wound, a temporary impediment to our growth. We adapt and grow as best we can, in spite of the discomfort. At some point in time, frequently in adulthood, the adaptation we made becomes dysfunctional, maybe even maladaptive. The pain of maintaining a dysfunctional pattern becomes unbearable. A call from deep within the psyche invites us to embark upon a healing journey to remember, integrate, and heal the wounds.

When we turn our attention to healing, a marvelous discovery awaits us. Locked away within the wound are valuable childhood gifts. Because of this, I like to think of our childhood wounds as time-release capsules. When healed, those innate talents that are gleaned from many lifetimes of experience—our inborn childhood gifts that we put away with our old baseball glove or favorite dolls—are remembered and released into our lives. The timing of the release is not an accident of fate, nor is the wound that set the process in motion. As author Demetra

George says in her book *Mysteries of the Dark Moon,* "The pattern of our fate is not imposed upon us by some external power but comes from the depths of our own souls."[5] The miraculous timing of this healing occurs at exactly the right time—when we have the wisdom, maturity, ability, facility, training, skill, resources, contacts, or connections to make our childhood dreams, the dreams of our soul, come true. Betrayal teaches you to release expectations. Trust reminds you to remain receptive to what you need next to fulfill the divine design, the pattern of your soul.

Trust is a learned skill. Have you ever seen a baby playing peekaboo? You cover the baby's eyes, then you suddenly pull your hands away, calling out, "Peekaboo!" The baby giggles in delight because you have magically reappeared. That is how we are when we begin our relationship with our spiritual Source of nurturance. We don't believe that there is really something or someone there for us, let alone within us. "If I can't see it, it doesn't exist." This response comes from much earlier stages of development. The animal part of us, the Pavlovian dog in each of us, thrives on predictability and wants Divine Mother to look the same and act the same every time, but Her form keeps changing. One moment, the Source of nurturance may look like our birth mother. The next moment, she looks like an image of a great, white wolf, a chair of wisdom, or a kind, dark-haired nurse.

The Great Mother changes every day, moment by moment. Across cultures, she is symbolized by the moon. Sometimes she looks like she's not there at all, during dark moon phases. However, we learn to trust that the moon is there, whether we see it or not. In psychosocial development, a baby learns that the primary caregiver keeps showing up. "There is someone or something there, even though I can't see them right now." Even when the object is not physically present, the baby has developed the ability to hold an internal image of the primary caregiver. The baby develops object constancy.

Our physical and social development trains us for our psychospiritual developmental challenges. As spiritual beings, we learn to hold an internal impression of our Great Mother, and ultimately, we strive to embody Her presence, to *give-forth* her love and wisdom. When we feel lost, we transfer our need for contact with the Divine Mother to a person, place, or thing that we expect will nurture us. We temporarily get caught in the projection of the Divine Mother as an object that is missing from our lives. We feel betrayed, but in reality, we betray our own nature, the part of us that knows. We temporarily lose ourselves in a game of peekaboo.

The emotional darkness produced by this experience of separation from the Source and the ensuing loss of Self during the dark moon phase of the betrayal-to-trust initiation is the nighttime, which puts us to sleep to bring us dreams. In the darkness, our deepest, most essential needs are revealed to us. Beyond the nightmare of one's fears, the dream of one's soul will be revealed. Intuition is the sliver of moonlight that brightens the night sky and helps you to see your way through the darkness. Instinctively, we are guided toward the fulfillment of our needs.

For example, Kate's healing of her mother wound graced Kate with compassion and sensitivity, which she now brings to her professional practice as a psychotherapist. When I met Kate, she had experienced over fifty years of physical abuse, starting in infancy with her deprivation of nourishment and constant hunger pangs, followed by painful hospital procedures, continuing throughout childhood under the guise of discipline, and culminating in her marriage to a man who was physically violent with her. When she was fifty years old, she divorced her husband, and by the age of fifty-one, Kate returned to school for a degree in psychology. During our therapy together, we traced the physical abuse and pattern of threat to her survival back to her congenital celiac condition, subsequent hospitalization, and near death during that first year of her life.

In the midst of one session, her higher Self, in the form of an inner voice, told her that she was a wounded healer. Kate intuitively understood that her tortuous past gave her personal insight and training that would help her help others move through their pain. This direct experience was more specialized training than she could have ever gained in school or gleaned from books. Currently, she has a full private practice in which she works with families and people dealing with AIDS, suicides, suicide attempts, murders, families who have lost children, and hospice staff and other helping professionals who suffer from burnout. With compassion, insight, and detachment, she has seen her way through the darkness and is gifted in helping others in their passage through the shadows.

Betrayal teaches us to distinguish between the death and birth phases of initiation. During death, we learn to let go. Our process of letting go depicts a way through the death experience. Before birth, we go through the same scary processes and repeat the same patterns, but we introduce a new understanding to the experiences in our life. Frequently, one recapitulates one's entire birth and growth process, including the tests and trials one has already surmounted. Having lived through death before, we know the value of release and acceptance. Thus, it is possible to go through it all much faster the next time around. Instead of death, this recapitulation becomes part of the birth of a new way of being.

For example, around the same time that June was doing her inner work on healing her incest memories, the apartment in which she and her fiancé were living was being torn apart and converted into two smaller dwellings. While she was growing in leaps and bounds internally, her external world was becoming more and more cramped. June received a very clear inner message that, even though the rent was low and there was a great view, it was time to move. Both she and her fiancé, Paul, wanted to buy a home and live in a less urban environment. On their honeymoon they went to Vancouver, Washington, where their $10,000 savings was more than adequate for a deposit on a house. It felt right, and they decided to move there.

The stress of June's move to Vancouver activated her patterned fear response. About six months after the move, I received a letter from her asking for referrals to therapists in the area.

> . . . Having that new incest memory while with you last October has continued to send me into a tailspin. My entire foundation has been shaken, and I don't know which way is up. I always felt so smug about having remembered all the abuse, and I could minimize the incest because it happened only once. Now, all of that has been taken away, and I feel so unsure of myself and unsure of what all happened.
>
> I'm also experiencing feelings on a new level. I feel terrified knowing that incest really happened to me—that I am an abused child. I feel like a child . . . it's not like it happened to me back then, but right now. Last night, as I turned over the entire matter to my higher Self, I cried, thinking I might have a child who could be abused like I was. I am so afraid of that, and I didn't even know it until last night. . . .
>
> . . . I cry, thinking about how I've always felt I had to be the one to take care of myself, all alone. I've been talking a lot lately

about how I can't do it all alone, that I need other people. So I reached out and got a sponsor. Still, it's hard to let in the fact—the truth—that I really do need people and that it is OK and healthy and human. . . .

Change will provoke a startle response. It is part of our animal ancestry, the instinctive fear reactions, the faint, fight, flight, and freeze responses that are wired into all mammals. Because of this, it is not uncommon to regress to earlier stages of development when faced with something new. The move to Vancouver triggered a regression to earlier stages of development in June's life, to a time when, as a child, she and her family moved in with her cousin's family. During that move, June's personal mother was not there for her. During this move, because she was temporarily caught in a fear reaction, June was not attending to all the ways that Great Mother was present in her life. She was only partly aware of the help that was already all around her, and the second half of her letter shifted in tone as she described all the good fortune and support she had experienced during their move:

> Paul has been very supportive for me. He suggested we read parts of *Courage to Heal* together, and we have. . . .
>
> . . . Within a week [of our arrival in Vancouver] we both had jobs. . . . After being here thirteen days, we found the house we wanted to buy. . . . The process took over two months. So we spent the remaining 6 weeks renting a room from a woman in AA. We got her name off a bulletin board for a room for rent. We have since become good friends. . . .
>
> . . . I found a list of what we wanted in a house that we had written in Oakland. We got everything we wanted. After reading the list last week, I wish I hadn't written "trees" in such large letters with an exclamation mark. We sure got what we asked for. We're planting vegetables in the tiny sunny areas. . . .

Support from the archetypal Source of nurturance comes through us primarily as self-knowledge and to us from external sources in the form of acknowledgments that uphold our deepest truth. Great Mother takes care of us by magnetically drawing to us what we need. June's letter abounded with lucky coincidences, from new friends and synchronicities to the purchase of her dream home. In her letter she described their 1,900-square-foot, two-story farmhouse with plenty of room for her art studio. It was built on a double lot resplendent with fruit trees and bushes, a grape arbor, raspberry bushes, a one-hundred-year-old rosebush, and six old-growth Douglas firs. The trees were especially important to June—during one of our more poignant sessions before the move, June and I spent some time under the redwood trees on my front lawn. We sat together in silence on the soft, pulpy ground beneath those majestic, imperturbable trees. Soon, her whole manner changed. Anxiety melted away into tranquility and calm. Trees were very nurturing to June.

Even though the underlying tone of her letter was one of anxiety about whether she would get what she needed from a therapist, the rest of her letter was filled with a description of the many mini-miracles of a life in which her deepest desires were being fulfilled. The right therapist was just a matter of time.

The pattern of June's personal process, including her fear and vulnerability, is part of her path. She is going forward, not backward. Movement through our patterns marks our ascension along the spiral path of conscious evolution. What you experience now, you have gone through before. That we all repeat themes is universal, yet the nature of the pattern, and how one responds to it, is distinctly unique to each individual. The patterns that you repeat mark your path—and are signs that you are on *your* path, and not someone else's.

Most importantly, you are not alone on your path. You have inner and outer resources that help guide you. Great Mother is one of those resources. Great Mother came to June in many forms: a loving husband, a book on incest, a job, new friends, a new home on a gorgeous lot, garden space, flowers, studio space, AA meetings, a sponsor, a massage therapist, and the trees she loved so much. In this sense, Great Mother was everywhere as long as June was not attached to the form She took when She came to answer her call. June's story demonstrates the magnetic power of archetypal Mother to draw to us all that we need to heal physically, emotionally, mentally, and spiritually. Every need contains within it the seed of its own fulfillment. Healing the personal mother wound teaches us to trust that fulfillment will come to us.

We intuitively know that an infinite intelligence is at work in our lives and is bringing us all that we need. We choose to merge with our highest Self and discover the highest good contained in our personal experiences rather than merge with our earlier, wounded self. We learn to recognize the flip-flops between these two states of consciousness as a creative tension that signals that we are in transition, the last stage before being born into a state of Self-integration. Rebirth is the final stage of initiation. Through the process of initiation, we discover our instinctive powers, talents, and strengths. We give birth to a new identity, one that brings meaning back to our lives. From this identity, we carve out a new role for ourselves. Observe how you are giving birth to trusting that Great Mother is present in your life by contacting your inner sense of certainty and Self-trust. Continue to build trust in yourself and what you know to be true.

As Tennyson said, "Out of the intensity of the consciousness of the individuality, individuality itself seemed to dissolve and fade away into nothingness." From this nothingness we are born. Direct contact with this inner state of consciousness, "where death was an almost laughable impossibility," dissolves our fear of the unknown. Though we cannot predict or control the stream of unpredictable events in our lives, contact with the Source within consciousness brings a sense of certainty to these uncertain times. Whatever the event or circumstance, it is governed by an infinite intelligence that expresses itself through us.

Contact with this inner Source nurtures one's ability to cope with the stress of living in a world in transition. Remember, transition is one of the phases of rebirth. We are birthing a new collective consciousness—a new form that is archetypal in nature. The deity is being born through us. We need Great Mother for this task in consciousness. Who else, other than Mother, is equipped to give birth? She is the vessel through whom birth happens. From her womb, humanity is being born in each of us. She comes to each of us as an expanded state of consciousness that draws to us exactly what we need, in exactly the right way, at exactly the right time. The heart of your experience is Her womb, self-expression is the birth canal, and realization of your heart's vision is Her creation being born.

Observe Your Feelings

If you have been conditioned to disregard your feelings, start by observing your body reactions to your memories. Emotions are "energy in motion." Emotions move through your body as sensations.

1. **Think of a betrayal memory that you would like to resolve.** As you review the memory in your mind, or perhaps as you tell a friend of your past experience, notice if you are holding tension in your stomach, jaw, shoulders, or chest. Observe how you are breathing: fast, slow, shallow, deep. Continue to expand on your body awareness by describing sensations like hot, cold, tingles, pressure, knots, butterflies, etc.

2. **Now ask yourself, "What am I feeling?"** Look at the Vocabulary of Feelings on pages 66 and 67. Begin by scanning the "mild" intensity words at the bottom of the page. As you find words that resonate with your inner experience, begin to look at the other words in that column. Identify your core experience by reading the title at the top of the column. For example, feeling unappreciated or let down is on the same continuum as feeling rejected or hurt; while feeling sad, low, blue, or down is on the depressed continuum; and feeling embarrassed, regretful, or remorseful is on the guilt or shame continuum.

3. **Trust your feelings.** They have the energy to move you from death to rebirth and Self-renewal. Continue your quest to discover deeper truths. Ask yourself, "What is at the core of this pattern?" and "What do I really want or need at the deepest level of my soul?"

4. **Once you have identified your feelings, begin to identify your personal patterns.** Include examples from your personal history and social traditions or cultural conditions that perpetuate the pattern. Explore the ideas and beliefs that historically support the pattern. Learn to witness your thoughts instead of believing them to be absolute truths.

5. **Speak what you know.** Tell a friend how you feel and what you have discovered about yourself. Learn to communicate your feelings with "I" statements.

Witness Your Thoughts

1. Observe your self-image by examining thoughts, attitudes, and beliefs. Identify righteous resentments or cynical generalizations about your betrayer or the betrayal. Your personal betrayal experience will lead you into the lap of your Divine Mother. Notice "poor me" feelings, or name times when you were victimized. Identify your negative underlying belief. Here are some examples.

> June: "When I told my mother about what my cousin had done to me, and she said, 'Don't say bad things about your cousin,' I had no one to turn to. *I'm all alone.*"

> Mary: "I'm afraid my lover will leave me. *I'm not good enough.*"

> Ken: "I'm so easily manipulated by a pretty face. I love getting seduced, and I hate it, too. *I'm so weak.*"

> Jake: "When I was born, I was supposed to fix my parents' marriage, somehow. *It's all up to me.*"

> Kate: "*You'll never make it. . . .*"

2. Ask yourself where that underlying belief came from.

3. Open your intuitive perception. Listen with your inner ear to the sound of the voice in your thoughts. Whose voice is it?

4. Open other intuitive channels. What do you hear, see, feel, and know to be true?

The Vocabulary of Feelings[7]

	Happy	Caring	Depressed	Inadequate	Fearful

STRONG	thrilled
	on cloud nine
	ecstatic
	overjoyed
	excited
	elated
	sensational
	exhilarated
	fantastic
	terrific
	on top of the
	   world
	turned on
	euphoric
	enthusiastic
	delighted
	marvelous
	great
		tenderness
		   toward
		affection for
		captivated by
		attached to
		devoted to
		adoration
		loving
		infatuated
		enamored
		cherish
		idolize
		worship
			desolate
			dejected
			hopeless
			alienated
			depressed
			gloomy
			dismal
			bleak
			in despair
			empty
			barren
			grieved
			grief
			despair
			grim
				worthless
				good for nothing
				washed up
				powerless
				helpless
				impotent
				crippled
				inferior
				emasculated
				useless
				finished
				like a failure
					terrified
					frightened
					intimidated
					horrified
					desperate
					panicky
					terror-stricken
					stage fright
					dread
					vulnerable
					paralyzed

MODERATE	cheerful lighthearted happy serene wonderful up aglow glowing in high spirits jovial riding high elevated neat	caring fond of regard respectful admiration concern for hold dear prize taken with turned on trust close	distressed upset downcast sorrowful demoralized discouraged miserable pessimistic tearful weepy rotten awful horrible terrible blue lost melancholy	inadequate whipped defeated incompetent inept overwhelmed ineffective lacking deficient unable incapable small insignificant like Casper Milquetoast unfit unimportant incomplete no good immobilized	afraid scared fearful apprehensive jumpy shaky threatened distrustful risky alarmed butterflies awkward defensive
MILD	glad good contented satisfied gratified pleasant pleased fine	warm toward friendly like positive toward	unhappy down low bad blah disappointed sad glum	lacking confi- dence unsure of yourself uncertain weak inefficient	nervous anxious unsure hesitant timid shy worried uneasy bashful embarrassed ill at ease doubtful jittery on edge uncomfortable self-conscious

CONFUSED	HURT	ANGRY	LONELY	GUILT-SHAME
bewildered	crushed	furious	isolated	sick at heart
puzzled	destroyed	enraged	abandoned	unforgivable
baffled	ruined	seething	all alone	humiliated
perplexed	degraded	outraged	forsaken	disgraced
trapped	pain(ed)	infuriated	cut off	degraded
confounded	wounded	burned up		horrible
in a dilemma	devastated	pissed off		mortified
befuddled	tortured	fighting mad		exposed
in a quandary	disgraceful	nauseated		
full of questions	humiliated	violent		
confused	anguished	indignant		
	at the mercy of	hatred		
	cast off	bitter		
	forsaken	galled		
	rejected	vengeful		
	discarded	hateful		
		vicious		
mixed-up	hurt	resentful	lonely	ashamed
disorganized	belittled	irritated	alienated	guilty
foggy	shot down	hostile	estranged	remorseful
troubled	overlooked	annoyed	remote	crummy
adrift	abused	upset with	alone	to blame
lost	depreciated	agitated	apart from others	lost face
at loose ends	criticized	mad	insulated from	demeaned
going around in	defamed	aggravated	others	
circles	censured	offended		
disconcerted	discredited	antagonistic		
frustrated	disparaged	exasperated		
flustered	laughed at	belligerent		
in a bind	maligned	mean		
ambivalent	mistreated	vexed		
disturbed	ridiculed	spiteful		
helpless	devalued	vindictive		
embroiled	scorned			
	mocked			
	scoffed at			
	used			
	exploited			
	debased			
	slammed			
	slandered			
	impugned			
	cheapened			
uncertain	put down	uptight	left out	regretful
unsure	neglected	disgusted	excluded	wrong
bothered	overlooked	bugged	lonesome	embarrassed
uncomfortable	minimized	turned off	distant	at fault
undecided	let down	put out	aloof	in error
	unappreciated	miffed		responsible for
	taken for granted	irked		blew it
		perturbed		goofed
		ticked off		lament
		teed off		
		chagrined		
		cross		
		dismayed		
		impatient		

Learn to TRUST

T — Turn inward for TRUTH.
- What is your truth?
- What do you need right now?
- Imagine how or what can fill that need for you.

R — Relax, Release, and Receive.
- Relax your body and mind to help you let go.
- Release attachment to outcomes.
- Release your expectations of who or what will fulfill your need, and how, where, and when it will get fulfilled.
- Remember to breathe. Like Lamaze childbirth instruction suggests, remember to do your breathing when giving birth.
- What else can you do for your body today that will help you relax and feel taken care of?
- Create a relaxation ritual.

U — Use Intuition to Understand.
- Identify and use your inner resources. Observe your thoughts, feelings, body sensations, and intuitions. Also, use your outer resources. (See Chapter 1 exercises for suggestions.)
- Purify your inner resources, then review your experience and your needs from this new perspective.
- Reach out to outer resources. Affirm: *"I know what I need."*
- Affirm: *"I am willing to ask for the help I need."*
- Learn to receive. Affirm: *"I am willing to receive the help I need."*
- Identify how and where you are already getting what you need right now. Affirm: *"I receive all that I need at just the right time, in just the right way."*
- Name one thing you did today that nurtured you.

S — Speak, Share, Stand Up.
- Ask for what you need. And keep asking a variety of resources.
- Don't get stuck on just one person, place, or thing as the only source to fulfill your needs.

T — Try again and TRUST.
- Keep doing your inner work.
- Refine your understanding and keep expressing yourself.

Chapter 3

Betrayal of the Father

Gateway to Self-Direction and Purpose in Life

Wound: If you suffer a father wound, your sense of purpose in life has been injured. You lack a sense of self that guides you to your greatest fulfillment in the world.

Truth: Each one of us is unique, born to fill a place no one else can fill, to do something that no one else can do. Self-expression, through the fulfillment of our creative potential, is our divine destiny—our mission or purpose in life.

Healing: Remember your vital dream, vision, or ideals. Let the Source of your vision inspire you to risk living your dream.

Not long ago, in another time and place, there lived a king. This was a real king, just as real as any of the few remaining kings who exist in the world today. One day, a son was born to this king. Oh, there was much rejoicing, celebrating the birth of the king's heir to the throne. The queen's musicians played, and the court dancers danced, and they celebrated the birth of this child. At the naming ceremony, the Brahman priests of the day looked at the stars at the time the child was born and looked at the markings on his little body and proclaimed, "This child has the signs of greatness. He will be a great ruler for your kingdom, or he will become a Buddha—an awakened or enlightened one—and leave the throne and your kingdom behind to become a great saint, one of the greatest to come to the Earth."

The newborn's father said, "Is there nothing that can be done to ensure that he will become king after me?" And his wise men said, "Oh, yes, sire. As long as he stays within the palace gates and never sees the pains of the world, he will remain within your halls. Then he is sure to become a great monarch." The king named his child Siddhartha, which means "one whose aim is accomplished." The king nurtured his son in every way and proclaimed, "Siddhartha must never be in want and he must never seek to go beyond the palace gates."

Siddhartha was raised in complete luxury and followed the ways of his father. But his father, King Suddhodana, was afraid that the predictions of the priests would come true and that his son and heir would become a wandering ascetic like the saints of his day and age. So the king built three palaces for Siddhartha: one for winter, one for summer, and one for rainy seasons. During the winter months, the young prince was entertained exclusively by female musicians. Siddhartha never left the palace grounds. The king trained him well in the art of statecraft, archery, riding, and all manner of worldly life that befits a king. Prince Siddhartha learned all the ways of a warrior, for in this country, like all countries, kings were warriors and rulers. At the age of sixteen, in the tradition of his time, the prince married his cousin Princess Gopa-Yasodhara. And so the son was prepared to succeed his father on the throne.

The overprotective father and the father who wants his child to follow in his footsteps are only two forms of the betrayal of the father. The overprotective father is usually the plight of girl children. The father who forces the child to take over the family business, be it owning and operating a shoe store, becoming a doctor, or ruling a kingdom, is usually the burden of boys. Killing a child with kindness is not the only form of soul death promulgated by the father. Frequently, betrayal of the father is harsh, brutal, or incomprehensible. I have known men and women who have suffered every variety of betrayal wounds. Some, like Saturn's progeny, had been swallowed whole, gobbled up by the authoritarian opinions and beliefs of their father's rule in the family. They had been physically, sexually, and emotionally dominated, threatened, coerced, and intimidated.

Then there are those who feel deceived, lied to, or like Ishmael or Esau, cheated out of their birthright. There are some who identify with Isaac, who was taught by his father Abraham that idolatry and human sacrifice were wrong, and then, years later, was bound by his father in preparation for slaughter as a sacrifice to God. Many sons and daughters feel forced to make sense out of perplexing contradictions and double standards that must be obeyed. Others suffer the pains of emotional isolation, physical desertion, or absenteeism. They, too, feel forsaken by their father, not unlike in the New Testament when God the Father forsook his son, Jesus, while he languished under the pain of crucifixion.

Betrayal of the father is essential. In that moment of being forsaken on the cross, Jesus was forced to discover and master resurrection for himself. He became the Master, Creator of Life. Resurrection, the personal creation of life from that which is dead, is the message of Jesus. It is also the mystery teaching of the betrayal-to-trust initiation. Like Jesus on the cross, we, too, experience betrayal to discover and master resurrection for ourselves. We must become potent enough to inseminate ourselves with new life.

There is a Creator of Life, a supremely dynamic, inspirational Source of energy, within the human soul. This inner authority guides the soul toward its right fulfillment. This is part of the secret teaching of the patriarchy and betrayal of the father. Patriarchal tradition says that authority is external to one's self and that this external authority will betray you. Paradox is the gateway to higher consciousness. Our fathers must betray us so that we break from the patriarchal tradition of looking to external authority to tell us what is right.

I was struck by the impact of the betrayal of the father when I read Chaim Potok's *The Chosen*. The passage where Danny describes his love-hate relationship with his father, a renowned Chasidic Rabbi, is a perfect illustration of the father's mystery teaching. Danny tells his friend, "My father believes in silence. When I was ten or eleven years old, I complained to him about something, and he told me to close my mouth and look into my soul. He told me to stop running to him every time I had a problem. I should look into my own soul for the answer."[1] Even if our fathers are wise enough to deliver the message hidden in the mystery, it still cuts us to the quick. Betrayal hurts, no matter how or when it is delivered. In fact, the delivery is part of what makes it a betrayal experience. James Hillman says that

> The father demonstrates in his own person the possibility of betrayal in even the closest trust. He reveals his own treacherousness, stands before his son in naked humanity. . . . I, a father, a man, cannot be trusted. Man is treacherous. . . . The father says, in short, I have betrayed you as all are betrayed in the treachery of life created by God. The boy's initiation into life is the initiation into adult tragedy.[2]

Action without understanding is treacherous indeed. Betrayal becomes the end if we do not engage the deeper levels of the psyche where we discover an inner Source of knowing (Mother) that inspires us to act (Father). Father without Mother reflects patriarchal traditions throughout recorded history. This is the "treachery of life . . . the initiation into adult tragedy" that perpetuates the five emotional ordeals associated with the traditional betrayal response.

Betrayal is an initiation of the soul. We need both archetypal Mother and archetypal Father on this soul journey in order to move beyond the death of betrayal and into a new life. Father is the inseminator. He inspires us to risk and provides us with the sense that we are protected as we move along our path in life. He affirms that we have a path. If we follow the path of initiation, betrayal of the father leads to life instead of soul death.

Let us consider Doris. Doris is a woman who had been physically beaten and verbally threatened by her alcoholic father throughout her childhood and teenage years. Her father was a trucker, and when he came home, the whole family would have to revolve around his drunken, violent tempers. She remembered that they moved to another state once because he had been involved in a brawl where a man was shot. She knew she came from an abusive family; the memory of sexual abuse, however, was still locked away in the safety of her unconscious.

Several months into our therapy, while undergoing guided meditation and regression work, she discovered some very painful memories revealing an incident of sexual abuse by her father. Her ability to deny and repress was shattered. She was devastated and repulsed as different memories surfaced. She realized that as a child she had handled much of her pain and fear by going into psychic and intuitive realms. She literally left her body. In the limitless expanse of the mind she had escaped the pain. Her psychic abilities helped her another way, too. She became fairly good at reading danger in her home situation, and she did her best to avoid both being the "reason" for the abuse and being around "when the shit hit the fan."

Doris began the first phase of initiation by separating her issues from those of her parents and the other family members. Using the tools and resources she already had, we used her nonphysical friends to guide and protect her as she broke through the denial into anger and grief. She became aware of deeper truths. In her early years, it had been safer for Doris not to feel, rather than to risk feeling pain and chance an accidental expression of emotion that would make her a target for her father's abuse. Doris soon realized that when she said, "It bothered me," she was really saying, "I'm angry." Acknowledging these feelings initiated new knowledge.

For Doris, expressing herself was part of her initiatory rebirth. She was learning to trust for the first time in her life. She learned that she could trust her inner feelings. Doris also reached for outer resources. In addition to therapy and work with her inner guides, she joined an incest survivors group to find out how other women handled their pasts. She was curious about whether they confronted their abusers and the nature of their confrontations. She also started to receive energy bodywork to heal wounds from these early childhood experiences and to help her relax into her present life—one in which she could have the power to confront her abuser, take care of herself, and protect her own children.

The first test of betrayal, the ordeal of righteous resentment and the desire for vengeance, is transformed through developing good communication skills. Doris began to practice communicating her thoughts and feelings to others. She started by setting limits with family members for the first time in her life. Her father was never allowed to be alone with her children. During one phase of the work, her father was not invited to, or allowed into, her home. That was her truth at the time; truth is relative, not absolute. As Doris integrated the other betrayal tests and teachings, her truth reflected deeper, more profound levels of personal healing and increased Self-trust.

With the second ordeal, the projection of the shadow, Doris looked at the things she did not trust about her father and then explored how and when she expressed those same negative traits. For example, both Doris and her father were escape artists. He used alcohol and she used fantasy to escape discomfort, and like her father, she also made many assumptions about what other people thought and looked for hidden motives behind their actions. Instead of examining her fantasies, she reacted to others based on her assumptions. This was like her dad, too.

With practice, Doris was able to differentiate between intuitive perceptions and psychological projections. She took intuition development classes from psychologically sophisticated instructors and learned how to use her intuition to develop deeper insight into the events in her life—to stop avoiding conflict and to confront and accept reality. She also began exploring out-of-body trips consciously, rather than as an automatic defense, and she developed her natural abilities as a medium.

Archetypal Father takes the form of both inner and outer guidance and assistance. Archetypal Father used synchronicity, coincidence, and opportunity to guide Doris to the next step along her path in life. For example, Bill, a friend of hers who died during the summer after our first year of therapy, came to visit Doris in the middle of the night a few months after he died. He woke her up and told her that she had a hormone imbalance and that a series of blood tests measuring her adrenal, thyroid, and thymus glands would help. Doris picked a doctor from the yellow pages and had the tests performed. The results from the tests that Bill had recommended indicated that Doris suffered from an unusual medical syndrome. Synchronistically, the doctor she had found in the phonebook specialized in, and published papers on, that particular area of medicine. This doctor was the perfect resource to take care of Doris. Through events like this, Doris discovered more truths. She could trust her perceptions, and with the help of others, she could take care of herself. She was not alone on her journey.

The discovery that Bill and her doctor were available to help her enabled her to question her unexamined generalization that men were untrustworthy. "Men" also included her husband, Lou. Doris had a lot of mixed feelings about her marriage. While Lou was a dedicated father, his alcoholism prompted erratic behavior and irrational mood swings. Doris married Lou to get out of her parents' home when she was eighteen. When she was twenty-three, Doris and Lou tried to separate for the first time. It didn't work. They got back together and had two children. Seven years later, and after two years of therapy, she decided that the only way to work it out was to leave him. Yes, she loved him, and according to a local psychic, they were soul mates. And, yes, she felt her karma with him was complete. She was free to be with him or not to be with him. For over a year she considered how, when, and if she and Lou could separate, and what impact that would have on their lives and the lives of their children.

Doris realized she could separate from Lou after she went through her first holiday season without the usual ritual of Thanksgiving and Christmas dinners in the company of her mother and father. After the start of the new year, she moved out. Living on her own, she went through many shifts and changes, coordinating childcare, dating, and life as a single parent. Another synchronistic event had a great impact on Doris. She met a younger man named Max. Max did not fit her old generalizations about men. He was attracted to her, respected her, and encouraged her to take risks.

Doris had been out of contact with her parents since before the holidays. Now, after living on her own for the first time in her life, she felt she could risk a visit. When she and Max met with her parents, Doris had another breakthrough. She found that she could be herself with them, that her boundaries were strong and secure. Physical separation was not the only way to be a separate individual. Doris could trust herself to be autonomous, separate, and whole. This realization allowed Doris to build a new relationship with her personal father. She feels comfortable accepting his advice on certain matters, like real estate, for example; but she does not have to give her authority away to him. She knows and accepts that her personal father has blind spots and is limited, and that she has limits, too.

Just as many men project aspects of the archetypal Mother onto the significant women in their lives, women frequently expect the men in their lives to be their guardian and protector—archetypal Father in the flesh. As one confronts father betrayal wounds, the men in one's life are free to be themselves instead of fulfill the role of Divine Father. When Doris felt the presence of a guiding force in her life and realized that this power did not come from her personal father, her husband, or Max, she began to reflect on her values and what she really wanted from life. Her dream included creating a family life that nurtured and supported all the individuals in the family.

After six months of separation, Doris and Lou decided to get back together. They wanted to create a family life for their children and support each other and their children's continued growth. They felt they could do this best together as a family unit. The past was complete, and now they could start anew. During the separation, while Doris found herself, Lou found that he could do laundry, make dinner for himself and the children, and based on the advice of his medical doctor, accept that he needed to stop drinking alcohol. For the first time, Lou and Doris felt they had common goals and a future they could create together. They both enjoyed being parents and valued family. Doris no longer needed Lou to be anyone or anything in particular. She accepted that he was a person on his own journey, just like her.

Initiation takes us through a conscious separation from, instead of a wounding rejection of, our betrayer. The path of initiation describes a way through emotional traumas. In the privacy of our own process, we can pass through emotional purification and symbolic death. Feelings of anger and grief are acknowledged and honored rather than unconsciously indulged or acted out. A personal commitment to growth, guided by a quest for meaning, value, and purpose, breeds a new perspective, a personal revelation. When one takes the time to turn inward and discover a deeper truth, understanding and insight are born. Birth is the phase when the teaching, or inner truth, is consciously brought forth through inspired actions. Like Doris getting the blood tests, choosing to move away from, and then back in with, her husband, or developing a new relationship with her father, step-by-step the action is congruent with one's inner experience. One acts in the world, rather than reacts to the world. Action (Father) joined with understanding and inner knowing (Mother) leads to compassionate action and mercy instead of treachery.

Healing mother betrayal wounds teaches us self-love. Healing father betrayal wounds guides us to express our love. According to Tibetan Buddhism, the Buddha has three faces: compassion, wrath, and peace. The wrathful expression slices through our illusions about love. But wrath without compassion can be malicious and merciless. Compassion without the wrathful aspect leads to soppy sentimentality. Peace is a place of equanimity, mindful detachment from the pushes and pulls of personal preference and external circumstance. Without the other two elements, peace may lead to lethargy. Wrath, compassion, and peace combine to support right action. These mysteries of the Father cannot be taught, only learned through experience.

The archetypal Father guides us to act with love and to express our inner love in our interactions with others through right action. The way to express love through action varies slightly from culture to culture, but the message is the same.

Christianity: "All things whatsoever ye would that men should do to you, do ye even so to them: for this is the Law and the Prophets."—Matthew 7:12

Judaism: "What is hateful to you, do not to your fellow men. That is the entire Law; all the rest is commentary."—Hillel, Talmud 31a

Brahmanism: "This is the sum of duty: Do naught unto others which would cause you pain if done to you."—Mahabharata 5.1517

Buddhism: "Hurt not others in ways that you yourself would find hurtful."—Udanavarga 5.18

Confucianism: "Surely it is the maxim of loving-kindness: Do not unto others that you would not have them do unto you."—Analects 15:23

Taoism: "Regard your neighbor's gain as your own gain, and your neighbor's loss as your own loss."—T'ai Shang Kan Ying P'ien

Islam: "No one of you is a believer until he desires for his brother that which he desires for himself."—Sunna

We must each internalize the teachings of the archetype of the Father on our own. Betrayal is a sacred event that has the power to move us to a personal awakening, realization, integration, and expression of divine love. Others can tell us the truth, but it is realized when we discover and experience it for ourselves.

Betty was catapulted into an all-encompassing experience of this universal love as she turned inward to heal the psychological wounds of her father's physical abuse. She came into my office one day full of anxiety, feeling overwhelmed by unnamed fears. Her eyes darted around the room. I noticed her scanning the crystal spheres and stones that were perched on the windowsill beside my couch, and suggested she choose a stone to hold. She picked up the rose-quartz sphere, closed her eyes, and we began our inner work.

She let her body relax and described feeling energy from the ball. She said she felt round, soft ripples enter her body through her hands, mix with the fear, break the fear up, and end in a point of no movement on her breastplate. There is always a point of stillness within us, a place where the energy is not moving. Kinesthetically, this point marks the spot of entry into the deeper levels of the psyche. It is the crossroad where mind and body meet to show us the path of the soul. For Betty, this point was in her heart. She saw and felt a cold, sharp, bladelike metal plate covering her sternum, protecting her chest.

She lifted the blade out, and it turned into a dark gray cloud. In the cloud she saw her father as a young boy. "I feel responsible for taking care of him," she said. Her panic returned with more anxiety. Then she described a new scene. She envisioned herself as a two-year-old child emerging from the center of a pool of water. Adult Betty was flooded with little Betty's two-year-old feelings. I reminded Betty that her consciousness had just merged with the younger self, and that a two-year-old girl was too young to be responsible for taking care of anyone. I asked her, "What happened at the age of two? How did this anxiety-responsibility pattern get set into motion?"

In a small, weak voice trembling with emotion, Betty blurted out, "When Dad slammed me against the wall." She began sobbing. Amid gulping tears and convulsive breathing, Betty began to explain the scene, which opened before her inner vision. "When I was about two years old, I was laughing and joyful and making noise. And my dad emotionally and physically slammed me against the basement apartment wall to shut me up. He was very, very angry and mean." A lightbulb went off. Betty always thought that she took care of others to show how much she cared for them. Now she realized that taking care of others was her weapon. She took care of others to control and manipulate their feelings, to protect herself from their feelings.

We continued our inner work. I reminded Betty, that the physical abuse, while not happening physically right now, was still happening in her psyche; and her psyche could provide her with someone who could psychically stop the abuse that her personal father directed toward her younger self. I asked her to imagine someone who could protect her from her dad. A ten-foot-tall, wide-bodied, brawny hulk of a guy appeared in the basement apartment. I also suggested she make contact with the Divine Father of her spirit—the creator of her joyful, exuberant, expressive self—the one who created her soul.

How can I describe the shift in state as Betty made contact with an experience of the Source of her joyful, exuberant spirit? Her face became smooth, and a delicate, relaxed smile graced her lips. Her breathing became deep and flowing. I could see her relaxing into the experience of being held by this energy that she identified as the Divine Father of her spirit. Waves of subtle energy moved out in concentric circles from the center of her chest with each breath she took. The rise and fall of her chest seemed to send forth gentle waves that washed over me as I sat with her.

Once we have an experience like this it never leaves us. We realize that, indeed, we are protected by a Source of love so great it is incomprehensible to our normal, ordinary mind. Whether we are conscious of this presence or not, it exists independent of our awareness. When we realize that this Source is much bigger than us, we feel relief, not concern. Betty called the Source of her experience "Heavenly Father."

She began a dialogue with her Heavenly Father.

"Why didn't I get to have a physical dad who would protect me instead of hurt me?"

"So you would seek me and find me," came the reply.

"Why did I have all that pain?" Betty prodded, not satisfied with that response.

"So you would learn compassion, so you would be able to know other people's pain, and so you would know your own depths." As she spoke these words aloud, I observed another shift in Betty's consciousness. She settled into the couch, sinking down. Then, after a few moments of silence, she said, "I feel myself to my core." As she shifted position a second time, a wave of discomfort seemed to cross her face. She addressed the Father of her spirit. "Do you love me? Why can't I let it in?"

"Because you have armor on your heart," he whispered into her inner ear. Her Heavenly Father brought her full circle, back to the initial image of a metal breastplate covering her chest. This breastplate may have blocked the pain of the blows she suffered in childhood, but it also shielded her from divine love in adulthood.

I sat with her in silence and then asked, "What is happening now?"

"I am lifting the metal plate up. The hinge at the center of my chest is giving way." Betty paused and sighed. "I am letting his love in. I feel so vulnerable and soft. He is filling my heart now. My Heavenly Father is all around my heart. He is protecting my heart, he protects me." We sat together in meditation, feeling this great presence of love and protection. Then Betty said, "He is always there for me. I remember growing up believing one God for the whole planet could never have time for me. But this is my Heavenly Father, and he created me so he'd have someone to love and watch over. He is never away from me. My God is always with me." Another wave of insecurity bubbled up. "Am I worth it?" she asked aloud.

She received her answer in the form of a revelation. "God created me—of course I'm worth it. I'm loved and accepted as I am, every particle of me. He protects and nourishes every inch of my heart—front, sides, and back. I don't have to be responsible for taking care of him either."

After these words, I suggested that Betty return to the basement apartment scene. I asked her, "What do you see now?"

"Superhero stands between me and Dad, just standing there. Little Betty is jumping about, running around, and making noise. I take little Betty in my arms. I hold her in my arms, while my Heavenly Father holds me in his arms. Dad watches, shocked! He is seeing how it is done—he never knew. Little Betty doesn't cry or lose her joyousness. She is loved and secure and taken care of."

I repeated these essential truths to Betty in the form of affirmations. "You are allowed to be in your joy. You are cared for. You are loved. You are secure and safe within yourself." I also added, "Since you are taken care of, you don't need to expect your personal father, your husband, or anyone in particular to be your Heavenly Father and take care of you the way that He can and does." She responded with, "My God is always with me. Always. In all ways. I can let go of needing to know what to do." She sighed and laughed and opened her eyes. She realized how much she had been trying to control and manipulate others by taking care of them. Now her heart felt protected from the inside out. There was nothing she needed to do. She felt free to act in new ways in her relationships.

Al had a similar experience after he made contact with the Father of his spirit. Al, an ambitious young executive, felt betrayed by his personal father. He felt he had a weak father. Al's personal father was a man who always aspired to be a lawyer but never finished college. All his life, Al could sense his personal father's fear of failure and anxiety about being successful. Even so, Al was treated like a prince in the family. Sent to the best schools, he eventually received an MBA from a prestigious university. Upon graduation, Al climbed his way up the corporate ladder, until one day, at the age of thirty-four, Al began to examine his personal ambitions. He felt disloyal. To succeed would most certainly exaggerate his father's failure. And what is the meaning of success anyway? How does the prince succeed to the throne if his father is not a king?

Robert Bly, in his book *Iron John*, explores father-son wounds. He identifies three expressions of the Father-King that are significant to the betrayal of the father. Those three elements are the Sacred King, the earthly king, and the inner King. The Sacred King rules the universe with the Sacred Queen. They live eternally in mythic realms, each in the magnificent full power of exalted male and female. According to Tantric traditions, the divine masculine and feminine are passionately embracing each other, joined together in ecstatic sexual union. Oneness is an expression of archetypal Father, King of the Universe, in the act of creation. We feel the afterglow of this divine love when we touch the sacred within ourselves.

Before we internalize the sacred through the vehicle of the inner King, we project it onto our fathers—heads of state, bosses, husbands, lovers—earthly kings. From what I've seen, the earthly father-king can't help but betray the Sacred. He is, after all, only human and subject to the conditions and traditions of his time. Just as betrayal of the mother is a biological imperative, betrayal of the father is a sociocultural imperative. "Under the title of Kaiser, Tsar, Emperor, Maharajah, Sultan, Bey—one after another, the kings fell, all through Europe and then throughout its colonies."[3] The earthly king's betrayal of sacred, eternal, timeless truths shocks us out of our idealization, and propels each of us toward the rediscovery of our ideals. We move from the trust of outer authority figures toward a search for our own ideals, our vision of the sacred within ourselves.

Let us return to the story of Siddhartha and King Suddhodana for a real-life example. Unlike archetypal Father, who guides us toward our greatest fulfillment in this world based on the pattern of our divine destiny, our earthly father's vision of the pattern of life is distorted by his worldly experience. When Siddhartha was born, his father saw the next king, not the next Buddha. King Suddhodana trained Prince Siddhartha in statecraft and warfare. He also taught him how to be a good king and husband. Our personal father teaches us about *his* life, not about life itself. As Kahlil Gibran writes, "Your children are not your children. They are the sons and daughters of Life's longing for itself."[4] One's personal father is not the master of one's soul, nor the master of one's life. Only life experience could train Siddhartha in the fulfillment of his destiny.

At the age of twenty-nine, while out driving with his charioteer, Prince Siddhartha beheld four sights that transformed his life. First, he saw an old man, bent with age, walking as best he could while leaning on his cane. The prince was struck by this aged man's tortured expression and general physical decrepitude. Siddhartha had never seen such a man before, and he questioned his charioteer. Siddhartha's charioteer explained, "All men and women are subject to the pains of old age if they live long enough." The prince reflected on this sorry sight. Lost in thought, he did not speak further as they completed their ride through the countryside.

The next time Siddhartha was out with his charioteer, the prince saw a man fallen by the roadside. Sick and weak, this miserable man lay deteriorating in his own refuse. Siddhartha, deeply moved by this sight, sought an explanation for such suffering. The charioteer said, "Sire, that man is sick. We are all subject to the afflictions of illness." Deeply perturbed, Siddhartha again reflected on what he had seen.

The next sight was a corpse. The dead man's body was beginning to decompose in the sun. Again, the faithful charioteer explained the situation, "This man is dead. We must all die some day."

The final sight that impressed the prince was the appearance of a wandering ascetic priest. He was wearing saffron robes and a deeply peaceful, serene expression on his face, even in the midst of all these worldly miseries.

Contradictions in consciousness cause us to ask questions. The questions we ask guide our quest and mark our path toward truth. Paradox ignites an inner Source of energy that has the power to simultaneously burn through the illusions of one's life and illuminate one's personal spiritual quest. The sights Siddhartha beheld—age, illness, death, serenity—juxtaposed with the complete material comfort and luxury of his father's court, led Siddhartha to question his lifestyle and consider the problems of humanity.

Something within us seeks a mentor, one who has gone before us and has mastered the way. We wish to be guided by this master. It is natural to wish to be taught the way to live. We continue to seek external father figures, authorities who we hope have the answers to our perplexing questions. When Siddhartha left his father's home in search of truth, he studied with the spiritual teachers of his time. He gave up his name and title, donned the saffron robes of an ascetic, and took the name Gautama. However, after learning all that the teachers could teach, he still was not satisfied. Gautama continued to practice their precepts in hopes of finding a deeper truth.

After six years of harsh asceticism, he realized that these severe disciplines did not lead him to the truth he sought. Gautama's fellow priests rejected him in disgust when he chose to break his austerities and accept a bowl of rice from a villager. Gautama was not disturbed by the moral judgments of his fellow priests. He was following the direction of truth, not dogma. The right way is a question of direction, not morality.

Infinite intelligence directs us toward our highest good, toward wholeness, a creative state of consciousness that is beyond the paradoxes. From this point within consciousness, one's destiny is revealed. Like Siddhartha Gautama's story indicates, we each have our own path to enlightenment. Life guides the quest for truth. The training we receive from our fathers, mentors, and life experiences are all part of a greater plan that brings us to our complete fulfillment.

For example, Siddhartha Gautama's training in his personal father's home as a warrior combined with the spiritual practices and teachings of his gurus to prepare him for his final battle—the inner battle between his higher Self and the limited self that blocked his soul from its complete fulfillment. At the age of thirty-five, Gautama received a revelation, the Four Noble Truths—life is suffering; suffering is caused by selfish desire; it is possible to become free from suffering; and the way to liberation is through the Eightfold Path: right view, right speech, right thought, right action, right mode of living, right endeavor, right mindfulness, and right concentration. This revelation brought him into his Buddhahood, and he spent the rest of his life living by and teaching these principles.

There is a Source within the psyche that guides and directs the soul along the path of destiny to its ultimate destination—complete Self-fulfillment. The inner King awakens as we open our inner vision to a Source of truth within. He invites us to embrace the light and the dark in our own nature, both our joys and sorrows, as passionately as the divine polarities do through the symbol of their sacred sexual union. This is a creative act. To become the authority, the author and creator of one's experience, one must discover a Source of courage, strength, and autonomy within. Bly says, "The inner King is the one in us who knows what we want to do for the rest of our lives, or the rest of the month, or the rest of the day. He can make clear what we want without being contaminated in his choice by the opinions of others around us. The inner King is connected with our fire of purpose and passion."[5] The inner Father-King empowers us to be able to take a stand in this world, even if it is contrary to the wishes of one's father, boss, or other earthly kings.

Let us return to Al for an example. Al's inner Father-King took the form of a stag. This King of the Stags demonstrated sensitivity, power, dynamism, protective leadership, a thrill of danger, and a love for life.

Then Al's inner Father shifted to a human form. A noble-looking, middle-aged man stood before Al. He had sparkling dark eyes and wore a great stag skin as a mantle and antlers as his crown. The Stag King taught Al that the secret of his power was "the power of presence." In his deep, resonant voice he spoke directly to Al, saying, "You are my son. You can be all that I am."

Al had a hard time believing his inner Father. Al responded with "I expect that you will want me to be inferior—to defer to your position."

His inner Father laughed! "The mighty remain mighty by bringing forth the best in their legions."

Something shifted for Al. He felt "present," like his Stag-King Father—alert, vital, and ready for life. Al realized that the Stag-King was different from his biological father. His father was competitive with Al and paradoxically wanted Al to remain inferior even though "Al should be successful in the world." Al's inner Father, King of the Stags, loved Al's spirit. Al was ready to inherit his spiritual legacy from his inner Father. This included the strength, sensitivity, power, and dynamism of his animal nature, the deer. Al's inner Father would be the one to train him to be a leader, a new kind of executive—one who empowers others to utilize their strengths.

Al reviewed his life and his concerns about success. He received a few revelations:

> I will know what to do, and do what is right.
> I will see the best path.
> I will use my strength to help, not harm.
> I can be protective without being destructive.
> I am an integrated male.

The archetypes act through us, instinctively. Al's inner Father will guide Al's success as an executive as Al succeeds from Prince to King in his own life. Al's spiritual practice springs from the act of realizing these truths through the process of living, and by trusting the process of life that will guide him to turn inward to discover deeper truths and outward in order to take a stand in life. When he goes within, he will find the inner King waiting for him. Personal integrity through creative self-expression is the way of archetypal Father. (See Exercise 3-B on page 89.)

For heroes and heroines of myth and legend, the practice of living life is a spiritual quest. The tragedies and comedies of life all have a sacred purpose. Betrayal of the father is a test to discover an inner Source of direction and purpose in life. There is a Source within the psyche that guides us and protects us as we follow our path in life. Tests and tribulations are living monuments to courage and character development. Gifts and rewards represent the revival of forgotten powers. Al brings forth a new kind of leadership through the practice of being present. Betty no longer needs to control and manipulate others to protect herself. She can practice living in her joy. Siddhartha Guatama Buddha lived and taught his truth—liberation from suffering.

Inner vision and outer action match. Action is not the result of a rationally calculated risk. Action is guided by archetypal Father. Like Buddha who came up with the Eightfold Path to guide his actions, we each have the capacity to know what is right. Right is not a moral judgment, it is a perception based on our inner sense of direction. We perceive clues and signals, as in a treasure hunt, that indicate we are going the right way. We all have people in our lives who are more than happy to tell us what to do, but acting from inspiration is the kind of action that is under the direct influence of archetypal Father. The biggest challenge is to develop patience until the right direction is made clear. Florence Scovel Shinn suggests that you make a direct request. "Give me a definite lead, let me know if there is anything for me to do." She reiterates, "Intuition is a spiritual faculty and does not explain, but simply points the way."[6]

The way frequently becomes clear through a series of synchronistic events. For Doris, it started with a dream, which she described during one of our therapy sessions.

> I had a dream that I found myself walking along a path. I knew I was in the Himalayas. As I walked up the path to the top of a mountain, I remembered a Tibetan legend. The legend says that when you find your heart stone this will signify that you are on your right path in life. Once you find your heart stone you may then search for, and collect, your truth stones.
>
> I looked down at my hands and I was holding a triangular stone. The stone was a creamy white-pink and almost translucent. I held the stone up toward the sun. As I did, a rainbow formed at the top of the triangle, much like a prism or crystal. I realized that this must be my heart stone.

I started searching for truth stones and found them, all triangular shaped and of different colors, scattered along the path. As I collected the stones, I remembered more of the legend.

All the stones are to be assembled on a thong to be worn as a necklace. There may come a time in your journey when you meet someone—someone you are particularly drawn to. Give them your heart stone. Once you pass on the heart stone, you must break the necklace and scatter the truth stones.

This dream was the beginning of a series of events that seemed to have a power of their own. Within ten days of her dream, Doris received a gift, a quartz crystal. It was full of rainbows, and when held to the light, splashes of color filled in the triangular face of the stone's point, just like in her dream. She knew this crystal was symbolic of her heart stone. This was a definite lead. Synchronicity is a spontaneous gift from the universe that links subjective inner awareness to objective outer world events. I suggested that Doris follow the advice of her dream and have the crystal made into a necklace. I gave her the name of a jeweler who works with crystals.

Between the time she gave Pete, the jeweler, her crystal, and the time she was supposed to pick it up, Doris came down with pneumonia. She suffered from fevers and delirium for a week. While she was recovering from her illness, Pete came by with the finished piece. He told her that as he meditated with her crystal, he received the image of a sun cupped in a crescent moon, and he decided to use this symbol in the setting for the necklace. He said he also researched the symbol and found that it sprang from a legend about a Chinese princess who left her family to make a pilgrimage to Tibet. Along with the finished necklace, Pete handed Doris a handwritten copy of the legend. It read as follows:

Lying not far southwest of Xining is the famous Ri Yue Shan—the Mountain of the Sun and Moon. There is a legend that when the Tang Princess Wen Cheng journeyed to Lhasa on a pilgrimage, she carried along an enchanted curved mirror in which she could see visions of her past and the home she had left behind.

She fell ill, and in the heat of her fever, she dropped and shattered the mirror, which turned into the Mountain of the Sun and Moon. When this happened, the Princess forgot her past and her distant home and went straight on to Tibet and Lhasa.

The legend wove together elements from her recent illness, her ongoing therapy, and elements from her dream about finding her truth stones in Tibet. The impact of these events convinced Doris of the efficacy of her chosen path more powerfully than anything anyone could have said to her. She felt a guiding force at work in her life. These events coincided with her thoughts of leaving her husband and breaking entrenched family patterns. She knew physical separation from her parents and husband was right action. The power of these events gave her the strength to risk and trust. She wrote the following in her journal.

> I would like to say, I have never been to Tibet, nor have I read anything about Tibet before my dream. Pete did not know of my therapy or anything about me. This experience is a warm, glowing gem that I can cherish throughout the rest of my life. The experience validated the hard work I have done to really shake loose the shackles of just surviving and really start to participate in this life.
>
> This experience also showed me in a big way how very much we are all connected. A physical manifestation of a dream gave me trust in myself and my greater Self. There is great magic in this physical realm.
>
> I truly do not expect anyone to know or understand the impact this experience has had on my life. This is a turning point for me. No one knows the dismal places I have come from within myself. The only way I can explain it, is that I was an actress playing a part for someone else. For the first time in thirty years I am free to be myself. My truth stones which I've been gathering are:
> You can change.
> You can be happy.
> There are rewards from being your true Self.
> Fear can be conquered.
> You can go against all odds and be the winner.
> All truths come from the heart.

Archetypal Father makes our path clear. The way opens. Though we might have to master our fear of change and take responsibility for the consequences of our actions, we are rewarded with an experience of personal fulfillment that is greater than anything we can imagine. The risk equals the reward. Both are great. The pains, traumas, paradoxes, and contradictions in one's life are as much a part of one's spiritual path as the obvious blessings and gifts. Both have the potential to lead us to our greatest good as we learn to read the signals and act in accord with our inner Self. Life wants something to be born into the world through each of us. It is up to us to risk living.

EXERCISE 3-A

Discover the Father of Your Spirit

1. What is the quality of presence associated with the Father of your spirit? Allow an impression, picture, image from nature, or figure from mythology to emerge within your imagination. Draw a picture or find a photo that expresses this quality of presence.

2. Reflect on your archetypal Father, the inseminator of spirit in your life, and your earthly father, the father of your body. Notice how your personal father and archetypal father are similar and different.

3. Notice how the Father of your spirit responds to you.

4. How do you feel after contact with your inner Father?

EXERCISE 3-B

Ask for Guidance

1. If there was ever a time in the past (recent or distant) in which you needed the wise guidance of your father, bring your inner Father into the memory and ask him for guidance.

2. Act on his guidance in your imagination, and notice what happens.

3. Imagine that you are given everything you need to act.

4. Observe if there is anything different about you. What is different?

EXERCISE 3-C

Follow Your Inner Authority

1. Give examples of the difference between doing what is right based on the moral judgment of external authorities and following the right direction based on your own inner authority.

2. How do you receive direction from this inner authority? For example: dreams, hunches, synchronicities, etc.

3. Take a vacation from moral judgment as learned from external sources. Practice being nonjudgmental toward yourself and others, and write about your observations in your journal.

Chapter 4

Betrayal of the Beloved

Gateway to Wholeness—Union between Self and self

Wound: If you suffer from a betrayal by your beloved, your sense of unity and partnership has been injured. Your heart aches, and you feel broken instead of whole.

Truth: Relationship, as a spiritual path, catalyzes personal discovery of an inner Self who knows (Mother) and directs (Father) each partner toward wholeness. The unconditional love between the higher Self and the ordinary self is reflected in the couple dynamic as creativity, commitment, cooperation, and intimate companionship.

Healing: Reunite with the One within who will never abandon you or mislead you. Move beyond the wounds of childhood inflicted by the betrayals of your mother and father, and discover your Beloved, your inner guardian and guide on your path to wholeness. Make the commitment to creatively cooperate with your inner companion; then make the same commitment to your outer companion.

Linda called me in crisis. Eddie, her husband of four years, had just told her that he didn't want to be married to her anymore. In jags of tears and sobs, she told me the story. He said he had met someone else at the professional training that he had been attending. He loved Linda. He said she was his best friend, but he just wasn't attracted to her anymore. The chemistry was gone. He wanted something else from marriage. Neither Linda nor

Eddie could make sense of why the marriage wasn't working. They spent the day together in each others arms, crying, talking, trying to make sense out of the circumstances of their life together as a couple. He said he had not yet had a sexual relationship with Alise, the infamous other woman, but he wanted to be with her and was ready to act.

Betrayal of the beloved usually evokes images of infidelity, a torrid entanglement leaving promises broken and dreams dashed. Sexual infidelity is only one form of the betrayal of the beloved. Unkept promises, failures to communicate, name-calling, shaming and blaming, emotional and physical abuse, withdrawal due to alcoholism or drug abuse, suicide and suicide threats, or divorce all usher in the experience of betrayal. Unmet security needs from childhood surface in the couple dynamic. When needs are not met, one or both partners act out and wound their beloved in the way they were hurt in childhood.

Personal mother and father wounds surface in the couple dynamic to be transformed. "She left without a word. I didn't even know our marriage was in trouble." Can you hear the unresolved mother wound here? Feeling abandoned and feeling out of contact with an inner Source of intuitive knowing are the symbolic clues. "He lied to me, purposely lied to me all this time—even when I asked him if he was seeing someone else. I knew it. I can't believe I was so stupid to go along with him." Feeling misled or misdirected, and following outer direction over one's inner direction indicates that unresolved father wounds are beckoning to be healed.

Our partners present us with potent life lessons. Relationship triangles often point to unresolved mother-father-child betrayal wounds. For example, Ken, from Chapter 2, who had an overbearing, domineering personal mother, felt constantly judged and criticized by her for his choice in sexual preference. When Ken sought contact with Great Mother's unconditional love in his sexual liaisons outside of his primary relationship, his partner Jim felt betrayed. Jim said he felt that Ken put him into the role of a restricting parent as Ken replayed his childhood role of a "lying little boy afraid of getting caught by Mom."

We can also remember Doris, from Chapter 3, who suffered from sexual, physical, and verbal abuse by her alcoholic father. She transferred distrust of her father to all men, including her alcoholic husband, Lou. Part of Doris's journey from betrayal to trust included separation from Lou and dates with another man, Max. By healing her personal father wound, Doris found that there was a greater force directing her life and it was not an external human agent like her father, husband, or boyfriend.

Intrinsic to the stress of a love triangle is the power to inspire an individual to recognize and heal his or her inner wounded child. Through direct contact with the Divine Mother within the psyche, one intuitively knows what one needs as well as who can and cannot fulfill that need. With the aid of Divine Father, we are guided to external sources that can fulfill our needs. We are empowered to act on our own behalf, in our own best interest. Divine Mother and Father unite within the psyche to give birth to the spiritual Self, the archetype of union and wholeness—symbol of the Beloved—one's faithful inner companion. The Self is a union of opposites within the soul: a union between light and dark, conscious and unconscious, one's immortal, expanded higher Self and one's mortal, ordinary identity, which includes one's personal history and idiosyncratic vulnerabilities.

Couples catalyze each other's discovery of wholeness as the personal provides entry into the transpersonal. Our personal wounds invite us each to make direct contact with an infinite Source of intelligence, love, power, and healing within the psyche. This state of consciousness, symbolically depicted as Divine Mother and Father in a passionately sexual embrace, figuratively making love, is a metaphor for the dynamic creativity and mysterious potency of the Beloved. The archetype of the Beloved evokes personal integrity by inspiring congruence between inner knowing and outer action. We tend to expect that our physical parents would have taught us how to act with such integrity. Or we wish that their marriage would have modeled integrity and wholeness through their union as a man and woman. Most likely, though, our parents raised us the way they were raised. Dorothy Law Nolte says it best in her poem "Children Learn What They Live."

> If children live with criticism,
> They learn to condemn.
>
> If children live with hostility,
> They learn to fight.
>
> If children live with ridicule,
> They learn to be shy.
>
> If children live with shame,
> They learn to feel guilty.

> If children live with encouragement,
> They learn confidence.
>
> If children live with tolerance,
> They learn to be patient.
>
> If children live with praise,
> They learn to appreciate.
>
> If children live with approval,
> They learn to like themselves.
>
> If children live with honesty,
> They learn truth.
>
> If children live with fairness,
> They learn justice.
>
> If children live with security,
> They learn to have faith in themselves and others.
>
> If children live with friendliness,
> They learn the world is a nice place in which to live.

Observe yourself. Notice whether you are repeating patterns from childhood. If you are acting like your personal mother or father with your partner, or feeling like a wounded child, you are being asked to rediscover the spiritual Mother and Father of your being—to rebirth and reparent yourself.

One's inner voice, the voice of intuition, speaks to the wounded child self within with words of tolerance, encouragement, praise, approval, and acceptance. This neutralizes and releases the criticism, hostility, ridicule, and shame that one suffered in childhood at the hands of one's personal parents.

Ego strength blossoms. As self-esteem builds, you reconstruct your personality. The ego becomes a sound vessel that can carry and contain the expanded energies of your true Self. In time, we grow beyond the divine parent-child relationship. One seeks to unite with the Beloved, with the Source of unconditional love within one's being. Egyptologist Isha Schwaller de Lubicz describes the process of attraction between the true Self and the ordinary self as a powerful draw toward the light within one's own being.

> You have within you a spark capable of burning up every obstacle to the realization of your true Power. For the Power of the Self is unlimited, and only the [wounded] Ego resists this power of the impersonal Self. . . .
>
> The union of the two is an irresistible Love, in which Height and Depth are united, in which they know not that they "give" themselves to each other, since their giving is a fusion, a rejoicing in Love, an ardent vibration; there is no longer any comparison, no longer any compensation; no longer "I" or "Thou," but only an intensity of Life in which all is mutual penetration and mutual knowledge.[1]

Betrayal of the beloved awakens the quest to find one's true soul mate, the faithful inner companion. The impersonal Self and the personal self giving themselves completely to each other within the psyche brings forgiveness to the soul.

Linda and Eddie's story is a remarkable demonstration of this journey of the Beloved. The sexual dimension of their marriage had been shaky for some time—ever since Eddie's mother was diagnosed with pancreatic cancer and died. During the two and a half years following her death, Linda was interested in sex and Eddie was not. In sex therapy, both Linda and Eddie learned that their relationship did not depend on sex for there to be a close bond between them. Sharing sexual expression was only one form of intimacy. To enhance emotional intimacy, their therapist helped Eddie express a wide range of very difficult feelings, including grief, anger, resentment, helplessness, frustration, and fear. Eddie also learned how to listen in a new way. He practiced listening nondefensively to Linda as she expressed feelings of disappointment and rejection. As their emotional intimacy continued to grow, exchanges of physical affection, including hugs, cuddles, and tender expressions of comfort increased.

Through this process of communicating feelings to each other, Linda realized that she had been relying on Eddie to give her a sense of herself as an attractive, passionate woman. In addition to his other feelings, Eddie felt burdened by this added responsibility. She came to understand that his lack of sexual interest was a statement about him and where he was emotionally, not a statement about her. She had personalized his withdrawal as rejection. Beyond the veil of her emotions, she perceived that she was, indeed, as attractive and passionate now as she had been before they were married. She started to feel sexually appealing again, with or without Eddie's approval. Whether or not they were having sex no longer determined whether she was sexy. Linda's image of herself did not depend on him.

They had been going to couples counseling with a sex therapist for almost a year when Eddie dropped the bomb about Alise and his desire to be out of the marriage. Even though Linda and Eddie's communication and friendship had continued to deepen, eroticism was still strained. Eddie was not yet interested in sharing sexual intimacies with Linda. His unilateral decision to leave the relationship was a real blow. They had both been working so hard, had seemed so committed to each other. To make matters worse, Linda was leaving town for a two-week trip to visit friends and family on the East Coast. Eddie, who had just gotten a recent job promotion, was not able to arrange vacation time, so they had decided months ago that she would go alone.

After hours of discussion on that fateful afternoon, Eddie agreed not to move out while Linda was away. Following hours of tears and discussion, they decided to take a break and rent a video. In the car on the way home, Eddie inquired, "How would you feel about me being with Alise while you're out of town?" Linda flew into a jealous rage, concluding her outburst with "I don't want you to be with her. If you're asking me what *I* want, *I* want you to be with *me!*"

I knew Linda quite well from our contacts over the last ten years. She attended several of my intuition development classes. We also worked one-on-one: I gave her annual birthday readings and private intuition development consultations. She trusted herself and her intuition explicitly and was courageous in acting on behalf of her inner truth. She knew that marrying Ed was the right decision. Even now, grief stricken, she did not doubt that decision, though when she was subsumed by the grief of the loss of her partner, Linda said she doubted whether she would ever love again. The thought of separating from her beloved marriage partner and best friend was wrenching.

By the next evening, Linda found the eye of the storm. She told Eddie, "I feel like you are asking me if it is all right with me for you to be with Alise. I can't tell you what to do. Though I don't want you to be with Alise, I'm not in control of that. You need to do whatever you need to do while I'm out of town. I can't control you. That's true for the marriage, too. I want to, and am willing to, stay with the marriage. Whether you want to stay or go is up to you." She felt calm and at peace, accepting the unknown.

How did she get there? Weeks before, she had preregistered for a workshop on crystal healing scheduled for the weekend before she would fly back East. She felt that it was her higher Self that had the foresight to put her in a situation that would help her turn inward and heal her grief and shock. Synchronistically, an old friend of hers from school just happened to register for the first day of the workshop. At lunch, Linda and her friend, whose husband had recently been diagnosed with cancer, shared the intimacies of the stresses in their respective lives. They talked about healing crises and facing loss and death. Linda found the discussion tremendously supportive and reflective of her present trials.

She left the workshop thinking to herself, "Trust, trust, trust—you don't know how this is going to work out, but, one way or another, it *will* work out. Trust." Then she remembered the acronym TRUST from our previous intuition development classes. She felt that the crystal workshop helped her turn inward and get in touch with herself. The crystal meditations throughout the day, plus the laying on of stones, which participants performed on each other, fostered relaxation and a release of some of her fear of the unknown. She realized she needed to continue to use the tools she had to get to a deeper truth before she took a stand and spoke her truth to Eddie. She didn't like the process, yet she was willing to trust the process, knowing that there was some intrinsic value in every experience in her life.

When she arrived at home, she secluded herself in her meditation room and did a crystal layout on herself. She was going mad with questions. She was trying to rationalize why Eddie was leaving her, but her inner voice led her in another direction. "In order to receive answers to your questions, you must shift the energy. To hear them through the distortion of your present state would not bring truth. Your fears, in the guise of grief, anger, and inertia, distort the truth. You have many fears about Eddie. Let them be for right now, and let us work on your body."

She was directed to use the crystals as she had been taught in class and by her wisdom Source within. She felt surrounded by a loving, guiding presence as she positioned particular crystals over the places in her body where she was hurting most—heart, stomach, brow, shoulder. One by one, emotions were released as she let go of the tension in her body. Floods of words and images, magnetized by her intuition, helped Linda come to a state of deep understanding about herself and the challenges she faced.

For example, her shoulder told her that she had a fear of doing or saying the wrong thing. She was guided to understand that she did not have the power to make or break the situation with Eddie. Her inner voice whispered, "There is a greater force at work in life. There is much outside of your control and much within it. Just as you have been able to master the tides of your emotions, these events are training you to be your own master. Just as these events are serving you now, they serve each and all. Let go of feeling a burdensome responsibility for the making of these events." She asked how and where this pattern was set into motion, the pattern of feeling a burdensome responsibility for events outside her control. She received an image of her personal father. Her inner companion, through the voice of intuition, told her that she learned this way of being from him. Images from childhood filled her inner vision—images like her father yelling at the newscaster on the television and engaging in inane arguments with her Aunt Sarah, who was sixteen years younger than him. His anger was an expression of his frustration, the result of ineffectual attempts to influence people and events that were out of his control.

Now Linda understood that feelings of responsibility were the underlying source of energy that pushed her father to be so aggressive as he tried to talk his sister-in-law out of her opinions. He always said he was trying to help Sarah grow up and live in the real world; his real world, one in which he impotently griped about the stupidity of world leaders to deaf, electronic ears on television. Linda also saw how his emotional outbursts distracted him from experiencing the helplessness he felt inside. It gave him the false sense that he was doing something to change outer events.

Linda saw how this pattern fed her father's low self-esteem. No matter what he did or said, no matter how responsible he felt, things continued to happen. Newscasters continued to report bad news. World leaders were still stupid. And Aunt Sarah did "whatever she damn well pleased." Linda realized that both she and Eddie shared this pattern of low self-esteem and high-responsibility codependence, and that it was becoming activated by this situation with Alise.

Linda knew that she was not responsible for Eddie's choice to be or not to be sexual with Alise. Nor would she be able to talk him into or out of whatever he decided. There were no magical right or wrong words. He had his own lessons to learn, just as she had hers. Linda felt she was being tested to be present with herself and all her experiences throughout this process and to set herself free from feeling responsible for events outside her control. She also saw that she was being tested to be present with Eddie as he went through his own process of transformation. She saw Alise as a catalyst, igniting a spark of desire within Eddie, a spark that seemed to have all but died over the last three years since his mother's illness and death. As Jean Houston writes,

> In our betrayal, the other becomes the instrument of God, bringing us to a tragedy that needs our ennoblement in order to understand it. . . . This is the mystery and miracle of love, and it changes the very fabric of reality, the very structure of our lives. When we are able to *give forth* [forgive], to give of ourselves beyond our protective shell and see the other in wonder and astonishment (regardless of how unskilled another's behavior might have been), then something evolutionary happens and we and the betrayal are not the same. Then love is restored, revealing the larger consequence and the deeper unfolding.[2]

Linda chose to trust herself and her inner guidance rather than be carried off by the drama of the circumstances. Instead of trying to change the situation, she chose to accept this situation as a challenge to be present with herself and her spouse. This included experiencing the process of being married to the man she loved, and who loved her, but who wasn't interested in her sexually and who was interested in someone else at the present time.

Marriage is a spiritual path. Linda's union with her husband is an outer reflection of the union between the exalted Self and the ordinary self "in which height and depth are united" through an "irresistible love." Eddie's process of being true to himself about needing to be with Alise brought Linda to her depths. One man's truth, in this case, was another woman's betrayal and call to initiation. Linda's experience of betrayal of the beloved was an invitation to seek and find her inner companion, the one who lovingly guards her and guides her to wholeness. Within the depths of her experience she touched heights, expanded states of consciousness which are, as Isha Schwaller de Lubicz said, "capable of burning up every obstacle to the realization of your true power."

When Linda returned from her vacation, Eddie picked her up from the airport. When they got home, he said, "You're probably wondering if I was with Alise. We were with each other twice. I don't know if you'll trust me when I say this, but I only want to be friends with her. I love you, and I don't want to lose you. I just needed to be with her. I can't explain it. But I don't want to lose our marriage."

The Goddess of Love is a ruthless teacher. As Venus-Aphrodite, the divine force of attraction is known for her irresistible magnetism. The goddess of erotic and romantic love is also the goddess of love spurned. Under the name of Apostrophia, "she who turns herself away," Venus-Aphrodite is repelled by those who would possess her. Love demands love, not obedience. Possessive romantic love, which demands fulfillment and obsessively determines to gain the affections of a love object, is an expression of lust rather than passion. Lust is a form of idolatry in which a mere mortal is deified. The Goddess of Passion and Desire abhors the worship of an image, a love object, or a false idol in place of devotion to Her. Passion arises from an immortal spark. The spark of the divine seems to have a life of its own as it inflames consciousness. Passion requires that one surrender to a greater force within one's being. This is the force of love.

Because of the confusion between lust and passion in romantic love, both Eastern and Western mystery schools have considered this to be one of the most difficult of initiatory tests. Ecstatic erotic rites and sacred prostitution were practiced in the temples of Astarte, Venus, Aphrodite, Hathor, Isis, Ishtar, and Vesta, as well as in the temples of Dionysius, Baal, Moloch, and Shiva. Both heterosexual and homosexual unions were offered as sacrifices to the divine. Sex was a sacrament and passion a prayer in which men and women sought physical union with the divine through the agency of trained priests and priestesses. Sexual excitation physiologically stimulates the pituitary and hypothalamus glands to induce subjective states of expansions in consciousness. Union with one's physical lover opens the gateway to union with the nonphysical Beloved.

It is a challenge that is all but incomprehensible to our modern way of thinking about sexual relations to fathom the arduous tests of initiation that priests and priestesses must have passed in order to become conduits for divine love and passion rather than instruments of lust and pettiness. Today, tantric schools, whose ancient mysteries are being disclosed to the modern seeker, reveal the intricacies of the science and art of erotic love. Many a warning still goes out to the uninitiated to watch for the perils of obsession and addiction, which are the pitfalls on this path to the divine.

The shift from personal to impersonal love is a delicate matter that we each learn, whether in past, present, or future lives, or through the test of romantic love. Linda and Eddie were both taking initiations in Aphrodite's temple of love. Eddie's sexual encounter with Alise invoked the archetype of Apostrophia, challenging Linda to transcend the traditional demands of custom and personal expectation. At the same time, Eddie was under the sway of the goddess's attractive force and was challenged to discover the subtle distinctions between lust and passion.

Even though Linda knew Eddie might sleep with Alise, there was also the possibility that he wouldn't. Something was irrevocably different and would never be the same again. Even so, Linda didn't want the relationship to end. Linda still loved Eddie and felt loved by him. She just needed time to grieve. Eddie held her close as she cried. He continued to stay present with Linda as floods of different feelings and thoughts surfaced over the next few weeks and months. They spent quite some time, together and on their own, processing these events.

As Linda and Eddie shared their ideals and disappointments about marriage, Linda grieved the loss of her illusions about love and marriage. Courageously, they asked themselves and each other penetrating, provocative questions: If their marriage was not based on monogamy, what other traditional values might be in question? What was marriage if it was not based on these traditions? What good could come from this series of events? The very structure of their lives together did, indeed, change as heights and depths were exposed and explored. Linda and Eddie discovered a deeper truth together, a vital dream of love in relationship, a vision broad enough to contain all that they had been through together. They decided that marriage was a personal commitment to be with oneself and another human being through the process of transformation—to be companions on the path. Indeed, something was irrevocably different, and both Linda and Eddie were ennobled in the process. Trust is a spiritual practice, not a spiritual accomplishment. To continue to risk in spite of opposition, counterinfluences, or discouragement is part of the practice.

The divine triangle of Mother, Father, and Child is not the only expression of the forces at work in triangles. As the archetypes of Mother, Father, and Divine Child raise the ego self to true Selfhood, one's perception of that archetypal constellation matures and expands into a triangle of Guardian, Guide, and Beloved.

The relationship between Guardian, Guide, and Beloved is an archetypal theme portrayed in the myths and stories of pagan European cultures, and it defines the soul's sacred quest for true love. The love triangle between husband, wife, and her noble knight is a creative modification of pre-Christian, Celtic rites of passage as they were adapted to the climate and customs of medieval Europe. Old English ballads, fairy tales, and legends—like that of King Arthur, Lady Guinevere, and Sir Lancelot—disseminate Celtic initiatory teachings. R. J. Stewart, an expert on Celtic myths and bardic lore, writes,

> the ambiguous sexual attitude of the courtly love of the medieval period is a reflection of the magical interplay defined by the Goddess, the Guardian and the Questing Traveler. These three figures are represented by the beloved, her husband and her courtly lover. . . .
>
> In mystical and orthodox traditions, the guardians are angelic agencies, far removed in nature from the fallen earth. . . .
>
> The hidden [Celtic] traditions assert that the Earth or Land is the highest state of all, that in which all conflicts are to be resolved, all actions purified, and all barriers to true enlightenment lifted. All this, if you know how to pass the Guardian.[3]

No doubt, the ancient Druidic spiritual foundation beneath much of European social custom fostered romantic liaisons between a married lady and her noble knight. Joseph Campbell, renowned mythologist and expert on medieval courtly romance, has said that "love and marriage" was considered an oxymoron during the Middle Ages. In order for love to survive the pomp and circumstance of medieval mores, where marriages were arranged out of necessity—for position, power, status, even lust—true love had to find another expression within society.

The archetype of the beloved and the quest for true love are just as potent today as they were during the Middle Ages. Acted out primarily at an unconscious level, as many as 69 percent of married women and

66 percent of married men report involvements in extramarital relationships.[4] Today's questing traveler, whether man or woman, seeks union with the divine, archetypal Beloved, just as our ancient ancestors did before us.

The third party is not always another person. The test of true love is evoked by anything that impassions or possesses you. For the artist, his or her creative project may complete the triangle. For others, it is a just cause, career, or work endeavor. Sometimes, children or one's family of origin sets up the triangle. Also, all varieties of addictions, including alcohol, drugs, or gambling, fulfill the role of the beloved. I remember one woman lamenting, "The racetrack is his 'other woman.' He spends Friday nights at the track instead of at home." Regardless of the form, the divine triangle has its part to play in awakening a person to the heights and depths of the mysteries of the Beloved.

As in the mystic tradition of Sufism, God is the Beloved, and the mystic, like a lover, seeks union with God. In Celtic mythos, the Beloved is the goddess and she represents the heights of ecstasy and expansions in consciousness. To find her, the noble knight is guided into a dark forest or must enter the depths of a cavern or cave. As he embarks on this underworld journey, the knight is bound to meet a guardian figure like a dragon, wild goat, wolfhound, or raven. The Guardian, who has the title of Dweller on the Threshold, stands between the seeker and blissful union with the divine, which awaits him on the other side of the threshold. "With one hand, the Guardian protects the Mysteries from penetration and imbalance, while with the other he protects the individual from contact with energies that he or she is unable to bear."[5] As an archetype, the Guardian marks the boundary and establishes limits. Blocks to intimacy in interpersonal relationships represent the Guardian at work.

Paradoxically, your inner Guardian helps you establish personal limits that simultaneously block you from intimacy and protect you from a union that could injure or wound you. In Celtic mythology, the Guardian presents tests to the seeker on the spiritual quest. The Guardian's tests reveal your personal blocks, fears, and limitations—those barriers to true enlightenment that prevent you from uniting with your creative Self. You must face and master your personal fears and limitations before uniting with the Beloved within. Mastering your fears liberates you from self-imposed restrictions. In this way, your inner child matures into full Selfhood. Then the mother-father-child triangle naturally transforms into the Guardian-Guide-Beloved Self.

You are both guided to the beloved Self within and guarded from premature union. At first, the Guardian, Guide, or Beloved is projected onto the various points of the love triangle. For example, in the case of the husband-wife-mistress triangle, when the wife feels blocked from union with her husband, upon whom she has projected her Beloved, she projects her Guardian onto the mistress. While the intruding mistress is identified as the block to intimacy in the relationship, she simultaneously evokes the internal blocks—the limitations of unresolved insecurities and other wounds—in the wife, who feels betrayed. On the other hand, the mistress holds the projection of Beloved for the husband, who seeks sexual union with a source outside the primary relationship. The wayward husband projects his Guardian onto the jealous wife, who seems to have the power to block the affair. Finally, for the mistress, the husband is the Beloved, and the wife the Guardian and barrier who prevents complete union. When any one person in the triangle internalizes the projected archetypes, the roles shift.

Let us return to the example of Ken and Jim. Jim found himself caught playing out the mother role with Ken. He knew Ken was seeing other men, and he knew Ken was lying to him. Jim followed his hunch about who Ken was seeing and contacted Seth, the other man. Jim's intuition was confirmed. Seth's presence in the relationship tested Jim's intuition, Self-trust, self-esteem, and ability to act on his own behalf.

Initially, the Guardian (projected onto Seth) was blocking Jim in his relationship with his Beloved (projected onto Ken). The psychic tension of the love triangle guided Jim to come face-to-face with his inner Guardian who took the form of psychological blocks—denial, fear, anxieties, self-doubt, and other self-limiting beliefs. After enduring the process of facing the inner Guardian and passing through his self-limiting attitudes, Jim was reunited with himself. His efforts were well rewarded with the return of Self-trust, self-esteem, self-love, and awareness of his personal boundaries. When Jim confronted Ken about seeing Seth and outlined his limits, saying, "A nonmonogamous relationship is unacceptable," Jim's role shifted and personified the Guardian for Ken.

The tables turn. The betrayer feels betrayed, and the betrayed becomes the betrayer. More obvious examples are found in cases of alcoholism or drug abuse. The codependent partner discovers that he or she has limits, communicates that truth, and takes on the role of initiator-betrayer. If the codependent person says, "l am not willing to live with your drinking (or drugging) anymore," the alcohol- or drug-dependent partner feels deeply betrayed and victimized. The normal reaction to confrontation starts with denial, then moves on to anger, rationalization, and depression. The cycle of sacred separation, purification, symbolic death, and, hopefully, new knowledge and rebirth, is set into motion for the intractable initiate-addict.

Jim took on the role of sacred initiator in his relationship. His statement put Ken to the test, but it was not really Jim's test of Ken. It was Ken's test of the soul—a challenge to come to his own truth, whatever that might have been. It only looked like Jim's test of Ken for as long as Ken projected the archetype of the Guardian onto Jim.

In couples therapy, Ken reviewed his own self-limiting patterns that perpetuated Ken's adoption of the role of the lying little boy. As mentioned in Chapter 2, Ken's direct experience of the Divine Mother's unconditional love in his inner work during our therapy together had a profound impact on his consciousness. He felt loved from the inside out for the first time in his life. His personal mother's judgments and criticisms about Ken's sexual preference had no power over him in the light of Great Mother's unconditional love.

This led to a startling discovery. Ken's choice of sexual expression was unconditionally acceptable. As he felt deeply loved and accepted for being exactly as he was, he awakened to a deeper truth: Loving other men erotically was an expression of his spiritual path. For Ken, sex was a sacrament and homosexuality was a form of worship. As I mentioned before, homosexual and heterosexual union between priest or priestess and worshipper was once a common form of religious practice throughout the ancient world. In addition to Indo-European cultures identified earlier in this chapter, there were also special divinities for homosexual worship in Tahiti, and the god Chin instituted homosexuality in the Yucatan. Though homosexuality became taboo since the dominance of Christianity and Roman rule, this form of union has a worldwide history contrary to our contemporary social mores.

Ken related to the stories of the Priests and Priestesses of the Sacred Flame. They were trained to arouse the heat of *kundalini* through erotic sexual passion as a form of divine service to humanity. The unmarried priests and priestesses were called virgins because of the purity of soul required to sustain one's sacred vows to keep the spiritual fires burning. The Romans, however, romanticized the purity of the virgin in efforts to control and suppress erotic forms of worship throughout the Roman Empire. The term *virgin* came to mean vows of physical chastity or celibacy instead of a purity of soul. A vestal virgin, if caught performing sexual rites, was sealed up in a cave and left alone to die a slow, torturous death. Ken felt that this story had resonance for him as well: Only today, sexual worship was identified with "immoral" sexual promiscuity. One suffered from social isolation instead of being sealed up in a cave; and, if one was not careful, one ran the risk of dying a slow, torturous death by the AIDS virus.

The archetypal Great Mother was telling Ken to trust his sexuality and the sacred, healing energies released through sexual union. As Ken healed his personal mother wound, he realized that her harsh criticisms were like a spiritual-warrior boot camp. If he had survived her slings and arrows, he would be ready for anything. Ken felt strongly that his sexual expression and sexual preference grew from ancient practices, and reawakening sacred sexuality within the gay community was part of his deeper purpose or mission in life. Ken's inner Father guided him to practice taking a stand on his choices and to tell the truth instead of remaining the lying little boy. He started with his lover Jim. Ken told Jim that traditional monogamous marriage, as a form, was not appropriate for him.

The archetype of the Guardian acts as an ego-boundary function in service of the higher Self. The Guardian requires respect. Sometimes it is important to push the limit, and sometimes it is important to accept the limit as it is. Whether to push or accept is not determined by anyone outside of oneself. Jim is not in a position to push Ken to be monogamous, nor is Ken in a position to push Jim to accept an open relationship. Making this choice is the function of the Guide. Inner guidance leads Ken to accept and act on the truth that ethical nonmonogamy is essential to the fulfillment of his spiritual path, a path that allows him to discover and unite with the Beloved in each sexual encounter. Conversely, Jim is guided to discover divine union through monogamy.

Monogamy, as a spiritual path, is a commitment to one, and only one, person. Numerologically, the number one represents independence, individuality, primal cause, and that original action that sets creation into motion. The mystery of multifaceted, multidimensional expression (i.e., the many ones merged into a single One) is intrinsic to the mystery teachings of monogamy. Monogamous relationship challenges each partner to respect the other's individuality, and to foster both independence and a sense of oneness within the primary relationship. This is achieved through actively initiating an exploration of the multidimensional facets within oneself and one's partner.

Betrayal of the beloved, like all betrayal experiences, returns us to our deepest sense of purpose in life. We are reminded that we each have a spiritual path in life that uniquely expresses one's true Self. We are here to live our ideals, rather than project our ideals onto a love object and presume that this person will fulfill our expectations. Through betrayal, we discover that we have an ideal that is not being fulfilled by our betrayer. Instead of dropping into perpetual cynicism and self-betrayal, this initiation challenges you to embody your ideal of love and to bring it to life. Become what you desire. For example, if you want respect, respect yourself and be respectful of others. One heals self-betrayal by taking a stand in life and by committing to the fulfillment of one's vital dream or vision by living it.

Through living our dream, we discover that we are all free to be ourselves in this world. In an odd, paradoxical way, betrayal teaches us to trust the process of life that brings us to truth and inspires us to live our dreams, regardless of the odds. In the words of W. H. Murray:

> Concerning all acts of initiative (and creation), there is one elementary truth, the ignorance of which kills countless ideas and splendid plans: that the moment one definitely commits oneself, then providence moves too.
>
> All sorts of things occur to help one that would never otherwise have occurred. A whole stream of events issues from the decision, raising in one's favor all manner of unforeseen incidents and meetings and material assistance, which no man could have dreamt would have come his way.

Ken and Jim both found this to be true. Within a year and a half of Jim and Ken's breakup, Jim found the partnership he sought. His new companion, Greg, shared many similar interests and the same sense of humor. They enjoyed stimulating conversations and soon discovered that they both dreamed of being in a successful, committed, intimate, loving, sexual relationship with a life partner who shared these values. More and more men were seeking this kind of relationship since AIDS intruded into the gay community. Greg and Jim were part of this new wave of expression among gays.

As for Ken, he enjoyed a wide range of erotic activities and became an advocate for creative safe sex. He encouraged the exploration of all varieties of safer sensual delights between himself and his sexual partners. Ken's commitment to himself and his community was to bring back some of the life, joy, play, and freedom that had been so prevalent in gay lifestyles prior to the threat of AIDS. Ken felt good about himself and his contribution to his friends and intimates. Expression of one's personal truth within one's community serves a greater purpose. The whole community benefits as individuals within the community follow their inner guidance and commit to living their dreams.

Every person we meet reflects our Beloved, evokes our Guardian's tests, and guides us towards integration and ultimate fulfillment. Sometimes we are guided to leave relationships. Sometimes we are guided to stay. Whether you leave or stay, you can expect that your inner Beloved will guide you to circumstances, relationships, and events that bring you to wholeness, the union of height and depth within the psyche.

Lover relationships that move beyond the parent–needy child patterns energize Goddess-God, cocreative partnerships. Choosing to live with your beloved betrayer-initiator is a soul challenge to stay true to your inner Self and to unite with your Beloved within. Move beyond the wounds of childhood inflicted by the betrayals of your mother and father, and discover your Beloved, your guardian and guide on your path to wholeness. First, make the commitment to creatively cooperate with your inner companion. Then you make the same commitment to your outer companion. As R. J. Stewart said, it is here "on Earth . . . the highest state of all . . . where all conflicts are to be resolved, all actions purified, and all barriers to true enlightenment lifted." Who is better qualified than your beloved friend and lover to initiate you and help you work through your barriers, resolve your conflicts, and purify your actions?

Margo and Cindy used the barriers in their relationship to recognize and work with inner blocks. Margo and Cindy had been together for about two and a half years when I met them. They had been married for just over a year and were living together in Margo's house when the betrayal-to-trust initiation presented itself. Prior to getting together with Margo, Cindy had maintained a long-term friendship with Tom, an older, male friend of hers who was now living out of the country most of the time. Their friendship included occasional sexual expression throughout the eight years that Tom and Cindy knew each other. The threat came when Tom, who had become an intimate friend of both women over the course of Cindy and Margo's relationship, invited Cindy for a visit to his home in Mexico at a time when Margo could not join them. Margo and Cindy came into my office with the "my way or no way" power imbalance. Creativity was blocked—they just couldn't imagine another way through this one. Yet their commitment to their marriage and their desire for continued intimacy was strong. This gave them a solid foundation to take the next step: to turn inward and release personal blocks to creativity and cooperation.

Margo's creativity was blocked by feelings of jealousy. Even though Cindy assured Margo that she loved and respected her, and that she had no intention of leaving the relationship, Margo's jealousy was not appeased. In our inner work, we explored the pattern supporting the jealousy. Margo had felt this intensity of feeling before. While she was focusing on her feelings, I asked her to close her eyes and intuitively pick a number without thinking about it. "Ten," she said. We investigated what happened when she was about ten years old. "That's when I began to play baseball," she reflected. It seemed that beneath Margo's jealousy was a more fundamental pattern associated with issues of competition. Margo was great at sports. She was always one of the first picked, even when she played with the boys. Competitive sports and varsity team sports in high school were a big part of Margo's early development. Winning was very important to Margo—being first and best.

In many ways, there was no way Margo could compete with Tom. She felt she was out of his league. First of all, he was a man. Second, he was retired and financially independent. However, for Cindy, there was no competition. Her loyalties were clear. Margo was Cindy's spouse and lifelong partner. Tom was a friend and the only man with whom Cindy pursued her bisexuality. Margo and Tom were separate and different, each with her or his own value. Metaphorically, Tom and Margo were playing in different ballparks. This new awareness took the edge off the sexual competition, but Margo needed to know that she was picked first by Cindy.

To be of secondary importance in Cindy's life provoked resentment and feelings of self-betrayal for Margo, the first and fourth stages of the traditional betrayal response. Meanwhile, Cindy was struggling with the fifth stage of the traditional betrayal response. She felt emotionally manipulated and controlled by Margo's moods, instead of feeling free to be bisexual. Cindy would retaliate with emotional distance and withdrawal.

This conflict was a challenge to discover a creative alternative in which both women were free to be true to themselves. Creativity is the mark of the Divine. Willingness to try something new, to reach for your ideals, and to risk becoming the person you want to be awakens the creative Source within you. I encouraged Cindy and Margo to cooperate more with each other and to take the time needed to negotiate a mutually satisfying solution—a solution in which Margo would come first and Cindy could go on vacation with Tom.

Before we began our process of negotiation, I told Cindy and Margo that cooperation would move us from conflict to creativity, because cooperation takes imagination, honesty, communication, and negotiation. Imagination bubbles up from a limitless reservoir of creative intelligence within the psyche. I explained that we have two helpers who move us along the path to unite with the creative Source of our being. The wisdom of the inner Guardian, on the one hand, tells us when to say no. The inner Guide, on the other hand, takes us to that creative solution that ennobles us and empowers us to fulfill our greatest potential and soul purpose. Honesty is essential. It means accepting your limits and expressing these limits to your partner. Communication requires that we not only say yes and no to our partner, but that we also listen to and respect our partner's inner guidance that brings him or her to say yes and no.

I defined negotiation as a process that means to "give to get." I asked Cindy what she was willing to give Margo, to show her that Margo was number one in her life, so she could go on the vacation. We brainstormed together. Cindy could spend extra time with Margo before and after the vacation; she could buy Margo flowers or give her verbal appreciation to indicate how valuable and important she was to Cindy; and they could plan their own romantic weekend, just for the two of them.

I asked Margo, "Would that work to show you how special you are to Cindy—that you are number one?"

"Yes," Margo replied.

"Cindy, can you do all these activities which we have discussed?"

"No," was her answer. The Guardian had spoken.

R. J. Stewart reminds us that the Guardian presents the test to those who seek to reunite with the Beloved, the creative Source. The use of the word no is not a personal rejection. Think of the word *no* as an invitation to explore and to become creative. The Guardian is bested through a battle of wits in fairy tales, not through domination or power struggles. Let your curiosity guide you through the Guardian's gate into the arms of your creative Self.

I responded to Cindy's no with an open-ended question. "Oh, why not?" I inquired innocently.

"Because, I'm afraid Margo will dump on me. Margo tries to control me by dumping on me, and I'm afraid of being emotionally manipulated if I spend too much time with her."

Commitment takes time and energy, planning, and follow-through. The three of us took the time needed to define "dump on" and discover that it meant Margo's bad-sport behavior—yelling, pouting, and being sullen and uncooperative. Margo understood how this behavior pushed Cindy away, and she realized that if she wanted Cindy to be closer to her, she would need to do something different.

Then Margo's inner Guardian spoke up. "I can't just deny my feelings and pretend they aren't there!" We all agreed that Margo had a right to express her feelings, but that Cindy was not the best person to listen and help Margo obtain some emotional relief. Margo agreed to talk things out with a close friend, call me, or use other resources. Cindy agreed to not provoke Margo's competitive edge by talking about her vacation plans with Tom.

Negotiation looks for a win-win solution based on consensus, not compromise. With compromise, everybody loses a little. In consensus, imagination is rewarded. Everybody comes out a winner. This additional information brought us to our win-win solution: Cindy would initiate spending extra time with Margo before and after Cindy's trip to Mexico. Cindy would make sure she did not taunt Margo or provoke insecurity and competition by talking about her upcoming vacation plans. Instead, Cindy would buy Margo flowers or give her verbal appreciation to make sure she expressed how valuable and important Margo was to Cindy. Cindy would be responsible for planning a special getaway for Margo and herself. In their discussions before and after Cindy's trip, Margo and

Cindy would focus on their upcoming romantic weekend, which was just for the two of them. Margo agreed that if she began to lose herself to competitive and jealous feelings, she would make contact with an appropriate outer resource and not dump on Cindy.

It is important to follow up on our agreements to see how well they work in reality. This process develops a quality reflected in one-on-one relationships: intimacy ("in-time-I-see"). Over time, we come to know ourselves and each other better. Since I wanted to use Cindy and Margo as exemplars in this chapter, I had a chance to find out how their follow-up discussion went. When I contacted them to get their permission to use their story, it was a year after the vacation-with-Tom catalyst for growth.

We sat together in my office reviewing what did and didn't work. When I asked them what happened, they laughed and told me quite a story. Margo began, "Everything was fine until Cindy left town. But after she left, I didn't hear from her. She didn't call, write, or anything. . . ." Cindy picked up the conversation at this point. "I called Margo when I got back into town and got a real earful." To make a long story short, we discovered, once again, that Margo's desire to dump is directly proportional to Cindy's lack of initiating contact, and Cindy's desire to withdraw is directly related to her anticipation of Margo's moods.

Every experience is a learning experience. This incident gave us valuable information for the next time, should the situation with Tom arise again. In addition to the previously mentioned agreements, if Cindy goes away with Tom again, it will be important to maintain some kind of contact with Margo. Something as simple as a love note, postcard, or phone call would get the message across. Cindy's actions have the power to affirm the deeper truth beyond Margo's fears—that as an outer companion and marriage partner, Margo is in first place.

Here's another example of using conflicts to stimulate creativity and new, nontraditional options in a relationship. Linda and Eddie found that, even after the tantric tune-up with Alise, Eddie was still uninterested in sharing sexual intimacies with Linda. It took another six months for them to each recognize, accept, and express their individual truths. Eddie was feeling asexual. Linda was feeling sexual. Yet there were many good points to their marriage. They loved each other, had great communication, and were physically affectionate with each other. They enjoyed each other's company, families, and friends. They also shared a lifestyle that brought them much comfort. Their home was a sanctuary separate from the hurly-burly stresses of their high-power careers. Tradition would have Linda betray herself and her sexual self-expression by remaining in a sexually monogamous relationship with Eddie; or she could betray her commitment to her relationship and divorce Eddie so she could be free to pursue a new sexual relationship. It seemed absurd to both Linda and Eddie to break up the relationship just because they weren't engaging in sexual intercourse.

Expressing personal values through action builds integrity. Linda felt alive and creatively turned on at a time when Eddie's creative and sexual energy was unavailable. They had a creative dilemma: how to act with integrity and respect both the inner companion and the outer companion. Linda and Eddie did find a way to be true to themselves and each other. Linda described it this way:

> We evolved into an arrangement, which we renegotiate annually on our anniversary. If I meet someone with whom I wish to explore my sexual expression, I will do so in a way that honors my commitment to my marriage and myself, and will keep this relationship private and separate from the sanctity of our marriage. This includes not provoking emotional insecurity or physical threats.
>
> This shakes down to:
> 1. Eddie does not know who, what, where, when, how, or if.
> 2. If he wants to know, and asks, I will be honest.
> 3. I will not bring any other person into our home, which includes our circle of friends and relations, as well as our physical home, especially the bedroom.
> 4. Sexual contact is within the context of safe sex.

Intimacy is a celebration of differences. Contrast is key. Intimacy urges a tolerance of differences, a confirmation of commitment, and an abandonment of the power struggle. They agreed that Eddie, had the right to be asexual if that was what he felt he needed; and Linda had the right to be sexual if that was what she needed. It so happened that Eddie's next two and a half years took him through depths of soul, which included job layoffs and career losses, the loss of physical health and well-being, and a confrontation with financial problems. Sex was the last thing on his mind. These outer events moved Eddie toward even deeper self-exploration, which led to a profound personal spiritual opening. Throughout Eddie's withdrawal into the depths of soul, Linda had her higher Self and a wealth of inner and outer resources to support and sustain her.

Commitment is born from the recognition of shared values. Linda and Eddie shared a value of being together through the process of transformation. Eddie was in the thick of psychospiritual death while Linda was experiencing the joys of rebirth—enjoying her new friends, continued success and increasing recognition at work. Linda and Eddie realized that they were experiencing different phases of spiritual transformation. They were willing to find a way to support themselves and each other through the process. Eddie had the right to be deep within himself, to hit bottom in his life, and Linda had the right to experience new heights, joys, and possibilities. They allowed each other the gift of sacred separation—the opportunity to follow the promptings of Spirit to guide them each individually. They were able to separate and go through the process of personal transformation without physically separating and ending the marriage.

It is not surprising to find that Linda and Eddie's resolution brought them to a new, nontraditional form that breaks with so-called "tried and true" traditions. The way they found worked for them. It allowed them to have individual integrity and remain together as a couple through these soul-testing times.

Fueled by integrity, commitment is the Source of energy that maintains and sustains a relationship over time. By their eighth year of marriage, Eddie's inner spark began to regenerate. He expressed new interest in work and career, physical health, social relationships, and sex with Linda. Their marriage motivated both Linda and Eddie to discover, follow, and fulfill their individual paths to wholeness. We make a commitment to ourselves first—to the fulfillment of the deepest values of our spiritual Self. Intimacy follows personal liberation, regeneration, and rebirth as a result of transmuting one's personal karma via psychic contact with deep inner resources. Linda and Eddie were stimuli for transformation and fellow travelers—companions for each other as they journeyed together along the arduous path of self-transformation.

Betrayal of the beloved trains us to be true to ourselves while simultaneously learning how to support another individual in the same process. Marriage gives us a safe place where we can practice living our values. We learn to risk being ourselves in our world. Freedom to be one's spiritual

Self in this world is risky. Our beloved outer companion provides us with a place to practice, experiment, receive feedback, and refine ourselves so we can turn inward, gain new insight, and try again.

One's spiritual practice is to become an example of what one's soul so deeply desires, to join with one's highest Self, rather than project one's desires onto one's human partner. We are here to bring the Beloved into this world, to demonstrate divine love in our human relationships—the irresistible love and union that exists between the higher Self and the evolving self within the psyche. We do this by allowing each other the freedom to be who we are as we each embark on our own remarkable journey of self-transformation.

Intimate partnership trains us to express unconditional love and to meet the Guardian's challenge to become ever more creative in our interpersonal relationships. The couple dynamic is a testing ground for the development of creativity, commitment, cooperation, and intimate companionship. These interpersonal skills enhance all the significant relationships in one's life. Newly found talents transfer to work relationships, family relationships, and friendships, as one practices living one's truth and vital dream within the context of one's community. The archetypes of the Beloved, Guardian, and Guide are working through us as we become agents of a social transformation of consciousness in service of the spiritual evolution of humanity.

Practice the Art of Self-Talk

1. Allow your Divine Parents to nurture your child within by practicing self-talk. Look in the mirror and give yourself the appreciation, approval, encouragement, praise, and acceptance that you seek. Remind yourself that you are learning and growing. Create a positive affirmation to hold in your mind as a mantra, as an antidote to negative thinking patterns. There is a Source of unconditional love in the universe that guards you and guides you toward wholeness. This One knows what you need in order to grow and empowers you to fulfill your dreams and get your needs met.

2. When you take a few moments of private time by sitting in front of a mirror, look yourself in the eye and get to know yourself. Smile at yourself. Frown at yourself. Make a few different faces, and come to know the many different faces that express different parts of you.

3. Now look deep into your eyes and make contact with your inner Self. Feel a warmth and compassion shining forth from your eyes in response to this contact.

4. Repeat each of the statements on page 117 aloud. Imagine that your higher Self is speaking to you. Repeat each statement two or three times. Notice how you feel.

5. Choose one of these statements that resonates with your inner Self and repeat it silently to yourself throughout the day as an affirmation.

AFFIRMATIONS

- Every day I respect you more and more. You are an incredible creation!
- I'm enjoying getting to know you. I accept you completely, in every way, exactly as you are.
- I love you, no matter what you do in life.
- I know that you always do the best you can, whatever the circumstances.
- Your best is good enough for me. I know you will do even better when you're able.
- There is a place for you to fill in the world, one that only you can fill. I will help you fulfill yourself.
- I have the power to undo all the harm that has been done to you in the past, which has blocked you from your right fulfillment. I undo all the harm that has been done. I hold you in a circle of divine protection.
- Judgments and harsh criticisms have no power to harm you.
- Only good comes to you. I give only good to you.
- I draw in everything you need to fulfill yourself. Today you can enjoy yourself.
- I want you to enjoy being who you are.
- I want you to express who you are and have fun doing it.
- Have a good time just being the way you are.
- There are no "mistakes." I will help you. Help me now by receiving the gifts I bring to you to bring to others.
- I accept you exactly as you are.
- I trust you.
- I praise you for your loyalty and service.
- You are fine just the way you are.
- You can serve me best by enjoying yourself and expressing yourself.
- I know what a stretch this is. Thank you for your perseverance and commitment to keep on keeping on.
- I enjoy talking with you this way. I want to talk with you like this often.
- You and I are creating the kind of relationship I have dreamed about and hoped for. You are not alone. I love you.

EXERCISE 4-B

Seek the Path of the Beloved

There are many paths to the Beloved. In astrology, sexuality and intimacy are defined by the fifth, sixth, seventh, and eighth houses. These houses are ruled by the four elements: fire, earth, air, and water, respectively. The fifth house, **fire,** is symbolized by sensual Leo the Lion. Key words include creativity, play, and fun, or recreational sex. Fifth house affairs are very hot at first, then quickly burn out. Eddie's sexual liaison with Alise might have fallen into the category of this fire path.

Sixth house dynamics bring **earth's** commitment to a relationship. Vesta combines with Mercury in the sign of Virgo the Virgin to symbolize commitment to the union of body, mind, and spirit working together in the service of a higher purpose. As already mentioned, the virgin is married to the sacred fires of spirit, first and foremost. Commitment to Self is key. Marriage to an outer partner is secondary, if this happens at all. Ken may travel this earthly path to the Beloved.

The one-on-one focus of the seventh house oversees both marriage contracts and business partnerships. Seventh house alliances are symbolized by the **air** sign, Libra, and have planetary associations with Venus and the asteroid Juno. Key concepts include monogamous partnership, cooperation, harmony, equality, and balance. The seventh house relationship path reflects Jim's values and visions.

Finally, eighth house ventures are ruled by Pluto-Hades, the Lord of the Underworld, who is at home in the **water** sign of Scorpio. The key word is intimacy, and this house emphasizes sexual, emotional, and psychic intimacy in the service of personal transformation. This describes the spiritual path chosen by Linda and Eddie, and Margo and Cindy. Different people have different relationship paths.

1. Which element or house best describes you now?

2. Have you followed different paths at particular points in your life?

3. Which path is most familiar to you?

Explore Your Blocks to Intimacy

Different blocks surface in our interpersonal relationships as signals to guide us back to our creative Source within. These blocks are the tests of the Guardian. Below are listed fire, earth, air, and water tests. Review the list and identify which, if any, are present in your alliance with your partner. Spend time exploring the nature of your blocks. Meditate on them, write in your journal, and share your insights with your partner.

1. **Fire:** Creativity is blocked. The two of you are not having fun together anymore.

2. **Earth:** You think about leaving the relationship, or you obsess on whether your partner will leave you. You doubt your commitment to each other.

3. **Air:** Cooperation ceases. There is a decrease in sharing ideas and negotiating a balance of power between you. Things seem unequal and unjust.

4. **Water:** Intimacy and companionship dwindle. Energetic connection between the two of you, as expressed through sexual desire, emotional closeness, or feeling psychically tuned-in, decreases. You feel isolated, resentful, vengeful, or betrayed.

Work with Your Inner Companion

External blocks are metaphors for internal barriers. If you find that you have any of the blocks identified in Exercise 4-C, take the time to consciously separate from your outer companion to rebuild TRUST with your inner companion and Guide.

1. Turn inward to discover a deeper truth.

2. Remember to release attachment to outcomes and relax your body and mind before you use intuitive resources to receive a new perspective.

3. Use your intuition to gain insight into what insecurities, wounds from childhood, old patterns, limiting beliefs, or expectations are blocking you from your full creativity, from being your most fulfilled Self in your present situation with your partner.

4. As you take your stand with your beloved outer companion, challenge yourself to be creative, committed, cooperative, and intimate in your communications with each other.

5. Remember to use feedback as a signal to turn inward to remove further blocks and discover an even deeper truth.

EXERCISE 4-E

Work with Your Outer Companion

Use your ideal inner relationship as a model for your interactions with your outer companion. Learn to communicate (listen and speak) as well as negotiate (give to get) as you move together from crisis to creativity.

1. Together, define the topic. Next, agree on a date, time, and place to explore the issue further.

2. Before this meeting, separately explore unspoken thoughts and feelings, including your hidden hopes and fears. Identify deeper wishes, wants, and needs. What blocks you from your creative Source within? Listen to your inner Guide and Guardian. (See Exercises 4-C and 4-D on pages 119 and 120.)

3. Imagine what your partner wishes, wants, or needs. Use your intuition.

4. Ask yourself, "What am I willing to give? How can I support my partner's fulfillment?" Remember that your partner has your greatest fulfillment in mind, too.

5. Imagine a few different scenarios in which you and your partner are both getting your wishes, wants, and needs fulfilled. Remember that the best is possible. We each were born to be fulfilled. Brainstorm and be creative! Include outrageous and silly, as well as practical, solutions.

6. At the agreed-upon time and place, share your reflections and ideas with each other. Remember:
   • Check out assumptions.
   • Ask for what you want.
   • Respect each other's no, but go for yes.
   • Present possibilities that bring mutual fulfillment.
   • Brainstorm together to expand possibilities.
   • Be willing to experiment, explore, and risk.
   • Use outer resources as needed.

7. Schedule a follow-up meeting to review and reevaluate the success of your solutions. Repeat steps 1 through 5, as needed. Continue to stimulate individual creativity, commitment, cooperation, and companionship between you and your outer beloved.

Chapter 5

Betrayal of the Body

Gateway to Surrender

Wound: If you suffer from physical illness or injury, your body does not respond to the command of your personal will as you imagine it should. You feel out of control, let down, limited, or disabled.

Truth: There is a force greater than you and your personal will at work in your body. Immortal Self expresses itself unconsciously through the wisdom of our bodies and consciously through the wisdom of our chosen attitudes and beliefs.

Healing: Consciously use the wisdom of your mind's thoughts and feelings to discover the mystery teachings unconsciously expressed through the metaphor of your physical body.

When I sat down to write the overview for this chapter, I came down with a horrible sore throat and cold. My writing day was clouded with an antihistamine haze. The next day I canceled my appointments with clients. I spent more time in bed. Actually, a sore throat was a relief for me. This was my first illness since I was laid up in bed during the previous spring and summer. I thought I just had swollen glands. It turned out to be shingles in my throat that infected my facial nerves. The right side of my head was in a constant vise-grip of electrifying pain for almost three months.

Prolonged illness presents a person with powerful life lessons. After five and a half weeks of "I'll be better in a day or two," an ears-nose-and-throat specialist verified the diagnosis of *varicella zoster* virus. I began to surrender to the truth that I might *not* be better in a day or two. In fact, no one knew when I would be better. Some cases, I was told, persisted for six weeks, some lasted up to twelve months.

While in bed, after trying everything I knew to reduce the pain, I finally asked myself, "What can I do?" My inner voice replied, "You can breathe. You can rest. And, if you are lucky, you can sleep." In truth, that was about all I could do.

Something happened as I breathed, rested, and slept my way through this illness. I became receptive to the help of others, especially my spouse. Everyone around me was so caring, so compassionate—my spouse, close friends and family, the homeopath, our family doctor, the specialist—everyone. Receptivity is a formidable lesson for someone as independent as I am—to trust that I do not have to do it all alone—that others are, and will be, there for me. Self-sufficiency is a value reinforced by Western culture. For many of us, to ask for help is tantamount to admitting some imagined defeat.

Wisdom of the body provides lessons for the soul and puts the spirit to the test. In my case, wisdom of the body had taught me to receive. Wisdom of the mind chooses thoughts that uplift, nurture, and support the spirit. One of my colleagues had said, "This illness seems like a contraction before you expand . . . like you are pulling way into yourself before you move out into the world in a new way." I held on to this idea when my mind taunted me with that famous betrayal-to-trust question, "Why is this happening to me?" How we answer a question like that brings either death, pain, and misery, or liberation.

The ancient Egyptians had an elaborate symbolic system for guiding the initiate's choice beyond death toward liberation and life. Within the funerary texts, in the "Papyrus of Hunefer," there is a scene called "The Weighing of the Heart."[1] One's heart is weighed on the scales of Maat, the Goddess of Justice and Truth. In one pan sits your heart. The other pan has a single feather. The feather is Maat's symbol. One's heart must be as light as a feather for the scales to balance.

The thought that there was a positive value to my illness, that I was like a spring being tightly compressed so I might be catapulted forward farther than before, lightened my heart. Other thoughts, full of self-blame, like "You've been pushing too hard and overextending," "You're not taking care of yourself," or "Your stress factor is too high" only brought about heavyheartedness and increased my pain and helplessness. I also noticed that looking for rational causes like "You were exposed to the chicken pox virus on the children's ward of the hospital in the spring," decreased my self-blame, but also disempowered me, leaving me a victim to circumstances beyond my control.

Objectively speaking, any and all of these interpretations may have been true. But the truth of Maat, that truth that lightens the heart and allows us to pass beyond the grief of death, is not necessarily based on rational cause and effect. The funerary texts counsel against heavyheartedness, which weighs a person down in fear, shame, or guilt. The mind chooses to eliminate destructive thinking and to observe the life lessons that remain. Some of my lessons were to receive the abundant love, caring, and support that is available to me, to slow down, to surrender, and to trust even more.

In the weighing-of-the-heart scene, digesting the value of one's experience is the job of **Anubis**, the jackal. He stands to the left of Maat's scales as he leads you to the weighing of the heart. Like the jackal who eats carrion, Anubis can stomach death. Anubis, sacred to the embalmers of ancient Egypt, exemplifies the wisdom intrinsic to the natural process of digestion, elimination, and assimilation. He and his priests knew the secrets of what to preserve and what to eliminate. Anubis, as a principle in consciousness, filters through the human psyche as an inner psychic structure that is able to digest our most rotten experiences. This includes digesting, assimilating, and eliminating those most foul or fetid thoughts and tainted, nasty feelings that prevent one from being lighthearted. Betrayal is a most putrid experience. Yet we have a natural ability to separate out elements within the betrayal experience that nourish and support the soul's growth and development. At the same time, we have the power to eliminate toxicity and waste material.

How we accomplish this miraculous feat is symbolized by Lord **Thoth**, the ibis-headed god. The sacred ibis of ancient Egypt is a graceful, strikingly beautiful white bird, accented by its bare black head and neck and the pitch black feathers in its wings and lower back. The contrast between dark and light is an appropriate metaphor for Thoth. He is a moon god, and he represents the reflective light of intuition that helps the mind soar beyond the dark night of the soul. This is the bird of the hieroglyph *gem*, which signifies "to find."[2] As consort to the Goddess of Justice and Truth, Thoth symbolically unites with Maat to find truth and justice. Thoth stands to the right of Maat's scales; you can see him recording each experience contained within the heart. Without value judgment, Thoth observes every thought and feeling, and he simply notes whether the scales balance or whether the heart pan hangs low.

If the heart is heavy, **Amam**,[3] the Eater of the Dead waiting at the base of the scales, gobbles it up. Amam, whose name literally means "the devourer," is a female monster with the head of a crocodile, body of a lion, and hindquarters of a hippopotamus. These are three of the most voracious, savage, and fearsome animals of ancient Egypt. A heavy heart indicates that you are being consumed by your base animal nature, your conditioned responses, and instinctive animal reactions. Adrenaline and other hormonal secretions pumping through the blood stimulate emotional reactions, those psychological defense mechanisms like the denial, anger, bargaining, and depression stages of mourning. All defense mechanisms are psychological representations of an instinctual fear reaction to a perceived threat to our survival. We faint, fight, flee, or freeze.

Ann, a sixty-two-year-old woman who almost died from kidney failure, told me of her journey from betrayal to trust. A veteran psychotherapist, she was trained in no-nonsense gestalt psychology. In the early 1980s, Ann began to explore tai chi and Taoist philosophy under the tutelage of a Chinese *sifu*, or teacher. Because her energy level was low, she began receiving regular acupuncture treatments from her sifu, who was also a traditional Chinese doctor.

For five years, Ann did everything she knew, short of seeing an allopathic physician, to work with her low energy. She tried taking vitamins and Chinese herbs. She also tried new diets, exercise, and acupuncture. Looking back on that time in her life, Ann reflected, "I was in so much denial that I needed my body to turn yellow, literally yellow from uremia, before I would pay attention. I just kept feeling worse and worse. For six months my friends told me that I looked yellow. I would just say that I was tired. I was dragging around without any energy. I don't know how I did it. I was just willing to live with no energy."

In addition to herbs and acupuncture treatments, her doctor repeatedly told Ann that she suffered from low energy, that in particular the energy in her kidneys was low, very low. "My Chinese doctor never says that anything horrible is happening, ever. You know, it's just not the way he looks at life. Toward the end, he simply said, 'No energy in kidneys.' I could not put two and two together and realize that I had kidney failure. The last few times I went, I finally said, 'If I don't get better by next week, I'm going to go and have tests taken.' He encouraged me to go and do that." Finally, at the age of fifty-eight, Ann went to an internist, submitted to blood tests, was admitted to a hospital, and placed on dialysis. Ann was diagnosed with kidney failure—end stage renal disease. Without treatment, this disease is fatal.

Ann's children were furious. They blamed the acupuncturist for almost killing their mother. Ann's interpretation was inspired by Maat's truth and justice rather than vengeance. Instead of blaming her acupuncturist, Ann said, "I needed to go that far before I would wake up and realize what I was doing to myself. It took me years to get the message that I have a choice about the quality of my life."

"It's like a dream I had," Ann said, as we continued to discuss her response to her illness. "I had a dream that I was stuck in traffic on the freeway approaching the tunnel going out toward my office in Walnut Creek, California. Everything was at a standstill—a total, dead standstill. I got out of the car and tried to see what the block was and all of the sudden I realized that I was going the wrong way. It was like a miracle in my dream. 'Oh, I don't have to be stuck in this traffic; I'm going to San Francisco, not Walnut Creek. I just have to turn around and go the other way.' I needed to almost die before I would turn my life around. My sifu was willing to let me die if that was what I needed to do to learn this lesson."

The choice of which way to go was her choice, not her doctor's or her children's. Ann chose to go toward life.

Emotional reactions to body betrayals are the domain of the soul and are to be weighed and measured on Maat's scale. Anubis, Thoth, and Amam provide the checks and balances. Through the intuitive self-observation attributed to Thoth, and Anubis's psychic, and frequently unconscious, digestion of the experience, one comes to find the truth that lightens the heart. These thoughts and feelings will lead you to liberation, regeneration, and rebirth. This is Maat's divine justice.

In our culture today, Maat, as a principle that stands for justice, law, and order, is misconstrued. Justice implies meting out punishment to the guilty while rewarding victims with retribution. Being consumed by Amam is not enough. Righteous vengeance is the order of our day. It is also the first test of the betrayal initiation. As we have learned in previous chapters, the antidote to righteous vengeance and resentment is TRUST. Who or what to trust is not determined by anyone outside oneself.

Ann considered her truth and spoke. "I learned so much through this whole process. Mainly, I have been learning to pay attention. For example, now I have to take medication twice a day. I have to find a way not to forget. I have to focus constantly. Daily. Like, maybe I could forget to take it once or twice. But, if the level of immunity goes up, then I'm in jeopardy of rejecting the transplanted kidney. So my body is teaching me to focus on what I'm doing, where I'm going, and what's happening—to live right here with my feet on the earth. Being here in this world is a big lesson for me."

As Ann spoke, I remembered a story told to me by my friend Rabbi Ayla Grafstein. She told me about her teacher Rabbi Zalman Schachter who was suffering from a variety of physical challenges and had said that "the physical world is the most holy of all the worlds." This is the world where it all

comes together. For Ann, an act like taking pills every day becomes a spiritual practice to remember—to be here, to pay attention, to practice living her deeper truth on a daily basis.

In the weighing scene, once your heart has found truth, you move onward in the company of **Horus**. Horus is the hawk-headed god standing to the right of Thoth. In the Egyptian story of the Trinity, he is the son of the Divine Mother and Father. Horus had been magically conceived by Isis and the dead Osiris. Osiris was cut up into fourteen pieces and scattered all over Egypt by his brother Set. Isis found thirteen of the fourteen dismembered pieces—all but the phallus. She put Osiris together and resurrected him. Even without a physical member, Osiris inseminated Isis, and she conceived Horus. Clearly, this was not a physical insemination. Horus was the birth of something other than the physical. Horus, the Hawk, is the dream child that takes form and becomes the soul of the initiate. He symbolizes the mystery of the spiritual life and the evolution of consciousness.

Egyptians, who were experts on immortal and mortal realities, created many words for the soul to describe the particular nuances of this concept. To the ancient Egyptian, physical to nonphysical described a continuum of discrete states, each with their own structure and function. *Khaibit, ka, hadit, khu, sa-hu, sa, ab, ba, sokhim,* and *ren* were, and still are, a few of the Egyptian words for "soul." Each describes different gateways to expanded states of consciousness.

In the weighing scene, the ka, which has the physical form of **Hunefer**, represents the soul. Notice that Hunefer is pictured three times in the papyrus. (See the figure on page 123.) First, he is being led by Anubis. Next, Hunefer is following Horus. Finally, in the upper register, we find Hunefer kneeling before the lord Ra and the company of Egyptian gods and goddesses. John Anthony West, an expert on ancient Egyptian lore, says that the ka

> is what today we would call personality: the pervading sense of "I" that inhabits the body but that is not the body. . . . There is the animal *ka* concerned with the desires of the body; the divine *ka* that heeds the call of the spirit; and the intermediate *ka*, which provides the impetus to those on the path for gradually gaining control of the animal *ka* and placing it in the service of the divine *ka*.[4]

The ka is one's self-concept as determined by one's body of personal experience. Our self-image changes as our awareness expands. The animal ka concerned with the desires of the body focuses its awareness on pain and pleasure. As behavioral psychologists have established, learning in lower animals and humans is based on a conditioned response to avoid punishment or pain and to achieve a reward or gain pleasure. This type of learning describes the personality of the animal ka. It contains all our pre-conceptions about ourselves and our world, such as self-judgments, praises, and criticisms as determined by conditioned responses learned from one's family of origin, cultural traditions, socioeconomic background, and personal history. One's self-concept includes a range of self-assumptions. An example is what it meant to Ann to see herself as sick and what she thought other people would think about her if she was ill. Anubis helps the personality digest and eliminate one's conditioning.

The image of Hunefer following Horus represents the intermediate ka in which the mortal animal self is tamed and serves the Master within—the immortal spirit. Notice the four figures standing on the lotus in front of Osiris. These are the Children of Horus. They are usually fashioned as animal-headed canopic jars that guard the viscera of the mummy, and they represent our instinctive gut reactions.[5] The Eye of Horus, seen hovering above the Children of Horus, carries in its talons the *shen,* symbol of eternity, along with a feather, the symbol of truth.

"All the urges of the passions express vital natural impulses," Isha Schwaller de Lubicz writes. "The human passions are life-impulses which have been perverted . . . and so skillfully perverted that it is very difficult to discover beneath their complications, the almost divine power which is their source."[6] Through perception of eternal truth, one gains insight into the spiritual nature of one's animalistic gut reactions. This is how the animal ka is placed in service of the divine ka.

To the Egyptian, the falcon is the symbol of the soul. Like the hawk who soars high above the earth and gains perspective on the terrain below, so the soul is free to fly beyond the physical and gain perspec- tive on life. Legend has it that immortality is a state of being in which the ka identifies itself with the *ba.* The ba is written hieroglyphically as a bird with a human head. It is the only Egyptian symbol that has a human head on top of an animal body. Typical Egyptian symbols are human bodies with animal heads. The ba represents an expanded state of awareness in which animal consciousness is surmounted by human intelligence. This is the state of consciousness associated with what today we call the higher Self.

Identifying with our Horus-falcon Self, we find that we have the wings to fly to the realm of the gods, as symbolized by Hunefer supplicating himself before the Egyptian pantheon. This is symbolic of an act of surrender to the Divine—a shift from "my will" to "Thy will." The immortality of the divine ka is the result of shifting the focus of one's personality. The personality that is identified with the ba, or higher Self, perceives life beyond the physical, and so it is immortal. A personality that is identified with our physical, animal body, is mortal and subject to a death and dying cycle. To follow Horus, the Hawk, is an evolutionary leap in consciousness.

In scientific circles, where the soul is a question for much debate, there are some brave enough to concede that there might be a mind separate from the physical brain. Spiritual realities are usually completely denied. Lack of awareness about transpersonal reality is a vestige from our animal roots. We need not berate ourselves for being unconscious or for being in denial. Self-awareness is an evolutionary leap. As a life form, we are fairly new to this evolutionary game.

Think about it. Scientific evidence indicates that Earth was formed about 4.6 billion years ago. It took about six hundred million years just to establish single-celled life forms. During the next few billion years, Earth was just one giant landmass until the seven continents that we know today took shape. Then, finally, plants, trees, fish, shelled fish, amphibians, reptiles, birds, and mammals appeared, about 570 million years ago. Humans have been around only for the last 1.8 million years. In other words, if we imagine that the whole world began a year ago, human beings only showed up on the scene about three and a half hours ago. Joan Grant tells the story like this.

> [When Ptah, Creator of Life, spoke to Life, his creation, he said,] "I have sent you forth into rocks, and into plants, and into animals. . . . Now I will make you bodies like my own, and for the first time you shall say, 'I am'; and in saying this must say, 'I am alone.' No longer can I lead you on your way. Now you must start upon a long journey, which does not end until you can greet me, not as your creator, but as your brother."
>
> And Life said, "We demand this chance, this right, to journey to your brotherhood."
>
> Then Ptah created man.[7]

We are a relatively new experiment in consciousness—a self-conscious being in an animal body. Our warm mammalian bodies are like a beloved pet that needs care and attention. We must take it out for walks, give it a healthy diet, and pet it and play with it to keep it healthy. When we tame and master the animal within consciousness, our body becomes like a loyal guard dog protecting the house of the soul. If not tamed, the animal self can become the wild beast terrorized by a perceived threat to its own survival. Life is change. Body changes are protective signals. The untamed personality becomes attached to maintaining constancy at all costs to avoid the pain of change. Fainters deny that there is anything to avoid and aggressive fighters go mad with anger when confronted with the contrary information. Flight personality reactions avoid the distress, while freeze reactions resist change. The spiritual warrior, on the other hand, masters these impulses and ACTs instead of reacts.

The recovery from addiction is one of the most wonderful examples of the wisdom of our immortal Self penetrating through the density of our conditioning. Addiction is a combination of a learned, conditioned response to life and a body response or craving. At some point, the wisdom of the body signals the necessity to change. Smoker's cough, hangovers, blackouts, the shakes, or other addiction symptoms all indicate that the physical body is changing. The guard dog is barking.

The habit pattern of the untamed mind is not Self-aware. It naturally denies the relevance of the body's perceptual signals. If we pay attention to the signals, we receive truthful, relevant information. During addiction, body and mind are at odds. The body is changing, and the mind avoids, resists, denies, and fights change. The separation between psyche and soma initiates a betrayal of the body.

Kim's story describes the shift from a conditioned response to Horus's evolutionary creative response. Kim was a twenty-six-year-old dual degree law student when she came to me to talk about her childhood adoption and to discuss her concern that she might be an alcoholic. We talked about David, another adoptee I knew. David's birth family was Irish Catholic, and he was adopted by a Jewish family in another state. David was diagnosed with alcoholism at the age of twenty-five and given about one year to live unless he changed his behavior. Ten years later, David finally met his birth family who lived in rural Iowa. He was not surprised to find that each member of the family was drowning in alcoholism. There was a story that his birth father had joked about dying naked with a can of beer in his hand, and, indeed, that was just how they found him.

Like David, Kim did not learn to drink in her adopted family environment. Yet she developed the habit of drinking about a bottle of wine a night to relax. Kim rarely felt drunk. She noticed that she could handle alcohol better than her friends, though she had occasional blackouts. These were times when she looked awake and normal to all her friends, but the next day, Kim's memory would be like Swiss cheese. Her memory was riddled with holes about what she said or did the previous night. Generally, though, Kim just felt a little buzzed. All these physical symptoms were signals from the faithful guardian and companion telling her that her body was changing and was no longer able to tolerate alcohol like it once did.

Kim's self-image was beginning to suffer, too. She described feeling like she couldn't trust herself. She would drink more than she intended and say things she wished she hadn't. Kim told me, "I only drink in the evenings. But, when I'm in a situation like a party or social gathering, I say in my mind, 'OK, now I know what's going to happen. I'm going to keep drinking and I hope that nothing bad happens. I hope that I don't say something stupid. I hope that I don't get really drunk. I hope that I just get somewhat drunk.' I never know exactly how far it's going to go. At the end of a party or social gathering, I'm left wondering if I went too far. Then I start ticking through my friends who were there and wonder and rationalize, 'Well, I don't really mind if so-and-so saw me like this.' I justify after the fact that it was really OK."

The terrible self-betrayal of addiction often includes obsession about what others think and is frequently followed by righteously resenting others for holding these assumed judgments. This righteous resentment, projection of the shadow, and self-betrayal are three of the features of a traditional betrayal response. Kim expressed it like this. "The worst is, I create in my own mind the image of what I think other people are thinking about me, like 'Oh, Kim's an alcoholic,' or 'Kim is out of control,' or 'She gets loud and obnoxious and provocative.' Fear of being called an alcoholic is typical of the generalization stage of betrayal. Remember, all this concern about image and what others think is symptomatic of the animal ka personality.

When I work with addicts, my first step is to help them become aware of their addictive behavior. I then educate them on the progressive nature of addiction and encourage them to make some choices about how they want to deal with their addiction. Kim had chosen to control her drinking, going through stage five of the betrayal-to-trust initiation.

After about five weeks of drinking one or two glasses of wine on weekends, Kim had a dream.

> I was on a plane. I was with a group of people who were all about my age, and we were all dressed in business attire. We were flying to some really important meeting that was going to begin right when we got there. In this dream, instead of my usual wine, I was drinking hard alcohol from those little bottles, and I was getting really drunk. I couldn't really walk straight, you know. I was weaving and wobbling up and down the aisle and slurring my speech. We were all standing around talking. I thought that we were all having fun.
>
> People started mumbling about me. This one guy talked in a voice loud enough for me to hear. He spoke to this one woman who was the leader of our group, and said, "What is she doing here? Look at her. She's falling all over the place. She's really out of control. She's a mess. She doesn't belong here." And the woman who was our leader said to that guy, "Don't worry about her, she's going to be OK. I know that she is out of control now, but I'll take care of it and it will be all right."

Kim woke up from that dream thinking, "Maybe it's time to stop drinking." We talked about the dream representing different parts of her self. Kim was especially struck by the woman leader in her group. She felt, for the first time in her life, that there was a part within her psyche that was completely aware of everything going on in all the different parts of Kim; and that this part of her could, and would, lead her. Something within Kim had the wisdom, love, and ability to heal the addict part in Kim and restore her to sanity. This is where Isis's magic came in—Isis, who collected all the dismembered parts of Osiris, resurrected him, and conceived Horus. In her dream, after Kim remembered her higher Self, a new awareness arose, and a shift in perception was born.

When a shift in perception occurs, though nothing may change outside of oneself, one's response to life is very different. You are able to respond to life in a new and creative way. Something truly magical does happen when you shift your attention from an external locus of control, like worrying about what everyone else is thinking, to an internal locus of control, like thinking about what is right for yourself.

For example, Kim's animal body now preferred sparkling water to wine. Though the conditioned response to a social gathering was "It's a party, so it's time to drink," Kim's Self-awareness guided her to recondition her thoughts and feelings. She consciously chose the new response and drank sparkling sodas. Also, Kim mentally said to herself, "I'm glad I'm not drinking. I'll never again have to worry about going too far and making a fool of myself because I got drunk."

I interviewed Kim six months after she stopped drinking. During this timeframe, Kim also quit smoking, lost ten pounds, and curtailed her tendency to exercise compulsively. We focused on the alcohol issue in our interview. We also noted that all these changes were related to letting go of compulsion, which stemmed from a natural animal fear reaction and responses created to cope with perceived threats. With regards to alcohol, Kim said, "I'm learning how to be around people, to be in social situations and not drink, and to feel comfortable. I am finally starting to feel that I don't need to drink."

"In the last week," Kim went on, "my husband and I were having hard times, and I was stressed about school and jobs and things. I had a lot of concentrated stress. It was really hard for me not to drink. I felt kind of walled in, and I didn't have any defenses. I couldn't go and get some wine or go and smoke a cigarette. I felt, 'Whew, what am I going to do. I have all this pressure on me and I have nowhere to go and no way to get out of this.'"

I asked her how she handled this situation. She said, "It was hard, but I called a counselor, and Stan and I started marriage counseling. I also dropped a class at school, and I tried not to worry so much about jobs. That is not something I really have a lot of control over. I've done my part. My résumés are out, and I'm going to interviews and all that. That is all I can do. I also reaffirmed that I was glad that I did not have something to drink. If I had had something to drink, then I would have had just one more problem to deal with—drinking. Now, a week later, I'm *really* glad I didn't drink."

Everything Kim did was a beautiful demonstration of how to ACT, instead of react. She accepted the reality of her situation. No matter what she might have said or thought, reality continued to remind her of her true situation. Instead of drinking and numbing out the pain of hard work, Kim experienced the reality of taking a full load of classes, job hunting, worrying about money, and making adjustments in her marriage relationship. She lived in reality, right here within the confining limitations of her physical body, and discovered what she truly needed. Since drinking no longer worked for Kim, she created new thoughts and behaviors to handle stress. She was willing to continue to create and explore alternatives.

Kim also learned to TRUST. For example, when Kim turned inward to discover the truth, she realized that she was experiencing a lot of pain and stress. She was overwhelmed. Kim relaxed, released, and received. She released her attempts to manage events that were out of her control and took action to influence those circumstances she could, such as dropping a class. Kim also used both inner and outer resources. She stayed in touch with her feelings and impressions, saw a counselor, wrote résumés, and went to job interviews. Kim took a stand in her relationship to her husband, as well as in relationship to her personal commitment to not drink and smoke. Finally, Kim made a conscious choice to release worry and to try again if necessary. This is an example of her leap of faith and her eventual trust in life's process.

Discrimination between old and new knowledge is the principle that allows us to be reborn. This process of discrimination is represented in the weighing scene by the image of **Osiris**, the only seated figure in the papyrus. Notice that he holds a crook and flail over his heart. This is the symbol of pharaonic leadership. A true leader goes to his or her heart to discover the truth. New knowledge comes from your heart. One's heart also determines whether to use the crook or flail: to be gentle, like the shepherd using the crook to herd the wandering lamb back into the fold; or to be fierce, using the flail to beat back the wild beast that would eat the lamb. The crook symbolizes the idea that to sustain the life created, you must gently bring in your new, or forgotten, vulnerable and disenfranchised parts. The flail is to tame the unruly parts of your personality that bring you death instead of life. (See Exercise 5-A on page 144.)

Betrayal of the body teaches us to surrender to the present moment, to weigh our experiences on Maat's scales, and, like Osiris, to resurrect ourselves and choose actions that support life. Kim used Osiris's crook and flail to help her make life-supporting decisions. Kim listened to the calls of her body that said she was beyond her limit. She gently brought in the part of herself that told her to call a counselor and drop a class, while she beat back the old conditioned and instinctive fear responses that denied her stress and pushed her to just tough it out and use alcohol or cigarettes to avoid or escape the pain.

I sometimes think that God created this animal body with its addictive habit patterns to train our creativity. We learn the difference between what we can control and what we can't control. Eliminating something tangible like a drink or substance trains us how to let go. Then we can face the tricky and sensitive challenge of breaking more subtle addictions like one's conditioned patterns of thought and feeling—the "I want what I want, how I want it, now!" syndrome. In freeing oneself, one joins Ptah as a brother, a cocreator in this universe. We master the conditions of our reality and use these conditions to support life. (See Exercise 5-B on page 144.)

Let us return to Ann's story for an example of how to forgo our conditioning. Ann's kidney failure story is such a perfect example of the difference between a conditioned response, which lacks Self-awareness, and the use of physical conditions to develop Self-awareness. One sunny fall day, Ann met me for lunch in a local cafe under the pretext of telling me about a couple of groups she was starting. We eventually began talking about our lives since we had last seen each other. At the time of our meeting, I was still rebuilding my strength from my bout with the *varicella zoster* virus. So I shared the impact of my Betrayal of the Body lesson.

Our discussion naturally shifted to a discussion of her own progressive illness. Our lunch meeting occurred about two years after her internist had rushed her to the hospital to begin dialysis treatment. Since her release from the hospital, Ann was placed on a waiting list to receive a kidney transplant. While Ann had much more physical energy than before, she was still making many adjustments to acclimate to her new situation, which included dialysis treatment three times a week. Over the course of these two years, her clinical practice had dwindled to five clients. Ann was in a real quandary. She felt she needed to build up her clinical practice, but was worried about what would happen to new clients if or when she received a kidney transplant.

Ann had already let go of her beautiful office in Walnut Creek, dropped her answering service, and began to see clients at home. Income from her private practice was just enough to pay her food and rent and a few other basics. Ann was feeling financially insecure. Insecurity is a challenge to trust. Insecurity will also feed self-betrayal. Together, Ann and I looked at options. What if the practice continued to dwindle while Ann waited to receive word on the availability of a kidney? Ann could sub-let her apartment, live with one of her daughters, rent office space from a colleague by the hour, or even make home visits. If worse came to worst, she could check out social services, or make use of community resources for seniors. Her phone machine could be set up anywhere, and Ann could continue to monitor calls from any location.

Physical illness or injury reveals the bare bones of what we really need in order to sustain life. A lot of what we think we need drops away. These perceived needs are based on the conditions of society, including one's profession, socioeconomic status, culture, family, or friends. Only those elements that truly support life remain. The key word is *life*. What is life-supporting right now? What does life want from us?

Initially, Ann had invited me to lunch as part of her marketing plan to promote some new therapy groups she wanted to start. "Client practice is low . . . build up your practice" was her typical conditioned response. During our lunch together, it became clear that there was another pur-pose—to move beyond the conditioning. Whenever we let go of a condi-tioned response, we go through an ego death at some level. This shift in identity, which is stimulated by the tension produced from changing our habits and conditioned responses, is very uncomfortable for one's self-image-ka identity. To get beyond the conditioned Amam animal survival response based on our appetites and fears, we move to Thoth and we observe what is. After talking about the realities encompassing Ann's life, she decided that preparing for her kidney transplant was her number one priority, even over making money to "survive."

When I met with Ann a year later, Ann told me that she was given her kidney transplant three weeks after our lunch together. Our lunch was a real turning point for Ann, one of the many mini-miracles that sup-ported her during her efforts to be true to herself. "I surrendered to the truth of what was. I was ill. I was not functioning. Everything was coming to a standstill. I thought, 'This is the way my life is right now.' I surren-dered to that. What a relief it was to accept the truth! This was a real turn-ing point for me.

"I felt like I had been traveling upstream for so long," she continued, "trying to get my group together, trying to get money, trying to get friends, trying to get a lover, trying, trying, and nothing was working. And suddenly, I saw another direction in which I could go. And, as I did during my dream on the freeway, I turned around and went in the new direction, even though nothing had changed in my life during that afternoon we spent together—nothing, that is, except my mind."

A year after the transplant, Ann's life was reviving. "I have so much energy now," Ann said, "I am learning to manage my energy. My illness has taught me to move from just surviving to creating. Energy to carry on is one thing, and this creative energy is something else. For example, I have always had a lot of different ideas, and I have rarely followed up on an idea. Now, I have an idea and I have the energy to do something with it—to act. For example, when I was listening to the Thomas hearings, I sent telegrams to the Democratic senator from Connecticut and the Republican senator from California to let them know how I felt. And I called ten to fifteen friends to suggest that they do the same thing.

"I've also created closer ties with my kids. And I've come to terms with my mother. This is a very big thing. I feel so happy that I have found a way to help my mom. Before, I kept pushing my mom away. I took care of myself by keeping her out. This worked on a survival level, but it didn't really nourish me. Helping my mom nourishes me, because, even though I can't stand her sometimes, I do love her. And now I have a way to show it. I fix her little house and organize her papers for her, and I feel so useful. I take much better care of myself. I notice that my body tells me my limits. My heart starts beating fast or I feel like I need to rest. I pay attention to these signals. As a result, I give energy to my mother within these limits, and then I don't get trapped in the toxicity of the relationship."

I asked Ann what was the most significant part of her whole experience. She paused quietly for a moment and then spoke. "Having tasted my own mortality and knowing what helped me through it—knowing how loving everybody was to me and how giving—I want to give back." Ann's client practice is double what it was the year before, she has received an invitation from a colleague to collaborate on a book, and she nurtures her family and friends in new ways. Ann is most certainly "giving back."

A few days after our meeting, I received a note from Ann with copies of an old business plan. Ann wrote, "Notice on one of the sheets of my business plan that I put a date of November 18, 1990, to have my business goals completed. I just noticed it as I copied these materials for you. Strangely enough (or not so strangely!), November 18, 1990, was the day of my transplant! I guess I had put down the wrong business but my higher Self knew better!" Ann's note was another example of the incredible magic that is present in our lives.

In hindsight, it is easy for Ann to see the workings of her ba Self in the events of her life. Our beloved inner companion, our own higher power, is present even while we are going through what seem to be dismal events. In time, we learn to trust that archetypal Mother will bring us everything we need. Inseminated by archetypal Father, the seed of Self-awareness grows in the body of our experience. We practice acting on our inner guidance, and that synchronistically leads us to our complete fulfillment here in this world.

In Egyptian mysticism, we are each Osiris traveling through the underworld, awaiting resurrection. Isis works in tandem with her dark sister Nephthys, the wife of Set, to bring Osiris back to life. It was Nephthys who sang magical hymns and sacred chants over the body of the dead Osiris. Together, Nephthys and Isis sing your soul's song, calling you to awaken and recall the dream of your soul—your deepest purpose in life.

Isis is the second figure behind Osiris, the figure with the hieroglyph of a throne on her head. Isis is the seat of power in the unconscious. Isis represents the principle of memory, creative imagination, and intuition. She brings our unconscious human potential into consciousness through dreams, visions, and psychic perceptions. Kim's "flying high" dream and Ann's freeway dream are good examples. Dreams sometimes contain precognitive elements, portending the future. For example, in Ann's dream, the suggestion to turn away from work and go to San Francisco is exactly what Ann needed to do when she caught pneumonia after her kidney transplant. Ann spent a few weeks convalescing in her daughter's apartment in San Francisco. Kim's dream could also have been precognitive if she denied the signals from her dream body and continued to drink. Using our intuitive resources enables us to remember a deeper truth. Part of the teaching in Betrayal of the Body is to awaken the memory of your immortal soul.

While Isis makes herself conscious through our dreams and intuitions, Nephthys is harder for us to understand. She, too, is part of the unconscious. Jung talks about the shadow and unconscious psychic functions and their impact on human consciousness.

> We are always discovering something new about ourselves. Almost every year something new turns up which we did not know before. We always think we are now at the end of our discoveries. We never are. We go on discovering that we are this, that, and other things, and sometimes we have astounding experiences. That shows there is always a part of our personality which is still unconscious, which is still becoming; we are unfinished; we are growing and changing. Yet that future personality which we are to be in a year's time is already here, only it is still in the shadow. . . . These potentialities naturally belong to the dark side of the ego. We are well aware of what we have been, but we are not aware of what we are going to be.[8]

Nephthys is the paradox of the unconscious that always remains unconscious. She signifies the deepest strata of the unconscious, those hidden creative elements within the psyche. Nephthys, the first female figure standing behind Osiris, has the hieroglyph of a chalice on her head. Like the chalice that holds liquid, Nephthys is a container for that which, as of yet, has no form.

When we are ill or injured, Nephthys frequently shows up as our darkest thoughts, or feelings of toxic self-pity or envy. In the Egyptian mythos, Nephthys is the personification of envy. No wonder she is married to Set, the betrayer of Osiris. Envy goes with self-betrayal, just as in wanting that which belongs to someone else, one rejects one's own gifts, talents, and resources. Nephthys bore no children by Set; self-betrayal through envy is fruitless. However, like the paradox of the betrayal-to-trust experience, the archetype of envy also contains some light. Embedded in envy is the seed of one's deepest desire. This side of the coin is told through the story in which Nephthys unites with Osiris and gives birth to Anubis, the jackal-headed god. Envy (Nephthys) gives birth to the innate ability to digest and eliminate

(Anubis) its own toxic elements once it is joined with the power of discrimination (Osiris). Then our deepest desires are called forth.

For an example, let's look at Lana and Peter, who experienced betrayal of the body when they planned to have a family and things didn't go according to plan. They were married in their early thirties. A nurse-midwife and real-estate agent respectively, Lana and Peter set their goals together: Get settled in their careers, buy a home, and start a family. When Lana turned thirty-six years old, the two of them stopped using contraceptives. Each month Lana would anticipate missing her period. To her great disappointment, she continued to menstruate as regularly as ever. For the next sixteen months, Lana began using thermometers and a variety of natural methods to establish and enhance ovulation times. All to no avail. Together, Peter and Lana explored all their options, from psychic healing to allopathic medicine.

By the time Lana was thirty-nine, taking fertility drugs was the final step in what felt like an endless, futile effort to have a child. "I would look at other people's children and at the babies I was delivering," Lana reflected, "and feel resentful. I was continually stunned by this indescribable envy. It just wasn't fair. I felt so much pain. I felt like a complete failure. My monthly period became a constant reminder of my failure to get pregnant." Peter said, "I felt like I wasn't really a man, somehow, just because there were no children in our family. I was incomplete in some way." Family tradition, cultural customs, social attitudes, professional beliefs, and even medical opinions supported the expectation that Lana and Peter would be able to, first of all, plan to have a family, and second of all, predict pregnancy.

When we have a betrayal of the body, righteous resentment is frequently turned inward against the self. "What's wrong with me?" is completely supported by our traditional medical practices. Insecurity, worry, and low self-esteem weigh the heart down. Amam begins to drool in anticipation of a tasty meal. Thoth's intuitive responses, on the other hand, observe the present moment. The ancient papyrus says: "You can digest this death. Observe your thoughts and feelings. Trust those, that lighten your heart. These will inspire your soul and bring you from death to life."

Turn inward to discover the deepest truth. Release your fear and righteous resentment by releasing attachment to results. Relax your body and mind. Receive intuitive insight. Use the tools you have. Use both your inner and outer resources. Then speak what you know and take a stand. Trust the process of life. Divine Mother and Father make their presence known in all the events in one's life. We are guided to all that we need.

For example, as synchronicity would have it, Lana was watching afternoon television one day and caught a talk show about the biological clock. The interviewer asked several women how they responded to their inability to get pregnant. One guest, an obstetrician by profession, explained how she and her husband decided to start using contraceptives again and made a choice to be child free.

Something about this woman and her story empowered Lana to realize that she had a choice. Peter and Lana discussed this option and began to imagine how their life might be if they chose not to have children. This option had merit for them. For example, they loved to travel, and not having children afforded them the freedom to travel without restrictions. Yet they kept coming back to the fact that both of them had such strong values based on home and family. A lightbulb went on. Peter, working in real estate, and Lana, working as a midwife, had both been fulfilling their dream in a way they had never imagined. Quite literally, Lana had given birth to many children, and Peter had helped numerous couples and families get a home for themselves. "Going after our dream was not only for ourselves, but for so many other people, too. And now we've begun to dream again—new dreams."

Peter commented. "Choice is so important. We have chosen to go on with our lives."

Together, Nephthys and Isis sing magical incantations and chant sacred hymns over the dead body of Osiris. Isis and Nephthys call Osiris to life. We each have a calling that speaks to us from the depths of our being. Nephthys reminds us that, though it is a natural reaction, we need not fear the dark part of our nature. There is something within the psyche that supports life and resurrection. In the darkness of our depths stirs the seed of one's potential that creates something beyond our wildest imagination. As Jung said, we awaken to an astounding discovery. We are "still becoming, we are unfinished, we are growing and changing."

Betrayal of the body through illness, injury, accident, or addiction are all tools to facilitate the death and rebirth of a deeper truth. As physical beings, we are limited by physical reality. As spiritual beings, we are able to touch unlimited states of consciousness. Osiris is in each of us. We act to awaken ourselves, and with the help of both inner and outer resources we live to fulfill a greater plan—one that benefits us and our community. One day at a time, sometimes even moment by moment, we create an opening for the gods to come to Earth through us and be embodied. Our actions encourage, inspire, and demonstrate the power and purpose of living our dreams in new ways here, in this physical world.

Observe Your Patterned
Response to Change

If nothing is changing in your life right now, create an innocuous change, like putting your socks and underwear in the bottom drawer of your dresser if they happen to be in the top drawer. Then, over the next few days and weeks, observe your reaction to this very simple change. Come to know the habits of your animal ka. Observe the attitudes, thoughts, and feelings that arise. Use this exercise as a stepping-stone for exploring other aspects of your conditioned self.

EXERCISE 5-B

ACT Instead of React

By working with our own fear responses, we are not trying to rid ourselves of fear in the usual sense of the term. Given that we have animal bodies, that would be a futile task. We are working with ourselves to recognize our responses, release them, and perhaps choose another, more creative and adaptive, response. This way, we gain mastery over the fear response.

1. **Accept:** Identify what is hard to accept about your limits. Identify what phase you are in as you are moving toward acceptance. Are you denying your limits? Are you resisting, avoiding, rationalizing, getting angry, or becoming depressed? Observe your personal history and other conditions that foster nonacceptance. Observe what is true.

2. **Create:** Now that you know what is real, imagine what you really need. Create alternatives to get these needs fulfilled. Ask yourself, "What action enlivens, instead of deadens, my vitality?" Imagine "next-time" strategies: "Next time I will . . ." By saying next time, you already begin to release the power the past has over your present experience. Know that you can do something different in the future. Commit to learn from the present instead of being conditioned by the past.

3. **Trust:** Fill in the blanks and develop your own methods for cultivating trust.

   To help me turn inward, I _____ .
   (e.g., close my eyes, meditate, take a day off, write in my journal)

   To release, relax, and receive, I _____ .
   (e.g., breathe, exercise, say the serenity prayer, do self-hypnosis)

   I use inner resources such as _____ .
   (e.g., dreams, feelings, perceptions, tarot, runes, creative arts, music)

   Outer resources that help me are _____ .
   (e.g., family, friends, doctors, therapists, books, meetings)

   Now that I know what is really true for me, my stand on my present situation is _____ .

   I realize that life will give me feedback on this stand I have taken. Others may even accuse me of being a betrayer or of betraying myself. Some feedback I've received is _____ .
   (e.g., comments from friends, body sensations, changes in my life)

   I take this feedback as an opportunity to discover deeper truths and develop my ability to TRUST. I turn inward and try again.

Chapter 6

Betrayal of Self

Gateway to Forgiveness

Wound: If you suffer from self-betrayal, you suffer from having betrayed your inner, creative Self. You cut yourself off from your true and primary Source of support, power, or guidance. You don't listen to your Self, don't act on what you know, or don't understand what is going on in your life.

Truth: Self-betrayal is at the core of most betrayal wounds. Self-betrayal is for-giving you an opportunity to know yourself much better—the truth of your reality as a human being, including your needs, boundaries, and limits, as well as your dreams, true capacities, and full potential.

Healing: Reclaim and redeem rejected or disowned aspects of yourself as you return to your transcendent Self—the One who contains all of what you are—and so much more. Having found your true Self, return fully to life by giving the gift of your Self to the world. Learn to forgive yourself and others for being human instead of only divine.

In Ancient Egypt it was said that there are only two paths in life—and each of us chooses one or the other. The first path is a lovely, simple path where each day is like the next. One wakes up in the morning, works all day, and falls asleep when it gets dark.

The second path looks much the same, only individuals on this path, after waking up in the morning and working all day long find that, in the darkness of night, there are questions that plague their soul that will not let them sleep! So these intrepid souls stay up all day and all night long—until an inner light dawns during the dark night of the soul, to show them a way through the darkness. This is called the path of initiation.

Which path are you on? How do you know? What are the questions that plague your soul, that keep you up all night? What are the questions that will not let you sleep?

"Why? Why is this happening to me?" "I've followed the diet to the letter, I've been so good, and I am still not losing weight. Why?" "Why does my husband love someone else? Why, what is wrong with me?" "I've fallen in love with someone else, what am I to do?" "Why is my family cruel to me? Why? What have I done to deserve this?" "I try to keep it together, but whenever she talks in that tone of voice, I loose it—I just fly off the handle. What's going on?" "My coworker stabbed me in the back—lied to the management about me to get the promotion. Now what?" "My so-called best friends shared my secrets, gossiped about me—how could they do that?"

At first it looks as though things are happening *to* us—victims of forces beyond our control. When we are out of touch with our own inner Self, external expectations take precedence over our own inner authority. We act as best we can, trying to meet the expectations as set for us by friends, family, social convention. We listen to the dictates of social conditioning, family, advertising, news media, education, religion. We enter into an implicit agreement to live according to these expectations.

We wake up in the morning and work all day long to meet the demands as best we can. In the darkness of discontent and emptiness, we go to sleep. We lose consciousness. We deny our inner perception of truth. Perhaps we live with a low level of anger, or find a way to rationalize our existence—"it doesn't matter anyway." We argue with ourselves and each other. We hope for reciprocity and resign ourselves to the belief that "life just ain't fair." Very depressing. Four of the five stages of symbolic death reveal themselves in this night-flight of the soul: denial, anger, rationalization, and depression.

Self-betrayal leads to many behaviors that sabotage our best intentions—there are just too many pushes and pulls on us. We cannot possibly satisfy everybody's expectations or requirements, let alone take time to discover what is right and true for us and that we *do* have an inner voice that can guide us through the darkness. This is the essence of self-betrayal: living from the outside in, what psychologists call having an "external locus of control," instead of living from the inside out and having an "internal locus of control." No wonder betrayal of the Self is at the core of most betrayal wounds.

Self-betrayal is in actuality a spiritual crisis. It is an experience of feeling cut off from our true Source of wisdom, protection, purpose, or value—the Creator within us. Sometimes the shock of betrayal catapults us into an entirely new state of consciousness. Shock can do that. For a moment, we break through the social conditioning. In an unexpected flash of insight, we understand how we got to where we are and know where we need to go. We get a glimpse of who we really are, and what we need to do to break free. This can be the gift of betrayal, a sudden and spontaneous return to a deeper truth—for a moment at least. Then doubt returns with its endless questions, and the profound soul searching starts all over again. Yet, the glimpse of a deeper truth can be the dawning of the inner light *if* we know how to integrate the new awareness.

In the ancient days, if you started on the path of initiation, you could go to the temples of initiation for further training. Within the temple there were two paths: the path of the outer temple teachings and the path of the inner temple teachings.

For those who chose the path of the outer temple teachings, they went to any number of temples that dotted the fertile Nile River valley. There the priests and priestesses of these ancient sanctuaries welcomed the initiates, and showed them how everything in the physical world is a manifestation of spiritual principle—with each temple dedicated to a specific God/Neter. Architecture, literature, science, and medicine were all sacred disciplines in the ancient world. And so the initiates learned how to live in a way that honored the sacred relationship between inner principle and its outer form.

Those on the path to the inner temple discovered how they themselves were a representation of spiritual principle, and how their very essence was an expression of a spiritual principle that was dedicated to a specific God/Neter. In order to be initiated into the inner temple teachings, each initiate had to find the temple without walls. Not everybody found the inner temple, however, because the inner temple is not physical. One had to look within, to the sanctuary of one's own heart. In the temple without walls, one dedicates oneself to Maat, Goddess of Truth and Justice, to seek out that secret, inner truth that liberates the soul. In the hallowed halls of the Double Maat, initiates surrendered themselves to the truth of who they are in essence and dedicated themselves to becoming the living example of divine principle in human form.

The Four Worlds:
Discovering Your Greater Self

Each of us has a secret Source that brings us back to life. It contains the seed of our pure potential, and we are the living manifestation of its truth. Life as a spiritual practice means we practice living life to our full potential. Anything less is betrayal of the essential Self. Following the mystical path of initiation has never been described as an easy path. This is especially so because it is said that we live not in one world, but in four worlds simultaneously. We are challenged to live to our full potential in each world concurrently. We live in a *physical* world, an *emotional* world, a *mental* world, and a *spiritual* world. Each world calls to us. The physical calls to us through our bodies and senses; the emotional through our feelings and values; the mental through our thoughts and beliefs; and the spiritual through our intuition, inner perceptions, and senses of truth and trust. We are here to discover the one Creator of all worlds, the inner Self who can live in harmony and balance in all worlds simultaneously.

When we focus on one world to the exclusion of the others, we can not help but betray ourselves in the other worlds. Because of this, most ancient traditions warn of the dangers on the path, and so I will share these dangers with you, so you can recognize them as they arise. The Kabbalah, the ancient Hebraic mystic tradition, describes them in a Talmudic parable about entering the orchard where the Tree of Life grows. The Hebrew word for orchard is *pardes*. The story is told about Rabbi Akiva (who lived during the second century A.D.) and three of his fellow rabbis, Ben Azzai, Ben Zoma, and Aher (also known as Rabbi Elisha Ben Avuyah). This is what happened as they entered the *pardes:*

> Ben Azzai glimpsed and died.
> Ben Zoma glimpsed and went mad.
> Aher cut the plants [and loses his faith].
> Rabbi Akiva emerged in peace.[1]

The word *pardes* provides an acronym, a symbol for the four worlds. Each consonant stands for a Hebrew word that describes four distinct

149

experiences, and each is associated with one of the four different worlds. Those Hebrew words and their English translations are:

P *pashut:* literal or simple
R *ramuz:* hint
D *drashah:* story, homily, allegory, or symbol
S *sod:* secret

If we take the story literally, it tells us that we have a one out of four chance at finding peace. Not great odds. However, the story is allegorical. It hints at a mystical, secret truth. Ben Azzai, Ben Zoma, and Aher are each metaphors of betrayal of Self from a physical, emotional, and mental world view. The first three rabbis describe what happens to us if we get stuck in one of the worlds, and try to live life from only that experience of reality. It destroys our faith, drive us mad, and can even kill us. Only Rabbi Akiva comes out alive, at peace, serene, with heart and soul open to all the worlds.

How did Rabbi Akiva do it? Living as a mystic, Rabbi Akiva is at home in all worlds because Rabbi Akiva was able to know the secret Source that is All. Akiva lived in union with the One that lives in all worlds. This infinite Source of knowledge and wisdom within reveals the truth about each world, and shows how to mediate between all the four worlds of experience—how to honor the truth of each world, and pay each its due.

For almost two thousand years, the story has been misrepresented and used as fuel to scare people away from living the mystical life. However, it is Rabbi Akiva's ability to open himself to these spiritual secrets that shows the way to peace. The sixteenth-century mystic Master Abraham Azulai stated that the mystic way will eventually eliminate war, destruction, and man's inhumanity to his fellow man. He went so far as to predict that, by the year 5760, we will live in a time in which the secret teachings will be taught publicly around the world to people of all ages. The year 5760 in the Hebrew calendar is A.D. 2000 in the modern Gregorian calendar. Today, we live in a time when the secret teachings from not only the Kabbalah, but from all around the world are available to all of us. Perhaps this will increase our odds of finding and living in peace with ourselves and each other in our lifetime.

First, however, we need to understand what these four worlds are, how they work, and how we might lose ourselves in each of them. Even more important, we must understand how we might reclaim our true Self in each world of experience.

The Physical World (Assiyah)

Literally, this translates as "the world of doing or making." This is a *literal* and *simple* world, based on the objective experiences of physical reality. This is where we experience the effects of our actions upon each other and upon all of life. We contend with the *objective truths* of hard facts.

Let's explore what happens when we lose ourselves in the physical world. Azzai, the Rabbi who gets lost and dies in the orchard, tried to interpret all his life experiences on a literal level. He tried to simplify the mystery of life by applying the limits of logical, objective, and concrete thinking to everything. In this world we may betray the emotional self with unsuspecting lies like "Sticks and stones may break my bones, but names will never hurt me." Or, conversely, instead of denying emotional reality, feelings become rigid, fixed, or stuck as we objectify our feelings into concrete things. Ideals and beliefs are also objectified or rationalized as God's truth, and spiritual mysteries may be paraded as religious dogma. "My God is the only true God because our sacred texts are describing historical facts, and they tell the true story of creation—all others are blasphemous lies!" Literal interpretations of scriptures are the source of all the holy wars and countless lives have been lost in these wars throughout recorded history. As the parable implies, literalism brings death.

Oddly enough, materialistic, literal thinking is also the foundation of scientific positivism, the primary philosophy of the twentieth century. If there is no physical proof, then it does not exist. Based on the null hypothesis, nothing is true until it is materially and objectively proven. Therefore, we used a nuclear bomb to end a war during World War II because, theoretically, the evidence said it should work, and we did not know how it would affect the environment until after the fact. We have used preservatives, additives, cigarettes, and pesticides because, initially, there was no evidence of danger. Since there was not enough evidence to say they "caused harm and death," we continued using them. Materialistic philosophies bring death and destruction to all life. No wonder Ben Azzai died in the orchard. He lived in a physical world that was disconnected from the other worlds, compartmentalized, unintegrated.

According to the Kabbalah, as we heal our relationship to our physical world we experience the gift of Divine Presence. This gives us the capacity to be physically present with ourselves and others in the face of differences, to stand our ground without aggression, and allow others to be who and where they are.

The Emotional World (Yitzirah)

Literally, this translates as "the world of formation or creation." This is an emotional world base on subjective, personal experiences, and it *hints* at what supplies the energy behind our motives: desire or fear, approach or avoidance. This is a phenomenological realm of discovering one's *personal truths*.

Magical thinking or wish fulfillment are forms of self-betrayal that belie the truth of physical reality. We deceive ourselves into thinking that the universe is based on our personal wishes, wants, and desires. Examples may include feeling punished by God when things don't go the way you want, or conversely feeling rewarded with boons and bounties for being "good." Both are examples of personalizing the impersonal world of Spirit. We betray our trust in the Creative forces of the universe. Whether we like what is happening or not, life is change. Circumstances are constantly forming and re-forming life—including our life—not because we are good or bad, but because we are connected to the flux of the Universe. These forces are archetypal and completely impersonal—not discretely "good" or "bad."

It is easy to lose ourselves and our connection to a greater awareness when we feel trapped in guilt and other emotional self-betrayal patterns. We risk going mad, like Rabbi Ben Zoma, when we live as though our feelings define all realities. Dealing with a constant barrage of positive and negative emotional projections makes us crazy. Ulterior motives are ascribed to everyone and everything. Life is laden with biases, value judgments, and prejudices. If someone agrees with you, you feel approved of, happy, or vindicated. If someone disagrees, you feel insulted, rejected, maybe even betrayed.

Identification with an archetype is a term coined by Carl Jung and describes another form of betrayal of Self. This happens when we personalize the nonpersonal world of Spirit. Perhaps you have known people who unconsciously believe that they are God of the universe. Codependent behavior is a perfect example of this form of self-betrayal. Living as though we have control over other people, or are responsible for what they think, do, or say is a sure way to drive ourselves crazy.

According to the Kabbalah, as we heal our relationship to the emotional world and bring it into a flowing relationship with other realities, we are given the gift of sacred relationship, our true foundation in life. We discover our deeper connection to the radiant splendor of our transcendent Self, the Self that is bonded to an ever-present, eternal Source within us. The link to our creative Self extends through our sexual, emotional, and intuitive nature in the form of honor and respect in all our relationships with others.

The Mental World (Briah)

Literally, this translates as the "world of creation" or "universe." It is non-personal and archetypal. It is experienced through the creative power of our thoughts, ideals, attitudes, and beliefs to describe universal principles in *symbols* and *stories.* In this world we tap into our universal Self that helps us create meaning out of our experience. We discover *universal truths,* such as the Golden Rule or $e = mc^2$.

In the *pardes* story, Rabbi Aher cuts the plants to help him find his way out of the orchard, so he won't go mad or die. Although he finds his way out, legend has it that he has totally lost his faith by the time he exits the orchard. The branches are knowledge and by cutting them he limits his knowledge. Like the blind men and the elephant, he thinks he has all the answers and cuts himself short.

Each time the experience of self-betrayal occurs it is an opportunity to claim and reclaim forgotten parts of ourselves. This is also true when we lose ourselves in the mental world of abstract reality, where we kill our faith with limiting ideas and beliefs about ourselves as well as others. The "could have, should have, would have, if only" type of thinking indicates Self-sabotage and the necessity to reexamine the origin of negative attitudes and punishing beliefs. Most often, negative attitudes are indicative of an imbalance between the emotional and mental worlds—we say one thing and feel another. When we say one thing and do another, then there is a clash between mental and physical worlds. In either case, we are out of integrity. The trap in this world is intellectualizing and rationalizing our experiences, getting caught in opinions and explanations instead of exploring universal truths.

In the archetypal world of mental reality, we may also project the Source onto an ideology and make a dogma into a god, thus replacing the Great Mystery of Life with an answer. Have you ever betrayed yourself by thinking you know the truth? Have you ever lost yourself to someone else's truth, to a cause, a committee, a board, a church group? Nationalism, industrialism, capitalism, communism, and all other *isms* are forms of self-betrayal. Or perhaps you expected others to share your ideals and suffered a devastating blow when your wife, workgroup, community, or party let you down.

The mental world is full of heros and villains, and we project these characters onto the important people in our life. As discussed in earlier chapters, we want our personal mother, father, or caregiver to be Divine Mother or Father, to be the Creator of Life. We wish for a "true companion," a Divine Friend, Sister, Brother, or Lover who will never make a mistake, always be there, love us unconditionally. We expect our leaders to be paragons of virtue. We seek to put all criminals behind bars. It is natural to seek guidance, support, protection, or sense of purpose from external sources. This is called projection. In essence, we project our concept of God (through the filter of our personal needs) onto reality. However, looking outside the Self, with the expectation that *it* will be our source of fulfillment, only fuels the experience of separation from the true Source.

Because of this, mental world betrayals are often experienced as feeling betrayed by God. Hence the profound loss of faith that coincides with this form of self-betrayal. God, from our perspective, has not lived up to our expectations. But God is not external to us and does not let us down like everyone else. God is a universal energy that exists in everything, including us. "God" is a universal metaphor for that creative force that gives meaning, purpose, and order to our universe and our lives.

To heal self-betrayal, we are required to rediscover our Creator within, our inner teacher who awakens us to the universal teaching, soul lesson, or deeper meaning hidden within our betrayal experience. The Kabbalah teaches that as we heal the part of us that has been lost in this world, we begin to gain the resources and gifts of discrimination without prejudice. We discover the right use of power and strength, balanced with mercy and kindness. This awakens compassion and appreciation for the sublime beauty of life.

The Spiritual World (Atziluth)
Literally, this translates as "noble" or "emanation." This is a *secret* and mysterious world of pure vibration. We experience it as emanations that radiate from an infinite and limitless, unnameable and unknowable Source of consciousness that is beyond anything we can imagine, name,

or define. This world connects us with our greater Self. The greater Self is nonphysical, nonpersonal, and far beyond our concepts or beliefs about it. This is the world that allows us to gain insight and wisdom into the mysteries of life, of who and what we are, and of our oneness with all existence. Here we awaken to profound *eternal, absolute truths.*

Clearly, we must ask ourselves, which "self" are we betraying, which self is lost? Our true Self is never lost, though we may have lost contact with it. Finding a way to live in all four worlds requires that you discover a way to:

1. Respect your own and others' limits or boundaries.
2. Recover lost and disowned emotions.
3. Recognize that there are larger forces than you at work in the universe.
4. Remember the mystery of who and what you truly are: a transcendent being with a spiritual destiny.

The physical world calls for us to be responsible to our physical needs by attending to the concrete facts, data, or information that support physical life. The emotional world asks us to honor our personal feelings as sources of information about our needs, desires, fears, and values. The mental world is more abstract and invites us to explore the universal teaching or symbolic message encoded in our experience by revealing universal ideals and principles as well as core beliefs or attitudes. The spiritual world summons us to become creators in our own life by making creative choices that express the integrity of who we are—aligning body, heart, and mind with a deeper sense of purpose.

When we pretend that we live in only one world, we betray the mystery of who and what we are—infinitely creative, spiritual beings living a very physical human life on this earth. Trying to live in only one world at a time and projecting that reality onto the other worlds can be devastating for the soul. Perhaps we betray the spiritual Self that understands the deeper mysteries of our life's journey. Or maybe we are blind to the signals sent to us by our emotional self that hint at our deeper values, needs, wishes, and fears, betraying the wisdom of our feeling nature. It is also possible to turn a deaf ear to the ideals and principles that guide us through life. And of course, many of us resist being in the physical world at all, with all its limitations, peculiarities, and conditions.

In essence, we abandon our true Self, the eternal Creator who lives in all worlds simultaneously. We lose contact with the core of our being, our own spiritual Source, by rejecting the Self within our consciousness that is big enough and creative enough to hold the paradox of all our contradictory feelings, thoughts, and experiences. Instead we fragment, compartmentalize, protect, and defend.

The pain of self-betrayal inspires a spiritual searching and yearning for our true Self until we discover and reclaim our birthright to simply be ourselves. It is essential that we develop the capacity to distinguish between the ordinary, conditioned self, and the transcendent Self that encompasses all of who we are. Eventually, we learn to recognize the parts of us that are impacted by personal history and previous conditioning. Ultimately, we strengthen our relationship to a Self-awareness that transcends history, personal and otherwise, because it taps into a greater Source of infinite wisdom within our being.

One of the ways I train clients to use their intuition to experience their true Self is to engage in a dialogue between their ordinary self and their greater Self. As a stepping-stone to developing the distinction between the ordinary self and the transcendent, greater Self, I have adapted the traditional gestalt therapy "double-chair" technique into an intuition training tool. I suggest that the intuitive, greater Self sit in one chair, and the ordinary, wounded, earlier self sit in another chair. With the aid of a guided inner process to expand the client's intuitive awareness, I encourage the client to move back and forth between the chairs—engaging in a dialogue between the ordinary self and the greater Self—until they can experience a distinction between these two aspects of being. Likewise, if I am consulting by phone, I ask the client which ear they are holding the phone to, and identify that as their "ordinary" consciousness. Then, following the same process as with the chairs, I ask them to switch the phone to the other ear, so they may "hear" the voice of their inner Self.

I use the acronym FORGIVE to guide my clients through this process. *Focus* on your current experience. *Observe* your ordinary awareness, such as feelings, desires, fears, thoughts, beliefs, perceptions, body sensations, and energy level. A shift in consciousness occurs when you *Request* insight in order to *Gain* greater Self-awareness. Next, you must *Integrate* the intuitive insight into a vision. You will *Validate* this vision (or not) through your *Experience* as you shift back to ordinary awareness.

F Ocus O bserve R equest G ain I ntegrate V alidate E xperience

A Meditation

F — Focus

Get comfortable. Close your eyes and focus on your experience.

O — Observe

Observe yourself, your body sensations, feelings, thoughts. Observe your body-heart-mind. This is your ordinary awareness.

R — Request Insight

Place your hands over your heart and ask for help. Ask the "right" question. Avoid "why"—it takes you into rationalization. If there is no response, chances are it's the wrong question. Try "who," "how," "when," "what," or "where."

G — Gain Greater Self-awareness

Take a deep breath. As you exhale, and clear your mind of all thoughts. With your hands on your heart open to an experience of a greater Presence—allow inner seeing, hearing, feeling, or knowing. Keep breathing and relax into greater Self-awareness.

I — Integrate Intuition

In a pose of receptivity, place your hands on your lap, palms up, and receive impressions. Use your breath to help integrate the insight, impressions, or intuitions by inhaling them into every part of your body. As you exhale, relax even more into the intuitive experience.

V — Validate Your Vision

Expand the inner perception into your thoughts and feelings. Use visualization or affirmations. See, feel, hear. Be receptive.

E — Experience

Experience your insight fully. Evoke it by envisioning how it would be for you to live from this perspective. Observe yourself. What does your ordinary self have to say about this? How does the experience "sit" in your body, heart, and mind?

If the energy in the body sinks or if muscles get tense, the wisdom of body reality is calling out to be heard. When emotions react and are unsettled, or thoughts get busy, it is a signal that we must continue the dialogue to open to heart wisdom, or the deeper truth of universal mind. Reactions in body, emotions, or mind indicate that we have not yet spoken the truth that has integrity in all worlds. I encourage individuals to explore these barriers through a dialogue between their greater Self and ordinary self by asking questions like "Greater Self, what is that tension in my stomach about?" or perhaps, "Universal Self, what is the lesson my soul is learning? How might I bring release and healing?"

For example, Dana and I had been working with inner development for some time. She had already moved beyond the "changing chairs" training wheels and could change her awareness by simply going straight to her heart for a clear impression of greater insight into her daily concerns. When it came to making some big decisions, her inner guidance suggested that she trust herself and the process. In our discussion she confided, "I do not trust myself enough yet to tap in to my inner wisdom consistently. It is a learning curve thing. I have my moments of clarity. And I have my moments of 'mistakes' still. So I do not feel confident. I haven't made peace yet with the reality that I may make mistakes, and that mistakes are part of the whole process. I see mistakes as 'I screwed up' and 'I didn't get it right yet,' as opposed to imagining that what I am viewing as a mistake is exactly right also. It is *all* all right—I do not have that fully integrated yet."

Like many of us, Dana had the mistaken notion that once we are "connected" with our true Self, life will be perfect—or we will be perfect. Like people who go to fortune-tellers to "read" their future, we expect that we can use our inner Source of wisdom to help us predict the future so we never have to make another mistake again. This is not trust. This is control—a reflection of the anguishing, internal struggle we feel when we are caught in self-betrayal. What if what we call mistakes are simply signals sent between inner and outer selves, a Morse code of stops and starts, dots and dashes, that spell out nonpunitive messages between infinite Self and ordinary consciousness? Mistakes initiate a dialogue between our ordinary awareness and expanded, creative parts of being to inspire our conscious spiritual evolution. Perhaps we can forgive ourselves for being wired to learn the hard way, through experimentation and trial and error.

Trial and error can be cornerstones of invention and creativity. Experimentation is part of the process of evolution. Thomas Edison, for example, tested over six thousand lightbulbs before he "invented" the commercial incandescent bulb that made him famous. What would have happened if he could not tolerate mistakes, or if he felt he needed to have it right the first time? Edison had less than three months of formal schooling, a father who called him a "dunce," and childhood teachers who said he was "addle-brained" and would never succeed at anything. We, too, may feel inadequate at times. We may complain that we do not have enough training, or perhaps we suffered name-calling and lack of support from significant people in our lives. Even with all this, there is an urge within each one of us to express ourselves, to be ourselves, to explore, experiment, risk. To trust.

Originality is an expression of our greater creative Self, filtered through the unique lens of individuality. What is self-betrayal? It is the anguishing self-doubt, internalized criticism, or expectation that we should be perfect, or at least different than we are. But self-betrayal returns us to our true Self. In the process we redeem our body wisdom, our heart wisdom, and our mind wisdom by returning to the greater wisdom of Spirit that lives in each world.

My own divorce was a test for me to "walk my talk." In 1993, six months after the first edition of this book came out, I felt like my marriage was ending. Matthew and I had felt that way before, but this time it was different. We were not sure what to make of our life together, our feelings, our marriage. Since I was leaving town for two weeks to go on a book tour, we decided to use the separation as a chance for us each to get clear, independent of each other, about the next steps for our relationship. Matthew dropped me off at the airport early Thursday morning. It took until late Saturday night for us to finally speak directly with each other instead of via machines and voicemail messages. Enforced separation signals that the sacred initiation of the soul's journey has begun.

Both Thursday and Friday nights, I'd had dreams about us separating. I'd asked for dreams before going to sleep—three dreams, in fact, just to make sure that my dreams were not reflections of emotional reactions or day-residue. I prayed for guidance on the proper course for our marriage and relationship each night before going to sleep. Dreams are one of the ways I ask for help and guidance from a greater intelligence within. Though

I was still waiting for a third dream to confirm the first two, by Saturday morning I was pretty certain that our marriage was ending.

On the phone, late Saturday night, Matthew told me that he had talked things over with friends during the days we had not been in contact with each other. His method of Self-reflection was to use the mirror of trusted loved ones as a sounding board to get a sense of clarity. By the time we finally spoke with each other, Matthew was clear. "I've decided that I want to end it." he told me. After a long pause he went on. "I have the image of a key and a lock. There's nothing wrong with the key, or the lock. It's just not a fit. It's not clicking. It won't open."

"Yeah," I said. I shared my two dreams with him. Though I was still "waiting for confirmation" with a third dream, I *knew* our marriage was over. I understood exactly what he meant.

"It's like there is a quality of happiness that we each desire—that we can't seem to provide for each other—and we both need to be free to discover it," I added.

We had been round and round the question so many times: that old, familiar impasse—our favorite barriers to intimacy—only in the past, feeling out of sync or disconnected from each other was an invitation to get closer, to share feelings, to express everything from resentments and disappointments to needs, desires, and dreams to each other. This time the release into openhearted love came when speaking the truth about ending our marriage. No more agonizing questions, trying to make things click. The key just didn't open the lock. Simple, clear, respectful. No nagging inadequacies or accusations. No blame. Speaking the truth without blame or anger was a big lesson for both of us.

Fascinating how one of the gifts of our marriage came to us in how we were choosing to end it. What a mystery life is.

Self-betrayal is one of the most challenging of all betrayal wounds. Haunting questions fan the flames. . . . How can this be? How do we know what is truly "right"? Can we act on it? Would it be a betrayal to stay in the marriage when we knew it was not able to take us to the place we each needed to go? Should we conform, compromise, do more, do less? How can we be sure that our decision to divorce is not just emotional reaction, frustration, hurt, or disappointment getting in the way of "making things work"? What do we really trust? These and similar questions are reflections of the turmoil of self-betrayal.

Instead of trying to answer those questions, I asked for confirmation or affirmation from deeper inner resources. I prayed for clarity that I might *know* the appropriate direction for us, and the next step that I might take to bring the greatest good to both of us. This had been my prayer throughout our nine years of marriage and twelve years of knowing each other. This time, I specifically asked for guidance in the form of synchronicities and dreams. I wished to be shown, without question, what would be right for me and us. Eventually, the inner light dawns, showing the way through all the muck and mire of the heavy heart and doubting mind, to the path of truth that sets the soul free. And sometimes we simply have to wait until it is truly clear. Lucky for me, I had two dreams before my phone conversation with Matthew, and by the time the week was up, I had two more dreams about us separating: a total of four dreams. I had my full confirmation and more.

If Matthew and I had chosen to stay in the marriage because of vows like "until death do you part"—and had interpreted that death literally, as a physical act—then we would have betrayed the deeper truth of the psychic and emotional death that our marriage had gone through. Not to mention the discovery of an even deeper creative truth about our ideals of love, life, and marriage. We loved each other enough to free each other and ourselves from the limits of our marriage, so we could literally be free to discover and explore the dreams of love that we both longed for and did not find with each other. I trusted our decision to separate as completely as I had trusted our decision to marry. In both cases I did not have a clue about what the future might hold—but I knew I was making the right choice.

Integrating the Four Worlds

The Celts talk about drinking from the four-sided cup of truth. The elixir of life is contained in a cup that unites all four truths together: the objective truth of concrete reality, the personal truth of one's subjective experience, the universal truth that creates meaning, and the absolute truth of eternal reality governed by greater spiritual Love combine together to bring forgiveness to all who might drink. As in the Kabbalah, we must integrate physical, emotional, mental, and spiritual realities.

It is interesting to note that some North American aboriginal cultures describe these same four worlds in terms of four directions on a medicine wheel. When we are out of balance, we need the medicine, or the power, of one of the directions to return us to wholeness. Some shamanistic and indigenous cultures also describe a process of soul-fragmentation: When a part of the soul splits off, gets caught in one world, or is out of balance with the whole. The sacred process of reclaiming and reintegrating these lost fragments is called Soul-retrieval, and it describes the process of calling the parts of oneself back home to the Self, to reestablish harmony, balance, and unity.

I had the good fortune to hear Ruth Turner, an Ojibway psychologist, expand on this concept of how we might reestablish harmony and wholeness when she presented material on the medicine wheel at a Canadian Psychologists Association meeting in 1998. In her session she described the power of the four directions and how we might apply different types of healing methods to various issues associated with each direction. The Four Worlds Development Project,[2] an intertribal North American aboriginal group of elders centered in Lethbridge, Alberta, Canada, teach that each of the four worlds brings not only tests, but also particular lessons, skills, and gifts.

Honoring Your Physical Self

To come into balance with our physical world experiences, we must pay attention to our body's physical needs and take care of our physical health. We can use tools such as diet, fasting, herbs, exercise, sports, dance, hiking, and other physical activies, along with rest and adequate sleep, to restore the physical body and reestablish a relationship to our physical energy. Take time to note which activities boost your energy level and what saps your energy. Taking care of your physical self includes maintaining not only your physical body but also your physcial home, work, and financial realities, as well as conserving our planet's resources. Eliminate energy depletion by limiting those activities or circumstances that deplete your vitality.

When integrated with the other worlds of experience, the physical world is here to help us take a stand and to practice recognizing our own and others' boundaries and limits. The Four Worlds Development Project teaches that when we live in harmony with this world, we share its gifts with others:

- Freedom to say no
- Ability to honor and respect yourself and others equally
- Integrity between words and actions

- Responsibility and discipline
- Commitment to the path of personal growth
- Ability to hear no without feeling rejected or hurt

Honoring Your Emotional Self

To bring our emotional world into balance with our other realities, we must pay attention to our inner signals and learn to restore trust in self, others, God, and the Great Mystery of Life. The emotional world asks that we explore our feeling nature including the origin of fears, hurts, and anger.

Ruth Turner suggests that emotional healing be attained through practices that show us how to release the pain of the past. We can use a variety of healing methods such as sharing circles, community support, counseling, and group therapy, including twelve-step groups (AA, Alanon, etc.). A more shamanistic or traditional approach might include soul retrieval or dream work.

The Four Worlds Development Project tells us that as we heal the part of us that has been lost in the pain of the emotional world, we retrieve emotional strengths, gifts, and resources to share with others:

- Freedom to love and be loved
- Emotional attraction to good and repulsion to bad
- Patience, compassion, and kindness toward oneself and others
- Ability to express hurt and other hard feelings without getting lost in them
- Ability to express joy and love
- Ability to set aside strong feelings in order to serve

Honoring Your Mental Self

To be in balance and harmony with the mental world, one must pay attention to one's innate intelligence and learn to acknowledge as well as bring forth one's own personal gifts or talents, while at the same time acknowledging the gifts, talents, and intelligence of others. Do practices that heal the mental world, such as taking time to study, explore, learn, and discuss your thoughts and ideas with others, especially with those wiser than you. Take time to find mentors, teachers, and elders; in time, become a mentor to others. Continue to take classes or workshops, write in your journal, or use meditation to speak with your heart. Open to the wisdom of your inner teacher.

The Four Worlds Development Project suggests that as we walk in balance in the mental world, we give forth its gifts:

- Freedom from hate
- Freedom from fear
- Healthy detachment
- Cultivation of wisdom
- Objectivity, clarity, and discernment
- Ability to honor one's heritage
- Appreciation of ancestors and elders
- Comfort with silence

Honoring Your Spiritual Self

To bring ourselves into balance with the spiritual world we must learn to honor and recognize truth, practice telling the truth (without blame or judgment) to others, and practice being an example for others. If you need to heal spiritually, there are a variety of spiritual practices that you can use to restore yourself. Explore the practices from your own tradition and feel free to use the spiritual gifts from other traditions if they help you heal, including ceremony, prayer, ritual, church service, sweat lodge ceremony, vision quest, or meditation retreat. Take time and space to quiet your mind and search your heart.

As we heal our connection with the spiritual world, we receive the gifts of spiritual insight, understanding, and the true wisdom that comes from experience. When living in harmony with this world, we give forth the following gifts:

- Freedom to tell the truth
- Increased Self-trust, self-worth, and intuition
- Ability to see clearly through complex situations
- Courage, innocence, and freedom from guilt
- Ability to focus attention on present time tasks
- Devotion to the service of others

Honoring Your Greater Self

Each world offers us resources that enable us to bring the gifts of our unique creative spirit into the physical world, to make the world a better place for life. Self-betrayals are *for-giving* us the opportunity to integrate, to give every world its due. We can consciously retrieve lost parts that we and our planet need to be whole. Eventually, we discover a transcendent Self that goes through all the worlds. This greater Self is like a shape-shifter able to travel in and through all the worlds of experience without losing itself.

The transcendent greater Self brings us the gift of choice. It teaches us to learn the difference between fragmentation and wholeness, between "my will" and "Thy Will" and it moves us to act on inner guidance from the integrity of our wholeness—heart, mind, and body working together with our spirit.

Harmony and balance with all four worlds requires that we walk the Path of Integration. There are tools we can employ to help us on this path, such as continuing to cultivate the Observer-Self. Neutrality reveals reality, and we learn to live in reality as it is. Practice accepting reality. Acknowledge reality. Appreciate reality. The practice of offering prayers of gratitude that honor life as a sacred gift, helps you stay connected with the gift that life is. Life then gives us the gifts of:

- Free will and freedom of choice
- Increased attention and concentration
- Ability to set realistic goals and meet them
- Self-responsibility
- Humility
- Willingness to initiate action
- Cultivation of perseverance
- Comfort with endings
- Ability to complete goals
- Willingness to be of service to others

We are called to be true to ourselves in each world—physical, emotional, mental, and spiritual. Each world calls us back to itself at different times to retrieve something, to learn something, to die, and to be reborn into an even greater awareness. As you assimilate its teachings, you are more able to allow reality to show you how to act by choosing to respond creatively to yourself and others.

I'd like to end this chapter with another ancient Egyptian story about the power and magic of time as a healer and that old adage of "Time heals all wounds"—but it is not our contemporary understanding of how "time heals."

Long, long ago, humans were calling out to the gods to help them, so they might be healed of their woes. They sought to learn the secrets of the universe, the secrets of magic, so they might have their desires fulfilled. And it was Thoth, the God of Science and Magic, husband to Maat, Goddess of Truth and Justice, who came to answer their call. Who better than Thoth, the ibis-headed moon god, the lord who sheds light in the darkness and knows the mysteries of the cycles and seasons of growth on our planet, to reach out to his younger brethren. It was Thoth who taught humans how every course of study had its outer, physical form, and its inner, nonphysical expression—how science and magic were two sides of the same coin. The Egyptians learned how disciplines like astronomy and astrology were one science, or the study of geometry and geomancy were both reflections of the science of architecture, and so the Great Pyramid was constructed as a testament to the ancient ways. Humans then sought to learn how to perform the mystery and magic of healing the woes of humanity.

And the God of Science and Magic called out, in a voice that pierced the darkness of night. "Humans, I will teach you the secrets of magic," he announced. "Magic requires three ingredients. Only three things: *Right time, right place,* and *right gesture.* With these three anything is possible." Thoth continued, "Right gesture is invoked when your intention is expressed in word and deed, saying and doing that which supports the magic you desire. Right place requires the creation of an environment that supports and expresses your intention. Right gesture and right place are for you humans to create. And as for timing," the Moon God paused for a moment, "timing is in the hands of the Gods."

So the ancient priests and priestesses were instructed in the ways of magic, just as you are being instructed. It is up to you to create the environment—to create the space or place for change, for healing. Likewise, it is your responsibility to do the appropriate gestures—the thoughts, words, ceremonies, and activities that bring about your healing. And then, when the time is right, like magic, the healing happens.

We must do our part for the miracle to occur. But we cannot control timing. Let me give you an example. I was scheduled to give a betrayal-to-trust workshop, and due to low registration we had to cancel it. Though we had done everything "right" (advertising, word of mouth, promotion, and so on) it just did not go. As it turned out, that was the day of the Oakland Hills fires, and everybody from my neighborhood was evacuated. When I called Matthew to let him know that I was OK, he told me that he had not even been allowed back into the neighborhood once the evacuations had begun. How lucky I was to be home, to pack up our kitty, some essentials (including the computer with this yet to be published book in it, plus a few other more sentimental items), load them in the car, and meet Matthew at friend's house on the other side of town. This was not the "right time" for a workshop. It was, thank goodness, the right time to be home, and I was in the right place at the right time doing the right thing. (Fortunately, the fire was finally contained just after midnight, about a mile from our home, and so our home was saved.)

There are greater forces that guide the growth of the soul—the same forces that guide the growth and evolution of stars and planets and all of life. We are not always privileged to know why the timing is on or off. "Timing is in the hands of the Gods." This is the final test of trust, and it teaches us patience.

Sometimes all three magical ingredients come together by accident—we are in the right place, at the right time, doing the right thing. This is called *grace*.

More often, however, the right time comes, and we are not in the right place, or perhaps we are not doing the right activities that might support our Self-healing, so we miss an optimal opportunity. For example, you may have tried to have a deep heart-to-heart with a friend or lover while waiting in line at the checkout at the grocery store. Even if it is the right time, maybe even the right gesture—it is definitely the wrong place! Or let's say you have the place all set up—privacy, no distractions—but you are lost in the pain of the emotional world, or keep jumping to conclusions and cutting yourself short (lost in the mental world). Wrong gesture—the magic will not happen.

Then it is the time to give yourself the gift of alternatives—to try other gestures. *Focus* on your current experience. *Observe* your feelings, thoughts, body sensations. *Request* by asking your Self, "What do I need right now for greatest healing? What gesture can I do that would be most appropriate?" *Gain* greater insight and *Integrate* your intuitions. *Validate* the vision you receive through *Experience*. FORGIVE yourself for the past, and create a new option in the present.

Maybe it is time to talk with a support group, write in your journal, get some emotional healing. Perhaps it is time to meditate, speak with your heart, read some inspirational books, review your journal, and explore forgotten insights. Or maybe your energy is low, and your body is calling to you to do some exercise—tennis, yoga, swimming—or just rest for a bit. You might also want to check to see if it is your spirit that is calling out for ceremony, ritual, and prayer. Drink from the four-sided cup of truth. Give each world its due. Take time to create a place for all of the parts of you.

Even if you feel like you missed out—missed the opportunity for the "great healing"—have no fear! Thoth, being a moon god, knows that time is cyclical. The right time is not a one-shot deal. The right time comes around again and again. Like the moon that moves from no moon to crescent to full, your opportunity for fulfilling the vital dream that brings you and everyone you know new life comes round again and again. Each betrayal of Self is *for-giving* us the chance to learn to make better and better choices over time. And it does seem to take time. So give yourself the gift of time.

You are larger than your wounds. You have the ability to listen to your Greater Self, to act on what you know is right or true for you, and to create meaning and value out of what life brings you when the timing seems "off," or when things do not go the way you expect. We must start by forgiving ourselves, and each other, for being human—ultimately forgiving the Creator for making each of us works in progress.

Choose Self-Renewal Over Self-Betrayal

1. Review the Self-Betrayal/Self-Renewal Checklist on page 170. Put a checkmark by all the styles of self-betrayal and Self-renewal that apply to you or that you would like to develop more.

2. Choose a prime self-betrayal pattern that shows up in your life—a time you feel off-center, disconnected, or fragmented. Instead of acting creatively, you may find yourself repeating reactive defensive patterns such as perfectionism, self-criticism, or asserting your need for control and predictable outcomes. You may act in a cavalier way, feeling superior, grandiose, or arrogantly righteous. Or conversely, you may feel inferior, insecure, or riddled with self-doubt, blame, or pity, and susceptible to stress, humiliation, confusion, or self-hate. Remember the last time you acted out this self-betrayal pattern. Observe body sensations, thoughts, emotions, or knowings.

3. Reflect on your results from the checklist. Out of the items you checked, circle three that most contribute to the pattern of self-betrayal. Likewise, circle three items from the Self-renewal list that could have helped you keep your integrity.

4. Now choose the primary form of self-betrayal from the three you have circled. Likewise, choose the most prevalent of your three Self-renewal items. The latter can act as your antidote to your primary self-betrayal pattern.

5. Imagine how your life would be if you lived more from Self-renewal instead of self-betrayal. How might you integrate this renewing quality into your life? What thoughts support it? What actions demonstrate it? How might these healing thoughts and actions impact how you feel? Write about the possibilities in your journal.

6. Make renewal of your Self a spiritual practice. Come back to this quality every day. Meditate on it. Pray for it. Imagine living from this place more and more in your life.

SELF-BETRAYAL/SELF-RENEWAL CHECKLIST

Some words may be interpreted as either self-betraying or Self-renewing, depending on which "self" is performing the act or interpreting the experience. For example "self-centered" may be an egotistical act, or it may be interpreted as "Self-centered," that is, being inwardly directed and following direction from one's greater Self. Some, such as "self-destructive," hurt both selves. Change or add to the words in each column accordingly, as you see fit.

SELF-BETRAYAL	SELF-RENEWAL
self-betraying	Self-accepting
self-absorbed	Self-analyzing
self-abusive	Self-directed
self-centered	Self-centered
self-aggressive	Self-assertive
self-defensive	Self-assured
self-destructive	Self-confident
self-contemptuous	Self-contained
self-complacent	Self-controlling
self-deceiving	Self-determined
self-denying	Self-disciplined
self-deprecating	Self-directed
self-important	Self-important
self-ish	Self-ish
self-conceited	Self-esteemed
self-doubting	Self-helpful
self-effacing	Self-improving
self-hating	Self-possessed
self-indulgent	Self-propelled
self-interested	Self-interested
self-regulating	Self-regulating
self-pitying	Self-respectful
self-protective	Self-revealing
self-righteous	Self-restrained
self-sacrificing	Self-sufficient
self-satisfied	Self-taught
self-serving	Self-sustaining
self-willed	Self-willed
self-sabotaging	Self-loving
self-repressive	Self-aware
self-defeating	Self-honoring
self-mutilating	Self-observing
self-reproachful	Self-caring
self-punishing	Self-healing

EXERCISE 6-B

Integrate Your Four Worlds

To determine if you are out of balance with your physical world, emotional world, mental world, or spiritual world, review the Five Gates of Power listed on pages 172 and 173.

1. Read the row that identifies signals that you are out of balance.

2. Move down the column to find the lesson you need to learn to restore balance in your life.

3. Choose the appropriate Self-renewing gestures to facilitate your personal growth and integration.

THE FIVE GATES OF POWER[3]

Gate	Physical World	Emotional World
Signals that you are out of balance	Unable to stay centered in the face of anger, fear, aggression, or negative projections of emotions	Unable to stay centered in the face of adoration, compliments, and positive projections of emotions
Lesson you need to learn to restore balance	Take a stand. Recognize your own and others' boundaries and limits without aggression toward others.	Restore trust in the self, others, God, and the Great Mystery.
Gestures and approaches for Self-renewal	Pay attention to your body's needs and watch your physical health. Use diet, nutrition, fasting, herbs, exercise, sports, mind-body practices, bath, sauna, etc. Notice what boosts and what saps your energy. Limit energy-depleting activities. Take care of business one step at a time. Balance rest, sleep, and activity.	Explore the origin of your fears, hurts, and angers. Learn to release the pain of the past through counseling, family therapy, listening circle, group work, Twelve-Step programs, healing centers, expressive art therapies, psychodrama, Gestalt, art, hypnosis, etc.
Gifts that you give-forth when you are in balance	Freedom to say no; ability to honor and respect yourself and others equally; integrity between words and actions; responsibility and discipline; commitment to the path of personal growth; ability to hear no without feeling rejected or hurt	Freedom to love and be loved; emotional attraction to good and repulsion to bad; patience, compassion, and kindness toward oneself and others; ability to express hurt and other hard feelings without getting lost in them; ability to express joy and love; ability to set aside strong feelings in order to serve

MENTAL WORLD	SPIRITUAL WORLD	THE PATH OF INTEGRATION
Unable to stay centered in the face of indifference, aloofness, apathy, or lack of concern	Unable to stay centered in the face of lies, deceit, treachery, falsehood, or betrayal	Unable to stay choice centered in the face of external pressure; relying on habit, fear, approval, or other external influences to make decisions for you
Acknowledge and bring forth your own personal gifts, talents, and intelligence, and help others.	Find the truth and tell it without blame or judgment. Practice being an example to others.	Establish equal power and capacity in each of the four worlds. Learn to distinguish between "my will" and "Thy will."
Study, explore, learn, and discuss, especially with those wiser than yourself, such as mentors, teachers, and elders. Attend classes, workshops, seminars, etc. Write in and review your journal. Use meditation to speak with your inner teacher.	Engage in ceremony, prayer, ritual, sweat lodge, church, temple, retreat, meditation, vision quest, dream work, etc. Take time and space to quiet your mind and search your heart. TRUST using intuitive tools for self-reflection, such as runes, tarot, I Ching, synchronicities, etc. Commune with your inner Self.	Develop witness consciousness through self-observation. Explore your physical, emotional, mental, and spiritual reality. Live in this reality and give each aspect its due. FORGIVE. Say the serenity prayer. Compose your own prayers. Honor life as sacred. Help center yourself by using vibrational healing methods, aromatherapy, color, sound, etc.
Freedom from hate; freedom from fear; healthy detachment; cultivation of wisdom; objectivity, clarity, and discernment; ability to honor one's heritage; appreciation of ancestors and elders; comfort with silence	Freedom to tell the truth; increased Self-trust, self-worth, and intuition; ability to see clearly through complex situations; courage, innocence, and freedom from guilt; ability to focus attention on present time tasks; devotion to the service of others	Free will and freedom of choice; increased attention and concentration; ability to set realistic goals and meet them; Self-responsibility; humility; willingness to initiate action; cultivation of perseverance; comfort with endings; ability to complete goals; willingness to be of service to others

Commit Yourself to a Spiritual Practice

1. Make a personal commitment to live with integrity. Look at your anti-dote for Self-renewal from Exercise 6-A and information from the Five Gates of Power in Exercise 6-B to turn your self-betrayal pattern into a spiritual practice that helps you restore Self-balance. For example, quit smoking:
   - Physical: Change brands, keep track of smoking habit, or do a cleanse.
   - Emotional: Check out a Twelve-Step program or join a support group.
   - Mental: Take a quit-smoking class or keep a journal.
   - Spiritual: Use your desire to smoke as a wake-up call to become more Self-aware.

2. Create a personal spiritual practice, an action plan that will reestablish balance in your life and that is consistent with your deeper spiritual purpose. Include the magic of time, place, and gesture. Identify everything you need (environment and gestures) to allow the magic to happen.

3. Practice that action as a spiritual practice for a set number of days. In yoga philosophy, it is suggested that if you wish to learn something new, practice it every day for forty days. To break an old habit and make a new habit, practice it for ninety days in a row. To become a master of the experience, it is suggested that you practice for one thousand days. This spiritual practice is your elixir of life.

Live with Integrity

To live with integrity, we must integrate physical, emotional, mental, and spiritual reality. To assess if you are living in integrity, notice if you are able to:

1. Tell the truth. Be honest to yourself and others.

2. Accept yourself. Know your personal limits as well as your greatest potentials.

3. Exercise choice. Say yes when you mean yes, and say no when you mean no.

4. Be congruent. Be sure that what you think, feel, do, and say all match and express your deeper truth.

Chapter 7

Betrayal of Society

Gateway to the Family of Humanity

Wound: If you suffer from a wound inflicted by society, your sense of relationship to the whole has been injured. You feel isolated and alienated, and powerless and helpless to effect change or get your needs met.

Truth: Unresolved mother, father, and beloved betrayal wounds are projected onto the collective. Your personal transformation makes you an agent of social transformation. Conscious commitment to be your most creative, fulfilled Self within the limits of your physical environment has a profound effect on everyone you meet. This contributes to the awakening of humanity.

Healing: Develop trust in your inner, knowing Self that directs you to ACT in your community, workplace, or social group. Let your enthusiasm and joy attract others who share your values and vision. Together with them, practice creating new ways to embody your shared ideals.

Ted was laid off from his job. He had worked with the company for three years. In fact, this company had stolen Ted from another company. When Ted accepted the job offer, he thought it would be a permanent position with job security, salary, pension, and other benefits. They didn't even give Ted the courtesy of two-week notice. In fact, they didn't even let him finish off the day. This is typical layoff protocol, whether in the unstable work environments created by mergers and acquisitions or due to economic recession.

Ted was in the middle of some orders when he was called aside and told to pack up and leave immediately. He felt bad about not being able to complete the work he began or deal directly with his customers and say goodbye. Ted was a loyal employee, working until each job was done. He earned the status of being the best-paid employee in his class. The company had tried to expand too fast and got hit with the recessionary economics of the 1990s. They realized they could save about $17,000 a year in salary and benefits by letting Ted go and hiring a couple of non-benefited, inexperienced employees.

Three days later, when Ted and his wife Judy came into my office, Ted was in a petulant mood. I asked Ted how he felt. "I feel betrayed," he said. "I feel like punching out my boss or blowing up the building or writing all my customers a letter." In almost the same breath, Ted was also quoting the serenity prayer. "God, grant me the serenity to accept the things I cannot change, the courage to change the things I can, and the wisdom to know the difference." After seven years of being clean and sober, Ted knew blowing up the building or punching his former boss was not the wise choice. Instead, Ted consciously chose to embrace the thought that a higher power was guiding him to something else, even though he had no idea what God had in mind for him. Individuals who have healed personal betrayal wounds, like those from Ted's alcoholic betrayal of the body, are Self-trained. Healings of previous betrayals teach an individual how to move from crisis to creativity in other areas of one's life.

Turning inward to discover the spiritual value, meaning, or purpose within a betrayal experience moves a person from the pain of death to the gates of an inner Source of wisdom, understanding, and Self-trust. With the aid of intuition, one begins to perceive the golden thread of purpose woven into the tapestry of one's life. All of life's experiences become synchronistic examples of the presence of a guiding force at work in one's life. When the infinite higher Self and the limited ordinary self are in union, creativity, cooperation, and continued commitment to one's higher Self guide one's actions in the world.

Society is our collective body and humanity is our collective soul. Just as our physical body is the guardian of the soul and points out the attitudinal limitations and restrictions that keep one from enlightenment, the constraints of society also challenge you to consciously use the wisdom of your thoughts and feelings to guide you to a deeper truth about your purpose in life and your contribution to the collective. The journey from betrayal to trust requires that we reawaken our dreams. As Henry Thoreau wrote,

> If one advances confidently in the direction of his dreams, and endeavors to live the life which he has imagined, he will meet with a success unexpected in common hours. He will put some things behind, will pass an invisible boundary; new, universal, and more liberal laws will begin to establish themselves around and within him; or the old laws be expanded, and interpreted in his favor in a more liberal sense, and he will live with the license of a higher order of beings.[1]

Ted's situation provides an example of how this process works on a personal level. During our discussion, just a few short days after the termination of Ted's position at his job, Ted and Judy realized that by combining his unemployment check and her salary as an accountant, their immediate survival needs would not be threatened. In reality, Ted could use this layoff as an opportunity to discover what he really wanted from life, as well as become receptive to what life really wanted from him.

I suggested to Ted, "Imagine, if you could do anything in your life right now, if money and time were not an issue, what would you be doing?" Ted said he always thought about finishing school, but now, at forty, he felt certain he was too old. I repeated my question, including, "If age was not an issue. . . ." In college, when Ted was nineteen years old, he majored in altered states: Quaaludes, alcohol, weed, acid, the works. After attending two years of school, Ted, like so many from his generation, turned on, tuned in, and dropped out. Before dropping out, though, psychology was Ted's favorite subject. Now, Ted and Judy were both active in Alcoholics Anonymous. In particular, Ted really enjoyed the service aspect of AA, working with newcomers and helping others on their road to recovery. The thought that he could make a career out of what he liked most—using psychology to help alcoholics and drug addicts like himself recover—was a novel idea.

In his book *Man's Search for Meaning*, Viktor Frankl, a Jewish psychiatrist imprisoned at Auschwitz during the Holocaust, shares his observations that life holds meaning even amid the most miserable and horrible conditions of a concentration camp. Inspired by prisoners who were able to move beyond the scope of their personal suffering, he tells remarkable stories of the influence of individuals who reached out to comfort others, to share, or even give away, a crust of bread, and to give faith, friendship, and love.

> *It did not really matter what we expected from life, but rather what life expected from us.* . . . [We] were being questioned by life—daily and hourly. Our answer must consist . . . in right action and in right conduct. Life ultimately means taking the responsibility to find the right answer to its problems and to fulfill the tasks which it constantly sets for each individual.
>
> These tasks, and therefore the meaning of life, differ from man to man, and from moment to moment. . . . Life does not mean something vague, but something very real and concrete, just as life's tasks are also very real and concrete. They form man's destiny, which is different and unique for each individual.[2]

Even under the unimaginable horrors imposed by living in a concentration camp, some prisoners attained an exalted level of human greatness and spiritual heights—the epitome of inner strength, spiritual freedom, and right action.

Right action flows from the center of one's deepest sense of purpose in life. The archetypal Father in the form of synchronicity prompts you along the path of your destiny. Your ultimate destination, to fulfill a task in life that only you can fulfill, occurs every day, moment by moment. Your personal history, including all your gifts, talents, and strengths, as well as your idiosyncrasies and vulnerabilities, uniquely qualifies you to apply yourself to the task at hand. There is no right or wrong way to fulfill the moment. Right is directional, not moral, imperative. It springs from your inner sense of purpose, your intuitive sense of direction.

Every experience in our life trains us to accomplish our next task. The task is defined by life itself. As I mentioned before, Ted's involvement in recovery from alcoholism trained him to "let go and let God." The AA's twelve steps and the process of recovery were only one part of Ted's life training that prepared him to fulfill life's next task on the path of his destiny. Ted's interest in psychology and his eighteen-year drug and alcohol habit were also valuable parts of the puzzle. Even being fired gave Ted the opportunity to practice living his principles and rediscover his deeper sense of value and purpose in life. If we look at the process of Ted's life, we can see how he had received all the training he needed to answer an inner calling. One's inner calling is personally meaningful, and, simultaneously, it fulfills a greater purpose in life that extends beyond oneself.

When Ted thought about returning to school, he came up against an invisible barrier. He was insecure about flunking out of school again. We talked about just taking a class or two to see if he still liked psychology. It so happened that the local state university had a certification program in Chemical and Alcohol Dependency Counseling. In addition to looking for work, and doing occasional handyman carpentry jobs for friends, Ted also studied psychopharmacology, one of the subjects required for certification as a chemical dependency counselor. Getting an A in this class convinced Ted that his brain cells were not completely destroyed and that he could, in fact, complete the certification program. Halfway through the program, Ted even began to consider finishing his bachelor's degree or going for a master's degree. Doors were opening instead of closing as Ted continued to follow and act on his dream.

Ted passed an invisible boundary. He was no longer limited by his old belief that he was a failure at school. His personal experience as an addict and alcoholic added a new value to his life's purpose. Instead, this self-destructive behavior could be interpreted as essential training to help him help others. Being of service is the quality in life that allows us to "live with the license of a higher order of beings," like angels in training, living on Earth and working in the service of the spiritual evolution of humanity.

Betrayal-to-trust is an advanced initiation rite. Healing your personal betrayal wounds cultivates your ability to turn to your higher Self for guidance. As individuals within the body of society more readily accept the death part of the cycle, spiritual birth and regeneration become more effortless, natural processes. Eventually, we learn to ACT (act, create, and trust) in harmony with ourselves, each other, and life itself. People are like individual cells that gather together to make up distinct organs in the body of society. Just as particular organs have their own physiological function and work in homeostatic balance with each other to maintain and sustain the overall health of the organism, so individuals of like mind and purpose gather together in groups and communities to add their part to the welfare of the whole. When the whole of society is transformed by the enlightened individuals within it, the whole body of society is regenerated and reborn.

Presently, our society is dying. Indications of existential despair and soul death abound. Massive layoffs and unemployment—whether due to a recession in bad times or corporate mergers and acquisitions in a good economy—combine with multinational corporations' employment policies, labor exploitation and dissolution of labor unions, poverty, prejudice, bigotry, war, famine, and crime. These are social diseases infecting the body of society. Dealing with the problem at the surface level leads to prolonged crisis management. Then, unresolved personal mother, father, and beloved betrayal wounds fester and are unconsciously played out in the social arena. "We've been misled," say the masses to their leaders. "We've been abandoned," cry the homeless. "We've been crushed, broken, taken advantage of, ignored, mistreated, and betrayed."

Separated into "us" and "them," we feel isolated, cut off from our own humanity. Separation kicks off the initiation. Emotional ordeals ensue. Angry and resentful, we rationalize our disenchantment and claim that our present social conditions are the result of failed economic strategies, international political maneuvers, social institutions, or governmental systems. Feeling helpless and unable to effect change, many members of society slump into apathetic depression. The second emotional ordeal disregards the presence of the positive potential in the entity identified as one's betrayer. One magnifies and projects only the negative. In betrayal of society, the betrayed individual disregards the positive potential in society and cynically escalates into the third emotional ordeal, generalization, where one projects the shadow onto the collective. We try to justify why people suffer: it's because they are/I am/we are black, Indian, illegal aliens, women, white men, poor, rich. Sometimes we conclude that "they deserve it," "they asked for it," "they're happy that way," "it's their karma"—all indications that societal betrayal wounds are activated and calling out for healing.

The fourth ordeal is the denial of one's vital dream. For example, the dream of the United States, "life, liberty, and the pursuit of happiness," is all but lost when high ideals are distorted and expressed unconsciously through a collective cultural shadow. Instead of life, liberty, and happiness, we unconsciously deaden ourselves to life's flow and are imprisoned[3] by laws and economic and social conditions that bring us grief instead of happiness. Society, as a whole, responds with more laws and rules, reflecting stage five of the traditional betrayal response. Attempts to control others or to protect potential victims against possible future betrayals only creates more fear and more victims.

181

Healing personal betrayal wounds trains an individual to be a transformative agent, to work within a higher order in the service of the spiritual evolution of social consciousness. Let's look at Paul's story as an example. Paul attended one of my betrayal-to-trust workshops. He focused primarily on father betrayal wounds during the group-sharing processes. Paul, a forty-four-year-old recovering alcoholic, discussed how his father was an alcoholic who physically beat and emotionally abused both Paul and his mother. He also confided that, by virtue of his being born the son of a black man in a white-dominated culture, he felt betrayed by his father. Paul was so passionate about the effect of racism on his life that he and a few of his friends created a group conscience and adapted the twelve-step format into a program that deals with racism and bigotry—Racism and Bigotry Anonymous.

When teaching cross-cultural psychology at Antioch University, I was always struck by how all my students from every culture in the San Francisco Bay Area—Filipinos; Amerasians and Asians; Hispanics from Mexico, Central and South America, Puerto Rico, and Cuba; Native Americans from a variety of tribes;[4] peoples from European descent whitewashed into the category of WASP; African Americans, including those descendants of people from the West Indies;[5] Sephardic and Ashkenasic Jews; Israelis; Iranians; Arabs; and South Africans—expressed being targets of prejudice. And they all made generalizations about their oppressors. The oppression of racism, prejudice, and bigotry is a symptom of betrayal. No matter how big or small the betrayal, an individual taps into the power of a collective force. We each have been betrayed, and we each have been betrayers.

Derald Wing Sue, an expert on minority identity development and the effects of racism on cultural identity, talks about a five-stage process in which individuals from minority groups resolve the pain of oppression. First comes conformity, characterized by feelings of ethnic or racial self-hatred and a desire to assimilate and acculturate. Next, the culturally different person experiences confusion and conflict when complete assimilation becomes an impossible task. This leads to the third stage, an active rejection of the dominant culture's values. "Desires to combat oppression and racism become the primary motivation of the person. There is an attempt to get in touch with one's history, culture, and traditions. Distrust and hatred of white society is strong."[6] Militancy and rhetoric lead to an experience of group-usurped individuality by the time the fourth stage is reached. Whether through the auspices of the dominant white culture, or through one's identified ethnic or racial subgroup, the individual feels a sense of loss of his or her individuality. During stage five, these conflicts are finally resolved. Self-awareness, selectivity, and flexibility construct a personal cultural identity that nurtures self-expression. "Cultural values of other minorities as well as those of the dominant group are objectively examined and accepted or rejected on a basis of experience gained in earlier stages of identity development. Desire to eliminate all forms of oppression becomes an important motivation."[7]

SUMMARY OF MINORITY IDENTITY DEVELOPMENT MODEL[8]

STAGES OF MINORITY DEVELOPMENT MODEL	ATTITUDE TOWARD SELF	ATTITUDE TOWARD OTHERS OF THE SAME MINORITY	ATTITUDE TOWARD OTHERS OF DIFFERENT MINORITY	ATTITUDE TOWARD DOMINANT GROUP
STAGE 1— CONFORMITY	Self-depreciating	Group-depreciating	Discriminatory	Group-appreciating
STAGE 2— DISSONANCE	Conflict between self-depreciating and self-appreciating	Conflict between group-depreciating and group-appreciating	Conflict between dominant-held views of minority hierarchy and feelings of shared experience	Conflict between group-appreciating and group-depreciating
STAGE 3— RESISTANCE AND IMMERSION	Self-appreciating	Group-appreciating	Conflict between feelings of empathy for other minority experiences and feelings of culturocentrism	Group-depreciating
STAGE 4— INTROSPECTION	Concern with basis of self-appreciation	Concern with nature of unequivocal appreciation	Concern with ethnocentric basis for judging others	Concern with the basis of group depreciation
STAGE 5— SYNERGETIC ARTICULATION AND AWARENESS	Self-appreciating	Group-appreciating	Group-appreciating	Selective appreciating

Notice how these five stages of cultural identity are similar to the five stages of symbolic death. One must *deny* one's own culture to conform. *Anger* is a natural expression of the conflicts one experiences when assimilation doesn't work. *Rationalization* fuels militant rhetoric and dogma. This naturally leads to a *depressing* loss of identity. Finally, in stage five one *accepts* and values oneself and others (even those from the dominant culture). Relationships are based on self-acceptance instead of self-betrayal.

Ultimately, Self-awareness and personal integrity are the determinants of relationship. This allows for awareness and acceptance of individuals from all other cultural groups. One accepts others for being who they are and where they are in their own process of growth. Relationships form on a person-to-person basis, instead using stereotyped generalizations or bigoted shadow projections and assumptions as the basis for understanding each other. Self-acceptance and acceptance of others promotes a new way of living together in our culturally diverse world.

Symbolic death attends the experience of purification in rites of initiation to awaken new knowledge that inspires renewal and rebirth. Unexamined generalizations and stereotypes perpetuate the third emotional ordeal of betrayal. Remember, betrayal will kill you, kill your faith and trust in yourself, and destroy your relationships with others. Symbolic death is the beginning of transformation. The mystery of death trains us to move from denial, anger, rationalization, and depression, toward acceptance. In death we discover our common humanity. All people suffer through the pains of existential loneliness, are ravished by rage from perceived injustice, and debilitated by grief or pain from the death of a dream. At the core, indeed, we are all one. The by-product of this experience of oneness is the release of racism, prejudice, classism, and the us-and-them consciousness that earmarks the third emotional ordeal of betrayal, and heals the self-rejection and self-betrayal of the fourth ordeal.

Through death, one comes to accept that there are greater forces at work in one's life other than those determined by one's personal will. Acceptance requires an act of surrender, a shift from "my will" to "Thy will." It takes an act of courage and inner strength to surrender rather than collapse into existential despair. Mother Teresa told a group of novitiates in India that complete, unconditional acceptance is the source of freedom in one's life. She talked about how, every day, she wakes up and prays to God that she will accept whatever God has in store for her that day. Whether she is to be a beggar on the streets, or is to live within the lap of luxury, she surrenders her life to the moment and prays to fulfill the will of God. The development of unconditional acceptance of ourselves and others is a radically new perspective. It is the foundation for social transformation, but it starts with self-transformation.

Progressing through the third and fourth emotional ordeals require that one moves beyond the rational mind that looks exclusively to the past to answer the painful question, "Why did I suffer?" One must seek answers from a creative, intuitive Source within, one's greater Self, which can provide new knowledge instead of old stereotypes. Every culture gives something very special to the family of humanity, and within every individual is a sparkling jewel that adds to this richness. To discover your jewel hidden in the shadows of betrayal is the test of this ordeal.

Use your intuition to discover the specific soul teaching, special gift, or challenge that is hidden in the darkness. Then, instead of betraying this gift, commit to its fulfillment by living your dreams. Paul, for example, following the instruction to go inside himself for guidance during an exercise on the second day of a betrayal-to-trust workshop, was given the word "grace." In relationship to his personal betrayal issues, this word made absolutely no sense to him. Intuitive information is sometimes like that. The sense in things emerges over time. During a break on the third day, Paul was browsing through *The Donning International Encyclopedic Psychic Dictionary* to look up "Holy Grail." Searching under the G's, Paul opened the book to page 259. Grail was not listed, but his eyes fell on the word "grace" and the phrase "grace of God." They read as follows:

> **Grace**—a level of consciousness in which all growth is effortless; an open, frank, joyful agreement between the soul-mind and conscious mind desiring growth which makes existence easy.
> **Grace of God**—a directive intelligence motivating everything to move onward and upward; the potential within every seed that motivates that unit or entity to become a perfect unit or entity of its kind.[9]

Paul had been raised by a mother who was the illegitimate daughter of a woman who had also been born illegitimately. Rumors had it that his father had been the doctor's son. Paul had generalized his parental personal betrayal wounds: being African American meant being illegitimate. Paul's inner guidance was telling him that rather than being illegitimate, he was perfect, by the grace of God. When Paul shared the magic and wonder of accidentally finding "grace" in the encyclopedia, he was expansive and exuberant. Like the passage on grace suggested, Paul felt open and joyful.

This state of consciousness opened Paul to a direct experience of effortless growth. Inner wisdom tells Paul that, through the grace of God, he will continue to move onward and upward until he expresses the perfection of that seed of potential that is Paul, the unique individual he is today.

Paul and I met for a private session after the workshop. We reviewed the suggested preamble that he and the group conscience of Racism and

Bigotry Anonymous had written. Paul had described himself as being stuck. "It's almost like I get a charge out of the anger," he reflected. In our one-on-one work, we identified the anger as a signal that Paul was "dying." I asked Paul to identify what part of him was dying, what he would lose if he truly recovered from racism. "One thing that appears is that I'd lose a sense of self. I'd lose my sense of being strong—strong and black and having it together." Paul was quiet for a moment, and then commented that if he let go of the anger "there is this sense that I'll be ostracized."

We did some inner work in this session. I asked Paul to close his eyes and make contact with the healing presence of his archetypal parents that were so strong and available to him at the betrayal-to-trust workshop. Paul felt contact with a radiant brilliance that was so effusive and penetrating that he broke down into tears and laughter. Meditating on this brilliance within him and suggesting that he let it permeate his being, I asked Paul to imagine, "What would it feel like to be fully recovered from bigotry and racism?"

Paul responded by saying, "It feels like all smiles. It feels like whistling as you're walking down the street, noticing nothing around you but brilliance. As others pass you, you notice the brilliance in them. Just walking down the street being with others and being with myself, trusting my brilliance rather than my pain." Paul considered this last thought, and after a moment, he commented, "Looking from here, I can see where a lot of my focus was just deep in the pain." Focusing on the pain perpetuated betrayal. Trust in this inner brilliance was the truth that set Paul free.

The unresolved betrayal wounds of every person on the planet collect energetically and psychically to form the mass consciousness. For example, Paul's personal familial wounds, plus the wounds of his personal ancestry, plus the wounds suffered by all those of African American ancestry who were enslaved in this country, plus the pain of all those throughout history who have ever been enslaved, dominated, or oppressed, all combine in the collective consciousness and reinforce one's personal experience of being oppressed, ostracized, or enslaved. There is a tremendous amount of collective energy gathered together in the mass consciousness. The tradition of dwelling in one's feelings of betrayal is very powerful. But the power of this negative collective energy is not omnipotent. It can be, and is being, released and transformed.

I like to imagine that the mass mind is like a giant balloon. Each and every one of us is blowing it up with hot air—that is, those preexisting opinions and beliefs formed by our cultural and religious traditions, personal history, and unquestioned expectations. As one begins the inward journey from betrayal to trust, one discovers one's inner truth, one's unique soul dream. From then on, instead of blowing air into the balloon, one makes a tiny pinprick. For example, every time Paul chooses to trust his brilliance instead of his pain, he stops blowing air into the balloon and pierces a hole in it instead. Even though everyone else in the world may still be blowing up the balloon, air begins to escape through the puncture. With enough little pinpricks, the balloon deflates. The power of the collective diminishes. At the same time, new images form, constructing a new balloon and letting fresh air in. The more individuals who share a new paradigm or common vision, like Paul's clairvoyant vision of each of us being expressions of radiant brilliance, the more the new collective image builds in potency and presence.

Having a vision of the future of our society is absolutely essential to our collective passage through betrayal to trust. Commitment to a collective dream heals the fourth betrayal ordeal. The collective dream of society is portrayed through the myths and folktales of its people. Cultures like the United States or Canada face a magnificent challenge. North American culture is made up of waves of immigrants from all over the world, along with a diverse group of indigenous peoples. The United States uses the "melting pot" image to describe the idea of blending cultures together, in contrast to Canada's "mosaic" image, in which individuals from diverse ethnic backgrounds add the distinction of their culture to the whole. Countries like these are in the unique position to discover an even greater creative and unifying dream, one that touches the heart and soul of people across the widest range of cultures. This reflects the distinct challenge of our global society: to discover a myth for our time, one that is great enough to contain the diversity of all peoples from both industrial and traditional lifestyles and cultures.

The rebirth of society calls for the discovery of a unifying, meaningful vision. To fulfill this collective calling, society's dream needs two essential components. First, society needs a dream in which each individual is ennobled by society. Second, we need to emphasize that society is ennobled by the individuals within it. One is ennobled by making a link to something or someone outside of oneself, so that one's individual contribution adds to the greatness of the whole. Then the future has value, purpose, focus, and direction. In the concentration camps, Viktor Frankl observed that "the prisoner who had lost faith in the future—his future—was doomed. With his loss of belief in the future, he also lost his spiritual hold; he let himself decline and became subject to mental and physical decay."[10] Our society is dying, but death is not the end. Our future is waiting to be born. Death initiates new knowledge, which inspires rebirth and reentry into society.

Personally and collectively, we circulate through the cycle of death and rebirth. Mythic time, which is also cyclic, describes the evolution of society in historical terms. Cross-culturally, there are four mythic ages metaphorically represented by the metals gold, silver, bronze, and iron. Ages rise and fall. Each great age is conceived during the dusk of the previous cycle. This next great age gestates in the increasing darkness of twilight as the passing age recedes into the dawn of the new age. Every culture and every society has a story of its golden age. Return to a golden age is a vision broad enough to touch the minds and hearts of all people. It has been the dream of humanity throughout the ages.

The next golden age will be a global affair, not a cultural or national entity like the golden age of the Greeks in ancient times or the Renaissance of the last millennium. The test of our time is to break through separation, both personal alienation and patriotic impulses that portray people from other nations as aliens, to use separation to initiate death and the rebirth of a new golden age. The universality of the next age is represented astrologically by the sign of Aquarius, which is ruled by the planet Uranus, symbol of unbridled creativity and unprecedented social change. Key concepts associated with Aquarius include friendship, community, dreams, innovation, creativity, individuality, originality, and humanitarianism. As a metaphor, the Age of Aquarius reflects the unique and original contributions of individuals who gather together in innovative societal groups or communities to creatively nurture humanitarian ideals.

The journey from betrayal to trust prepares us for this collective mission, this group soul dream. Within the heart of every individual who passes through the five soul tests of betrayal, trust is born. Trust builds communication, compassion, intuitive perception, commitment to one's dream, and spiritual freedom to be oneself and act on and fulfill one's dream in this world. These are the skills we need to build a new golden age that nurtures the individual and sustains humanitarian ideals. Righteous resentment challenges you to discover and express your deeper truth. You cultivate compassion as you accept your own negative traits and release unconscious projections onto others. Cynical generalizing requires that you intuitively commune with your greater Self and use your innate intuitive gifts to perceive your unique relationship to the whole, rather than project unresolved fears onto groups of people.

Then you can no longer deny your own vital dream, inner talents, or resources. The fourth test nurtures your commitment to Self-fulfillment. Express your innate talents and embody your vital dream, mission, or purpose by taking a stand in life. The fifth test cultivates spiritual freedom to encourage you to recognize that you and every person you meet is free to act in the world as we each live our dreams. This builds trust in the process of life, which, through conflict, guides you back to your inner resources to continue to return to your greater, creative Self, as well as to reach out in new ways to others as we strive to resolve our conflicts together. As we creatively cooperate with both inner and outer resources, we naturally come together to collectively create a golden age for humanity.

Across cultures, a golden age is a utopian time of peace and prosperity for all. It is a time of harmony, laughter, and joy between men and women in society. The golden age is a time of creative cooperation, in which each person, whether child, adult, or elder, is valued. Each person naturally contributes his or her part to the betterment of the age. Mythological sources say that, during the silver age, the seeds of discord are sown and laws are instituted to maintain society. While drastically less idyllic than the golden age, prosperity, luxury, and happiness are still plentiful. The bronze age brings with it the beginning of social conflict and marital discord instead of harmony, and we find the invention of weaponry, money, conventional marriage, and social class. By the iron age, massive weapons are invented to settle conflicts, and discord is the order of the day. Mircea Eliade, in his book *Cosmos and History,* tells us that it takes twelve thousand years to cycle through the four ages and return to a golden age.

According to the Vishnu Purana, particular signs indicate when society has degenerated to the last great age.

> Society reaches a stage where property confers rank, wealth becomes the only source of virtue, passion the sole bond of union

between husband and wife, falsehood the source of success in life, sex the only means of enjoyment, and when the outer trappings are confused with inner religion.[11]

This final cycle is called the Kali Yuga by the Hindus.[12] In Hindu theology, Kali is the goddess of death. She typifies the ruthlessness of the archetype of the betrayal of the mother. Paradoxically, Kali, mother of death and destruction, is also intricately interwoven with the principle of life and birth. Death and birth are both transition times and serve as metaphors for transformation—the transmutation of darkness into light. During the death part of the cycle, our own denial blinds us to the light of awareness, and we transit through our anger, rage, grief, and fear.

We are inside the womb of Great Mother right now, and it is dark in here. Labor begins as individuals within the body of society come to terms with the betrayer in one's own nature. The destroyer lives within each of us. For example, in betrayal of society, it is easy for us to point the finger at the Germans during World War II, or at the Iraqis during the Persian Gulf War. It is easy to see the shadow in the "enemy" outside of ourselves. The challenge is to recognize and integrate the shadow within. The first difficult step is to ask, "How am I different from the German people during World War II who pretended not to smell the stinking odor of burning flesh reeking from the death camps, when I pretend not to see the poverty-stricken homeless who are shivering with fear, cold, and hunger on the streets?"

Whereas the Germans projected the shadow onto Jews and Gypsies, in our country the indigenous peoples of this great land suffer from the results of our methodical annihilation of Native American cultures. All people of color hold the burden of the shadow in North American society, not just the Native Americans.

The darker one's skin, hair, and eyes, the more one is the recipient of the projection of darkness, as indicated by the demographics that allot a disproportionate number of African Americans, Native Americans, and Hispanics to the lower economic classes, the prisons, and the emerging caste of poverty-stricken untouchables in our supposedly classless society.

It is hard to look at how we, too, are betrayers of humanity. As one harnesses the killer within who strikes out of fear of the dark—fear of the unknown—one learns to direct this destructive force in constructive ways to consciously destroy whatever it is within one's being that destroys one's awareness of union, harmony, and greater purpose. Betrayal reactions create separation and destroy unity. In the journey from betrayal to trust, we have learned that blame, whether self-blame or pointing the finger at others outside oneself, only fuels the betrayal fires, enflaming righteousness, resentment, and continued suspicion. Trust is all but lost. We are not here to cast blame when we review the state of humanity as revealed through our social systems. We are here to transform societal betrayals by recognizing them, too, as sacred events that unlock the mystery of our own creative power.

For example, Alfonso Williams, who found himself among the ranks of the homeless after moving to the San Francisco Bay Area, was so dissatisfied with the shelter system, that he founded the United Volunteers for Homeless Persons and Families (UVHP&F).[13] "When I moved from Traveler's Aid to the Richmond Rescue Mission, I had a temporary job working at the *Oakland Tribune* newspaper agency for $5 an hour. At that rate, it would have taken me months to save up enough money to cover my first month's rent, plus my last month's rent, and a security deposit on a place to live. Because I had a job when I went to the shelter, I had to get special permission to come in late. Normally, you can't come back until 7:30 at night, and you have to leave the shelter at 6:00 in the morning. You get a morning meal and an evening meal and a place to sleep. In between, you are out on the streets."

Shelters are short-term crisis facilities offering temporary housing for eighteen days. Alfonso described how one's life in a shelter gets fixed on survival, focusing on how to handle the ten-day waiting period before one can return to the shelter for another eighteen days. Rather than nurturing a person's innate creativity, self-worth, or other inner resources that would support an individual in his or her search for permanent employment and housing, Alfonso says, "The shelters are adding to the problem instead of solving it. So, living in this situation, I got to thinking, 'There's got to be a better way.'"

After the shelters, Alfonso rented a room on Third Street from a fabulous seventy-three-year-old lady who became more like a foster mother to him rather than a landlady. For the next two years while Alfonso lived on Third Street, he and a friend who shared his dream started the UVHP&F. Alfonso put together a board of directors and hired an accountant to prepare the necessary papers to apply for nonprofit status. Once they achieved federal and state nonprofit status, Alfonso and other members of the

UVHP&F came up with the first and last month's rent, and security deposit to rent and convert an abandoned thirteen-room hotel into low-rent, single-occupancy dwellings. A man of both action and vision, Alfonso sees unoccupied housing all over the city that could potentially be converted to transitional housing facilities for the homeless. "There is plenty of housing. Owners can get rents and pay their property taxes, and homeless people can get off the streets."

This statement reminded me of a story I read about Jubilee West, a low-income housing development in West Oakland, California. Jubilee West was founded by two nuns who were working in West Oakland. Sisters Joanna Bramble and Pat Sears, like Alfonso, noticed a lack of affordable housing in the neighborhood where they were working. "There are homes that used to rent for $85 a month, that are now $450 a month," said Sister Joanna in a 1985 newspaper interview. "There are people here who live on less than $10,000 a year. What happens to these people who have rented here all their lives?"[14]

To correct the situation, sister Joanna started a nonprofit organization called Jubilee West, modeled after a similar grassroots community organization in Washington, D.C. With money raised by the nonprofit organization, and with grants from Clorox, Safeway, Southern Pacific, and the San Francisco Foundation, Jubilee West buys properties, then fixes them up and offers low-rent housing to community residents. Jubilee West presently owns eighteen buildings. Residents pay only 30 percent of their income in rent, and the remainder is subsidized by the federal Section 8 program.

A neighborhood screening committee meets with, and selects, prospective newcomers to become residents of the neighborhood and members of Jubilee West. Members of the Jubilee West community put in 150 hours of work a year supporting Jubilee West community programs. In addition to renovating housing units, Jubilee West distributes free food and clothing to the needy, trains peer counselors for their extensive youth program, and offers drug and alcohol counseling as well as college prep counseling to younger members of the neighborhood. They also run a job-training and placement program, recreational youth programs, and a local thrift shop.

Ideally, Alfonso envisions UVHP&F also owning properties and expanding their services. For now, Alfonso's dream is "to operate a series of transitional housing facilities, and make the public aware of why the problem of homelessness exists, and what we can do to change it—to help break the trend of people going from shelter to shelter." Ideally, with the aid of volunteers and by networking with existing social services, Alfonso envisions UVHP&F providing a variety of services to people in transition: job training, job placement, literacy education, and counseling for substance abuse. He has already begun in small ways by inviting Alcoholics Anonymous volunteers to chair meetings at the thirteen-room facility.

When we met, Alfonso was living in a three-bedroom UVHP&F home in a low-income area in Richmond, California, with three other housemates, one of whom was a nine-month-old baby boy named Eldrige. During our interview Alfonso told me that he was recovering from the denial of his appeal to the Richmond City Council to keep the converted hotel available as a UVHP&F transitional housing facility. He lost the vote four to three. Opponents claimed that since the property was one thousand feet from the Richmond Rescue Mission, property values would decrease. His use permit was denied. Alfonso was forced to close down the thirteen-bed facility. Not long after, Alfonso received a phone call from social services in Antioch, California. They were interested in more information about the UVHP&F, and they talked about the possibility of starting a facility in that city. Alfonso's initial response to losing the thirteen-room facility was one of disappointment. In our next conversation a week later, he suggested that the rejection might be a blessing in disguise.

Rejection is not a personal rejection. It is a message from the Source of wisdom that guides and directs one's life. When we experience a rejection in life, it is an expression of being out of the flow of one's destiny. Life itself gives us all the feedback we need: It tells us when to go forward or change direction and return within ourselves for redirection. Going with the flow is not a passive way of life. It takes an act of trust.

Mihaly Csikszentmihalyi, author of the national bestseller *Flow: The Psychology of Optimal Experience,* has made a lifelong study of the positive aspects of human experience and that which psychologically creates a sense of joy, creativity, and meaningful involvement in life, a state he calls "flow." Csikszentmihalyi identifies flow as the source of happiness in life. Contrary to the myth of our time, this state is independent of externals like income, social status, career, or position. Flow is an internal state of consciousness that reflects a sense of personal challenge, skill, concentration, and such total involvement in the present moment that one is able to lose feelings of self-consciousness or boredom. Time seems to stand still. "Purpose, resolution, and harmony unify life and give it meaning by transforming it into a seamless flow experience."[15]

Rebecca is an example of a person who moved into the flow of life by making the shift from just kind of going along with life without purpose or personal motivation, to becoming deeply involved in personally meaningful pursuits. Rebecca came to one of my workshops about a year after her father died. Rebecca had always been daddy's little princess. Now she felt lost and directionless, not knowing how to cope with the legacy he left her.

In a private consultation, Rebecca shared her personal story with me. Six years before, when Rebecca's father became ill and was unable to run his company, he sold the company, and Rebecca received $250,000, her share of the stock. A year later, upon the suggestion of her father's financial advisors, Rebecca bought a house for herself, but she also continued working as a clerk in a local health-food store as though nothing had changed. Sometime during that year, Rebecca met and married her husband, Sam, a man who had been born to working-class immigrants and had become a college professor. After Rebecca and Sam were married, Sam encouraged Rebecca to go back to school. She earned her master's degree and then had twins. The direction of her life always seemed to be inspired by events outside of herself.

A year after her father's death, Rebecca again felt like a boat cast to the high seas without charts or a compass. Her father had never trained her or her mother in the intricacies of his financial affairs. Rebecca was stereotyped as a Southern belle, so her father's financial advisors made light of Rebecca's inquiries concerning the distribution and management of her father's estate. They did not take Rebecca or her mother seriously when it came to managing her father's twelve million dollars in assets. Rebecca was at a loss.

When Rebecca met me for another private session six months later, she had quite a story to tell. As synchronicity would have it, Karen, Rebecca's hairdresser, just so happened to be dating Robert, a good friend of Sam's. Through Robert, Karen knew that Rebecca had inherited some money. It also so happened that one of Karen's other clients was an inspiring woman named Tracy Gary. Tracy Gary started a self-help program called Managing Inherited Wealth (MIW). MIW was specifically designed to meet the needs of women like Rebecca. One day, while cutting Rebecca's hair, Karen told Rebecca about Tracy and gave her a contact number.

Under the aegis of Resourceful Women, MIW is one of several self-help programs for women of wealth. "We are a community of women with shared values; we are activists in pursuit of health and learning and change—for ourselves and for the planet—and we are passionate about our original vision: that women who learn about money and money management will change the world."[16] At MIW, Rebecca met other women who understood the confusion, guilt, and the many cultural taboos about women and money in our society: having more money than her spouse and friends, the challenges to one's self-esteem when the work ethic of our culture says that you are what you do, and coping with the projection of envy and entitlement from others who think money solves everything. Rebecca also needed help with the headaches that came from the logistics and practicalities of choosing and managing investment professionals and investments that would work for her and her values instead of for self-serving professionals with no social conscience.

At MIW, Rebecca learned how to hire her own financial planner and use this person to confront her father's financial advisors. Through the Women Donors' Network, another one of Resourceful Women's innovative programs, Rebecca learned about social-change philanthropy. Rebecca had been born into a family tradition that valued giving. For example, long before his death, Rebecca's father had set up a million-dollar endowment fund through a public agency in Atlanta. Rebecca was determined to take over some of the allocation of funds for grants. With the help of the Women Donors' Network, Rebecca learned which questions to ask and what procedures to follow to start taking control.

"I have these resources," Rebecca shared with me privately, "and I feel I have a duty and obligation to use this money in a way that would alleviate pain and suffering and improve the quality of people's lives." I asked Rebecca when it was that she first realized that giving to others was an important value to her. She said it had always been true. "When I was eight years old," Rebecca said, to elucidate this point, "my girlfriend and I formed the Good Deed Club. We would do good deeds for our families.

When our families were visiting together, we would bring our mothers cookies or watch over and play with our little sisters."

When Rebecca told me this story, I thought about Carl Jung, who built his dream home in Bollingen in the latter part of his life. In the documentary movie *Face to Face,* Jung said that every child finds him or herself involved in an activity that is so consuming and enthralling that time stands still. Meaningful passage through adulthood, suggests Jung, depends on reintegrating some of these forgotten experiences from childhood. The creation of a golden age also depends on living more and more from this sense of flow that brings happiness into one's life.

Another mini-miracle in Rebecca's life occurred about two and a half years after her father's death. Some of the people to whom Rebecca had given five-thousand-dollar grants kept mentioning a woman named Ellie. "You've got to meet this lady. She funds all the things you fund," they would say to her. A friend from Seattle connected Rebecca with a Bay Area woman who was seeking funds to start a women-oriented healer's magazine, and Rebecca was invited to lunch. It so happened that Ellie was also at this fundraising luncheon. Ellie, who helped her husband, Frank, manage his family's five-million-dollar endowment fund, was also dedicated to social change philanthropy. It also turned out that Ellie lived, literally, around the corner from Rebecca and that her youngest child was the same age as Rebecca's twins.

Rebecca and Ellie quickly became friends. Two years later, through Ellie, Rebecca was invited to a national conference for funders of social-change philanthropy. She made contact with a national group of other people who all shared Rebecca's values and visions. Rebecca found herself at home with a group of kindred spirits who, like her, were all dedicated to improving the conditions of the family of humanity.

We are each part of larger communities, and every one of us has something to contribute. Linking up with like-minded others who share your inner vision builds community that breaks through the alienation that pervades our culture. Like Rebecca and Alfonso, follow your heart. Let the flow of life guide you to join others who inspire you to fulfill your dream. Trust your inner Guardian and your Guide. Your Guardian reminds you of your natural limits. Respect your limits and accept the limits of others. If you feel rejected, identify what you can do now to take care of yourself as you stand steady in your vision and continue to move on. Trust yourself, and let harmony, purpose, and resolution guide you to the fulfillment of your dream.

There is a divine design at work in the world and in your life. Infinite intelligence works through each of us. As we each get more comfortable saying yes and no and speaking our truth to each other, there will be less need to fight, resist, deny, or discredit each other. One can simply say no without a lot of wounding explanations, justifications, or rationalizations. Remember, the perceived betrayals we cause in each other's lives are not intentional. Rather, they are expressions of our common human experience of psychological woundedness that stems from each of us being works in progress. Trust brings us into contact with inner resources that heal the pain of being human and moves us to discover new outer resources. Trust that all experiences are God's way of guarding you and guiding you to the highest good and ultimate fulfillment of your divine destiny—your complete fulfillment as a human being.

As more individuals heal personal betrayal wounds we can apply our inner and outer resources toward creatively resolving betrayals of society. Collectively, we have all the resources we need, including human resources, creative intelligence, technical skills, equipment, and financial resources to make our greatest dreams come true. Even during the worst economic times in the United States, the richest people have continued to get richer, and their greatest gains have been made at times when the lower economic strata suffer the most. Puncture the mass-mind balloon that holds the idea that there is not enough for everyone. Instead, know what you can and cannot do. Decide what you will do and ACT. Be true to yourself and trust your limits. This builds integrity. Be careful not to over-commit. One little step in the direction of your dreams is enough to move you along the path of your destiny. You are not alone! We each give just our part—and that is plenty. Together, we have all the resources we need to fulfill our dreams here and now.

Like Rebecca, you may find an opportunity to join with others who are dancing in the same dream as you, and they may already have the music playing. Or, like Alfonso, perhaps it is up to you to find the musicians and conduct the orchestra, to take the risk and present your plan to others. Either way, you will be guided every step of the way: You will discover whom to speak with, and when and how to present your dream. Sometimes you may be guided to speak. Sometimes you may be guided to keep silent. Use all your new skills. Honor your intuition and when it feels right, speak what you know in your heart of hearts.

There is a power in collective consciousness. As a group dream builds and is actualized by members of the group, it impacts the whole society. By joining together with like-minded others, we can nurture our new collective dreams and change our society. All sectors of society have institutions that are beckoning to be transformed—service organizations, health organizations, educational systems, religious institutions, corporations, entertainment fields, the arts—they all need support in order to reflect a greater purpose that is in harmony with a new collective dream: the birth of humanity and a new global golden age.

Some of us are working together to change society from the inside out. Examples like Sisters Pat and Joanna, who at first worked within the structure of the Church and then founded Jubilee West, demonstrate that we can work with existing institutions to build a new dream for our society. Paul and his group of twelve-step buddies who came together to form Racism and Bigotry Anonymous is another good example of expanding existing social structures to address current issues and nurture humanitarian ideals. Others of us, like Resourceful Women or UVHP&F, are being guided to found new organizations, institutions, or agencies—to join with like-minded others to build new, innovative structures for an emerging society. Finally, each of us nurtures change in simple, quiet ways through our daily interactions with every person we meet. Every member of society provides some degree of support, information, or professional assistance to others who may be in need. As we embody our dreams, we become the eyes, ears, hands, and feet of the archetypal Mother and Father guiding their sacred child, Humanity, into maturity.

During these times of transition, contrasting forces in consciousness catapult us beyond the paradox of our experience of Earth as it is—with its history of betrayal through violence, torture, human oppression, and struggle—and the incredible vision of all that it can be: a world of personal fulfillment, humanitarian love, international and intergalactic cooperation, harmony with nature, simplicity, peace, and prosperity. The pain of transition is not in vain. Birth of the next golden age is imminent. It is no fantasy. It is reality ready to happen. Healing our personal betrayal wounds trains us for this global enterprise.

EXERCISE 7-A

Rediscover Your Dreams

1. Remember your dreams from childhood.

2. How do they fit in with your life right now?

3. Which dreams continue to inspire you?

Discover Your Dream for Humanity

1. As you imagine yourself living your truth and fulfilling your personal quest, use your intuition to perceive how you affect those around you.

2. How do you wish to affect others?

3. What is your deepest wish for humanity?

4. What is your contribution to society?

5. Risk telling at least one other person your personal dream and your dream for humanity.

6. What are concrete actions you can take, little baby steps, which move you toward the fulfillment of your dreams?

7. Identify at least one action you can take that demonstrates your commitment to your dream, and do it.

Create a Psychic Shield

1. Find pictures from magazines and other publications that include language, images, and symbols that represent the following archetypes:
   - The Mother: support and nurturance
   - The Father: protection, direction, guidance, and synchronicity
   - The Beloved: wholeness, unconditional love, and union
   - The Guardian: energy that sets limits, respects boundaries, and honors your body
   - The Guide: inner truth

2. Find an image or phrase that represents your dream for humanity. Use this as your central image.

3. Take the images and phrases and create a collage that is symbolic of your true energy within that you give forth to the world.

4. Meditate on the power and presence of these archetypes as they work through you, guiding, directing, and protecting you as you live your dreams.

Chapter 8

Betrayal of the Planet

Gateway to a New World

Wound: If you are devastated by earthquakes, volcanic eruptions, blizzards, cyclones, tidal waves, floods, lightning storms, forest fires, heat waves, drought, or famine; or exposed to toxic wastes, air pollution, nuclear or ultraviolet radiation, ozone depletion, acid rain, groundwater or ocean pollution, deforestation, endangerment of species, or overpopulation, your sense of independence has been injured and you need help from outside resources just to survive.

Truth: Natural and man-made disasters give people of all nations the opportunity to act collectively. Resolution of our previous betrayal wounds prepares us to be compassionate, humane emissaries.

Healing: T — Turn inward to discover your deepest truth. To Thine own Self be True.

R — Relax your body and mind and release fear, then receive intuitive guidance.

U — Use the tools you have, both inner and outer resources, to gain greater awareness.

S — Speak the truth. Share your dreams. Take a stand.

T — Trust the process that continues to return to your Source within.

Did you know that 500 million people live near active volcanoes worldwide? In Colombia, in 1985, a volcanic eruption triggered mud slides and floods that destroyed the city of Armero. It is estimated that between 22,000 to 25,000 persons were killed in this disaster. In June 1991, Mount Pinatubo erupted in the Philippines, sending a cloud of ash and gas into the stratosphere. "A gray-green mushroom cloud of ash and smoke rose 10 miles in the sky. . . . Another big explosion threw fist-size lumps of pumice as far as 25 miles. By the weekend, the volcano had erupted 26 times."[1] This time, thanks to the early warnings of volcanologists, about 18,000 people were evacuated. Only eighteen people were killed and fifty injured. Volcanologists can play an important part in an early warning system to save human lives and unsuspecting livestock. Volcanologists are a self-selected international group of scientists impassioned by the ferocious display of fire and earth. Many live to travel from live volcano to live volcano. In so doing, they fulfill a personal mission and potentially contribute to the welfare of people and animals who live close to active volcanoes. Officials in the Philippines heeded the warnings of the scientists, and a total of 84,000 people successfully fled from the disaster. Unfortunately, in Columbia, local authorities did not listen to the advice of these outsiders.

Like all natural disasters, volcanoes have an immediate impact. They also have long-term effects. According to Paul Handler, Ph.D., the publisher of *Atlas Forecasts,* aerosol spray cans and industrial pollution may not be the primary cause of the greenhouse effect. He says that a lack of volcanic activity created the global warming trend that concerned scientists and industry during the five-year period prior to Pinatubo's eruption in June 1991. When the stratosphere is clear of tons of dust and sulfur dioxide gas, like the emissions from Mexico's El Chichon in 1982, more solar radiation penetrates the atmosphere and hits the ground. Then the earth warms up.

Pinatubo sent twenty million tons of ash and vapors into the air, producing a natural aerosol that keeps as much as 7 percent of the solar radiation from penetrating Earth's atmosphere. This resulted in exquisitely gorgeous sunsets and a radical shift in climate. Over the next few years, climactic changes due to greenhouse gases from Pinatubo's eruption had a huge impact worldwide, including:

- A decrease in some key world crops due to late spring and early fall frosts
- Longer, colder winters
- Recurrence of severe African droughts
- Below normal precipitation in the tropics.[2]

In astrology, volcanoes are an expression of Pluto, the Lord of the Underworld, symbol of death and rebirth, and a symbol of the transformation of mass-mind consciousness through destruction and renewal. Ultimately, by regulating Earth's atmospheric temperature, volcanic activity regulates life and death on our planet. Volcanoes regulate the weather; which regulates the occurrence of droughts, dust bowls, tropical rains, and floods; which regulate crop production; which regulates famine; which regulates overpopulation, life, and, ultimately, death.

Dr. James Lovelock noticed this self-regulating, self-regenerating organismic nature of the ecosphere and came up with something he called the Gaia hypothesis. The Gaia hypothesis, named after the ancient Greek earth goddess, suggests that our planet is itself a hypersensitive living organism.

> Gaia has many features in common with the physiology of warmblooded animals. Rivers and oceans act like the blood in an animal's circulatory system. The atmosphere acts like the lungs. All the components of Gaia can be likened to the cells and tissues that aggregate to make up a complete organism, and each component has its unique part to play in the functioning of the whole.[3]

We are only one part of life on this planet. We tend to think we are the most important. But if you met an army of red ants in the Amazon, and it came down to a vote, your opinion would easily be outweighed.

I am reminded of discussions with my former spouse, Matthew. During the early years of our marriage, we each had the revelation that "where *I* put my attention is important to me." We noticed that we both felt that way at the same time, and we each had different opinions and priorities. Before marriage, both Matthew and I were lovers of solitude. We chose our wedding date based on how much longer we each needed to live alone. After he asked me to marry him, we both went inside ourselves to ask for a number to represent the number of months we would each need to complete living alone before living together. Miraculously, we both chose the same number. We set our wedding date for three months hence, thinking we'd be ready and prepared for married life. I don't know if there is such a thing as being able to prepare for the shift from being alone to living in union with another. Six months after our wedding ceremony, continuing to make the shift from "I" and "mine" to "we" and "our," we came up with a startling awareness. Imagine both of us saying these same words to each other, "This is our house and I have a right to be here." This is akin to the shift in awareness that we human beings are making as we come to recognize that we are sharing our home planet with many other life forms. This is *our* home.

Another lesson of my marriage included learning how to dance to the subtle harmonies of being together and separate at the same time. When we first started living together, we'd often unwittingly step on each other's toes. Over the years, we learned to respect and appreciate the gifts our differences brought to our union. For example, I never took the time to accurately balance a checkbook, so I compensated by keeping a large "cushion" of funds in the account to keep from bouncing a check. Matthew, on the other hand, was consistently accurate, down to the penny. Yet, time management skills and retirement planning eluded him.

Awareness of our natural gifts and idiosyncratic blind spots progressively evolved into a natural division of labor. Somehow, through our union, we harmonized and balanced each other. Alone, we each had our own convoluted coping mechanisms to survive. Together, we each received even more than we could alone. The idea that I did not need to keep such a large cash reserve locked up in a low interest account, because since the book was balanced I knew where I stood, opened new opportunities for me to use our resources more wisely.

Metaphorically speaking, I learned that when I am in union with my beloved, more of my resources are available to me now, and I can invest these resources where they will give us an even greater return. We are interdependent, as opposed to independent of or symbiotically dependent on each other. The same can be said of life on this planet. Earth is our beloved. When in union and harmony with it, we shall act together cocreatively and synergistically. Through our interdependence, we each invest our personal resources to give us all an even greater collective return.

The archetypes, like Mother, Father, Beloved, and Self, act within the human psyche as inner resources, in our outer world as natural resources, and in our universe as unknown resources. Archetypal forces are our guides, guarding all of life. Life within us directs us to act in this world, to be links in the flow of resources between inner and outer, physical and nonphysical, known and unknown worlds. Earth is our collective body. Humanity is our collective soul. Our collective destiny is to serve. We are children of creation—children of the Earth taking our initiation into a greater, unknown universe.

Earth is home to all kinds of life forms, and we all have the right to be here. No single form is more important or better than any other. Union results from a synergy between the parts and the whole. Our atavistic human anthropocentricism does not allow us to feel this harmony and union. Life on this planet is interdependent, in a state of beloved union with all of life. It has its own agenda, and human life is but one small part of it. For example, just because you might not like to live in a sewer or garbage heap does not mean that these habitats are unfit for life. In fact, they are swarming with life. Rats, cockroaches, flies, larvae, and bacteria of all shapes and sizes are quite content to live off of human refuse. Each expression of life, from microbe to mammal, has a very specific focus of attention as well as a particular function to fulfill in the greater picture. We all embody and express universal archetypal forces. This is how we serve. When we look only at the survival level, the illusion that each species acts separately and independently of others is created.

Throughout the short time in which humans have lived on this planet of ours, we have felt that our survival has been threatened by natural disasters. We forget that natural disasters are natural. We respond to them as though they are an anathema and we humans have been personally betrayed by God. "How could this happen? All we've created—our homes, cities, our very lives—are destroyed!" Earthquakes, volcanic eruptions, blizzards, tornadoes, hurricanes, typhoons, tidal waves, floods, lightning storms, forest fires, heat waves, drought, and famine, and now overpopulation upset our tenuous, harmonious relationship with our environment. We are like children betrayed by Great Mother, afraid that Gaia will no longer support and sustain us.

Has Earth betrayed us? Or have we betrayed Gaia? Regardless, betrayal of the planet is a sacred initiation, an expression of our spiritual and physical evolution. The first stage of initiation is separation. In this case, we feel separate from nature, instead of in harmony or in union with it. We perceive this separation as real. Earth is objectified, what Martin Buber calls an "I–it" relationship instead of "I–thou." In the pattern of initiation, separation is followed by rites of purification, including ritual tests and trials. Natural disasters evoke emotional ordeals, which follow the patterned betrayal response. We tend to judge the shifts in life's flow from a perspective of betrayal rather than trust. We are suspicions of the shift. Historically, we have responded to natural fluctuations in the ecosphere as though we were being punished for some unknown, supposed wrong. We project the shadow onto nature, make sweeping generalizations about it, and use scientific data as well as religious dogma to justify our fears and suspicions.

By the fourth stage of the tests and trials of this planetary initiation, we wander about lost, expelled from the garden. Union with nature is lost. We suffer the ordeal of ultimate agony when, by the fifth stage, we act out of fear, control, and manipulation. In the past one hundred years, we have become masters at controlling our environment. All of Earth's natural resources, air, water, and energy systems are viewed as raw materials to be manipulated to help us cope with every perceived threat to our existence. For example, by harnessing electricity, our air-conditioning and heating systems reverse the seasons for us. We have warmth in the dead of winter and cool breezes during the scorching summer seasons. We manipulate the very elements of our planet through atomic fission to provide the energy to manage our collective comforts as we attempt to mold Earth to meet our needs.

Acting from betrayal perpetuates betrayal. In the pattern of initiation, initiatory ordeals are designed to kill you. That is why death is the third phase of initiation. The constricting patterns of the past are doomed to die to make way for new growth. In our personal inner work, when we resolve mother, father, or beloved betrayal wounds, the death is symbolic. In betrayal of the planet, death is both symbolic and physical. Our manipulations of Earth's resources betray our own continued existence on this planet. When we act against any part of nature, we act against ourselves. When we destroy any form of life on the planet, we destroy a part of ourselves.

Let's look at our relationship with trees as an example. Trees are a vital part of the production of oxygen on this planet. We use trees for lumber to fuel the building and construction industry, the paper industry, and, of course, for heating our homes. In Oregon, there are many tree-planting and harvesting companies. After World War II, lumber companies began to use an herbicide called 2,4,5-T to increase production. Between 1973 and 1977, eight women reported having eleven miscarriages following the spraying of the forests. These same women had full-term pregnancies when no spraying was done. Their doctors had no explanation.

In 1978, these women asked the Environmental Protection Agency (EPA) to investigate. In 1979, the EPA put a temporary ban on the use of 2,4,5-T because it contained the deadly toxin dioxin.[4] Ten years before the EPA investigation, dioxin was known to cause birth defects in animals as well as to kill lab animals in doses as low as a few parts per billion. Even so, 2,4,5-T was used on ranch lands, in rice fields, and in timber areas, no doubt contaminating the entire food chain in areas affected by the spraying. However, we did not put a ban on this herbicide until there was evidence that human life was at stake. Since we see ourselves as separate from nature, we did not understand that control and manipulation of nonhuman life affected us as well.

Environmental dangers accelerate the death phase of the initiation by perpetuating a betrayal of life on this planet. Hazardous and toxic wastes, air pollution, nuclear radiation, ultraviolet radiation, ozone depletion, acid rain, groundwater pollution, ocean pollution, deforestation, the inadvertent creation of endangered species, and the overpopulation of human beings are all the result of the blind manipulations of our industrialized, modern world. Paradoxically, even though we see ourselves as separate, or think we can act independently from the system of life on this planet, we cannot and do not. From the perspective of Gaia, perhaps human beings are simply doing their part. We are like bacteria on the face of Earth just doing our natural catabolic and anabolic processes,[5] destroying and reconstructing life. Collective awareness of loss of human life, through a collective agency like the EPA, stimulates the feedback loop. Destructive catabolism temporarily ceases, and constructive anabolic processes are mobilized. Planetary biosynthesis continues.

That is one possibility. Another possibility might have something to do with our ability to be Self-conscious and spiritually aware. As the ancient Egyptians said, human beings contain all life forms within the field of human consciousness: minerals, plants, animals, and a higher consciousness of the Self. Contained within our ancestral memory is the wisdom of the Earth. As Self-conscious beings, we are being initiated into the mystery teachings of the Earth. With practice, we can draw from our four and half billion years of evolutionary experience on this planet to remember these teachings of evolutionary transformation. Mythologically, this process of evolutionary transformation has been described as the pattern of initiation that moves from separation, purification, and death, to new knowledge and rebirth.

Nature gives us our own nature. She whispers her secrets to us. To hear them, we must become very still and turn inward to discover the truth. We are not alone on Earth. Humanity is waking up to our many neighbors and relations, our evolutionary ancestors who share this world with us. Examples like those in Chapter 2, including Mary who found her Great Wolf Mother or June who was nurtured by the trees, along with Al's Stag-King Father in Chapter 3, show us how to discover the wisdom of our spiritual and physical ancestors and how to use inner awareness to guide our actions in the world. Living on Earth as spiritually Self-conscious human beings trains us to be present; to be genuine and real with ourselves, each other, and all of life. Following Earth's example, we can practice the art of presence to simply be here as life continues to evolve.

We know something about our world from both inner and outer resources. Metaphysically, as Self-conscious beings, we have the ability to observe both our inner world, the nonphysical world of psyche-soul, and our outer, physical world, which we generally call reality. For example, as we look out into our vast universe, we measure the speed of light emitted by distant stars. From this data, we observe that our universe is still expanding.

We have been able to place ourselves in our expanding universe. Our four-and-a-half-billion-year-old Earth, that revolves around a star we call the Sun, is part of a solar system that revolves around a galaxy called the Milky Way. It takes our sun 225 million years to complete one revolution around our galaxy. During the last two and a half spins around our galaxy, life as we know it began to evolve from one-celled organisms into plant and animal sea creatures, to later become fish, birds, amphibians, reptiles, mammals, forests, fields, fruits, and flowers.

Just as there is a natural and progressive expansion in our universe, we have observed a natural and progressive evolutionary process at work on this planet. The macrocosm is reflected in the microcosm. Human life has been around on this planet for a small fraction of time compared to the age of our universe. We are young. Self-consciousness, as expressed through humanity, is very new, and like the rest of the universe, still evolving and expanding.

At the present time, our human response to change is still quite rooted in our animal ancestry and expressed as instinctual faint, fight, flight, and freeze adrenal reactions. Emotionally, we feel betrayed; and we also know, through our greater Self-awareness, that betrayal is just part of a process that stimulates an expansion in consciousness. On both the personal and the universal level, betrayer and betrayed are one. Both serve the evolution of consciousness in our expanding universe. The mass mind is still dead asleep to this mystery.

For the collective consciousness, the impact of man-made disasters is so devastating and frightening to us that we go into an immediate denial response. It is hard to accept that we are betrayers, especially when the betrayal appears to be on a magnitude that could destroy life on our planet. Yet we have learned that if we break through the denial of death and wade our way through anger and depression, acceptance follows. After acceptance, the birth of something new is possible. No matter how large the disaster, we can open to new knowledge and rebirth.

I'd like to shift for a moment and tell you a story about Ellen, a colleague of mine. The last time I saw Ellen, it was at a gathering of friends. Ellen showed up late, after almost everyone else had gone home. I hadn't seen Ellen since before her citizen's diplomacy trip to the USSR in 1986. When I saw Ellen at the gathering, I barely recognized her. She looked quite frail and was walking with a cane. I asked her what had happened. Though medical doctors could come to no hard and fast conclusions or diagnosis, Ellen was convinced that her health condition and continuing slow physical deterioration were caused by exposure to nuclear radiation. Her visit to the Ukraine in 1986 coincided with the Chernobyl disaster. She told me that Kiev, one of the cities on their tour, was downwind from the nuclear explosion. Kiev is eighty miles south of Chernobyl. About a year and a half later, I bumped into a mutual friend of ours. He told me that Ellen had just died.

Chernobyl was a terrible disaster, of which we are still experiencing the aftermath. Something like Chernobyl not only affects human life, it affects the plants, animals, insects, underground waterways, streams, fish, the entire web of life, and, therefore, the entire food chain in affected regions. There is another important consideration. Nuclear radiation is also carried on the winds that blow across city limits and beyond state lines or national borders.[6] On April 26, 1986, radiation equivalent to ten times that of the bomb that was dropped on Hiroshima burst into the air when one of Chernobyl's four nuclear reactors ruptured. The next day, radioactivity was detected 720 miles away across the North Sea in Sweden. Also, on April 27, the winds shifted, taking the radioactive cloud over Warsaw, Poland, on to Eastern Germany, and as far south as Italy and Greece.

The explosion and the fires that followed sent 12 million curies of the most dangerous forms of radioactivity into the environment during the first twenty-four hours. (Just 17 curies had escaped during the Three Mile Island accident.) Another 38 million curies were emitted during the next ten days, especially between May 2 and 5, when gases from burning graphite carried radioactivity into the air.[7]

The winds shifted several times over this ten-day period.[8] By early May, radioactive fallout was detected in Canada and the United States.

There are an estimated four million people in Byelorussia, Russia, and the Ukraine whose health needs to be monitored so we can begin to understand the impact of such an overwhelming exposure to nuclear radiation.[9] There are both psychological effects and unknown physical effects, maybe even genetic mutations, which must be monitored for a long time, even for generations to come.

When my spouse and I were visiting Japan, we went to Hiroshima. I vaguely remembered that a radioactive isotope has an outrageous half-life. For example, it takes thirty years for Strontium-90, and up to .7 billion years for Uranium-235, to decay and become only half as dangerous. As we left the railway station and entered Hiroshima, in the back of my mind I wondered if the ground we walked on was safe. "Probably no worse than dental x-rays or a chest x-ray," I mused to myself. Then I wondered what it would be like to live in this city populated with new buildings constructed over a city that was irradiated to death.

Today, Hiroshima is a city dedicated to peace. I wish every person in the world could go and visit the Peace Museum in Hiroshima to learn about the effects of radiation poisoning and see the bizarre shadow of a human figure burned into the concrete from the sudden exposure to that great blast of light and fire. After visiting the Peace Museum, Matthew and I met a young Japanese man who was also visiting the city. The three of us stood together looking at the remnants of a blackened skeleton of a building in the center of town. In addition to the city's estimated population of four hundred thousand people, this building was completely incinerated by the A-bomb. Now its remains stand as a monument to the horrors of nuclear warfare and as a call to peace between nations. Perhaps, in the not too distant future, our nuclear reactors will also stand as memorials to our past.

The Japanese youth who stood next to us did not speak English. Through sign language, he offered to take our photo for us in front of the building to capture a memory emblazoned on our minds and hearts. A memory to share with our friends in North America. When he returned our camera to us, he pointed to himself and then pointed to the burnt-out building. Then he spoke one word, "Nagasaki." He wanted us to know that he was from Nagasaki. He reminded us that Hiroshima was not the only city to suffer from the devastation of nuclear attack. Both he and his city will be remembered.

Remembering means not falling into the forgetfulness of denial; it means that you are willing to feel the depth of the pain and move all the way through it by means of awakening to new knowledge. James Hillman says that forgiving is not forgetting, "but the remembrance of wrong transformed within a wider context."[10] The pain of man-made disasters demands that we awaken and learn something from these experiences and that we share what we have learned with others so we do not blindly re-create the pain.

In response to the Chernobyl catastrophe, Margaret Anstee, the United Nations Coordinator of International Cooperation for Chernobyl, has drafted a document that includes a section entitled "Lessons to Be Learned from Chernobyl."[11] The document is part of a master plan that was put before governments and the international community to educate the world community about the economic, social, and humanitarian consequences of the disaster. We have much to learn from Chernobyl. In addition to learning about the danger of nuclear reactors and nuclear energy, new learning concerns the impact of fallout on countries a long way from the source of the disaster, as well as discovering how to tend to the physical and psychological needs of millions of victims of radiation poisoning, all of whom require contin-uous monitoring or acute medical attention. We are also learning about the enormous damage to the environment. "Twenty percent of the farm-land of Byelorussia alone can no longer be cultivated. And countries as far away as Sweden and Wales had to kill irradiated livestock."[12] As Margaret Anstee said in her plea for international cooperation and sup-port, we are also learning how to cope with an accident of these propor-tions when it does occur.

I had an opportunity to hear Joanna Macy speak after she returned from a trip to villages around Chernobyl in April 1991. During her presentation, she painted a sad and gruesome picture of ghost towns, contaminated food and water, and people slowly dying due to the destruction of the body's immune system. She told us about children who, when they are not sick in bed, have lived their entire lives since 1986 by watching the world through their windows. These children are never allowed to play outside, pick wild berries, swim in a stream, or even sit on the grass. Simply put, Joanna said, "[The catastrophe at] Chernobyl is every day. The effort is to try to believe that this is so . . . to believe our world. I knew my life would be changed by visiting Chernobyl. Mostly, my life is changed by the sense of solidarity [with these people]."[13] More than anything, an incident like Chernobyl undeniably teaches us that all of life is interconnected. The suffering of any one of us is not in vain as long as we don't fall into a denial of the suffering. Rather, when one acknowledges the truth of another's experience, even if it is painful, the suffering of any one of us affects all of us. This is solidarity.

Another lesson learned from an experience like Chernobyl is that we need each other. We are all so incredibly vulnerable. Instead of trying to protect ourselves and our vulnerabilities by using the traditional betrayal response of looking for someone or something to blame, or by isolating ourselves from each other, we can come together in a new way. For example, for the first time in the history of the United Nations, the Soviet people appealed to the world community and asked for massive assistance after the Chernobyl disaster. We are learning to accept our interdependence. Betrayal of the planet reminds us that we must act together for the good of all.

Natural and man-made disasters give us opportunities to be present with each other in new ways. I learned this through experience while living in the hills of Oakland, California. I was witness to two natural disasters in two years—the earthquake in October 1989 and the firestorm in October 1991. I was struck by the many ways in which people came together to help each other through these difficult times. Communities drew together.

For example, one client of mine, Susan, a bookkeeper with a high school diploma, came to our scheduled session five days after the fire. On Sunday afternoon, the day of the fire, Susan and her apartment manager made plans about how to evacuate the older adults who shared their apartment building if the fire spread to their part of town. Susan packed a suitcase, photos, and other personal items and put them by the door. By the late afternoon, seeing that the fire was not moving toward their apartment complex, Susan went down to the closest Red Cross evacuation center to volunteer her services.

213

Though Susan's apartment was not under immediate threat from the fire, smoke was pervasive throughout the area. In our session on Friday, Susan told me that on her way to the evacuation center, "It was very smokey. As a matter of fact, my nose was bleeding from the smoke. I remembered from my experiences after the earthquake in 1989 that the Red Cross always needed towels. I brought an extra set of towels with me and handed them over to the emergency first-aid station. Then I signed up at the mental health station as a volunteer. They said, 'At this point, there are more volunteers than clients.' So I gave them my name and number, told them that I lived just five minutes away, and went home."

Susan and I talked about the different ways people take care of themselves when they are in a stressful situation. She shared her strategy. "For me, if there is some way I can be around people and can be helping, doing something functional, or utilizing my specific talents, that is when I feel the best." In addition to working as a bookkeeper, Susan volunteers at the local suicide prevention center on a weekly basis. Both the 1989 earthquake and the 1991 firestorm gave Susan an opportunity to use her crisis intervention skills to be of service. On the Tuesday after the fire, Susan checked into the Red Cross after she finished work at 3:30 in the afternoon. At the Oakland Tech Evacuation Center, Susan took a three-hour disaster-training course in family service assistance and then was put to work until 1:30 the next morning.

"I took incoming inquiry calls. I would match volunteers to victim's needs. First, you interview disaster victims and write them vouchers for clothing, food, or whatever is identified as the immediate need. The Red Cross has arrangements with supermarkets, and a victim can go right to the store and use the voucher like money to buy food and supplies. Your financial status doesn't matter. The Red Cross wants to help victims get back into their routine lives as quickly as possible. So, for instance, if you are a construction worker and you can't go to work because you don't have boots or tools, you get a voucher to replace these items."

"On Saturday, I will be working at the family service center," Susan went on. "There are lots of forms that need to be filled out." Then she quickly followed this observation with the thought, "What was really interesting, was during the training, the message I got was 'Yeah, there are a lot of forms, but remember what these forms represent. This is a person's life.' The victims are telling you that they lost everything. So, yes, we need to fill out the forms; and, yes, we need to deal with it; but I never ever forget the real priorities. You are dealing with a person first. When you greet them, when they come in, you need to treat them with the greatest respect and care. You can never forget that."

Susan's story is just one illustration of the remarkable sense of solidarity that was felt throughout the Bay Area during both the firestorm and earthquake disasters. I heard about many innovative, individual responses as well as all the traditional ways of helping, such as making financial donations to organizations like the Salvation Army or the Red Cross. Some of us offered free professional services. Others donated clothes, food, blankets, towels, or shelter as we helped each other recover from the disaster and rebuild our lives.

In my circle of friends, for example, a few of us organized a ritual for Hannah, Frank, and Amy after they lost their home to the fire. We asked our extended circle of friends to bring typical wedding gifts to the ritual to help the family start over as they settled into their new home. They lost virtually everything to the blaze. On the morning of the fire, Frank smelled smoke at about 11:45 as he roused himself from bed. By 12:15 that afternoon, the family packed their two cats and a dog, themselves, and whatever they could grab into the cars and drove away with flames closing in upon them.

Hannah described to me how this sense of solidarity extended far beyond the Bay Area. "I just never realized how much love there is. That has been wonderful. People, from dear friends to anonymous strangers, have been so kind. For example, I made a call to get Amy something from a clothing catalog and I had to explain to the woman why my credit card didn't match my address. In the process, I told her about the fire. And the woman on the phone said, 'Oh, God bless you dear!' She's sitting in Kentucky somewhere. I was so touched! She talked to me and said she'd pray for me.

"Her heart just opened!" Hannah remembered, as we sat together basking in the warmth of this sincere and spontaneous exchange of care and empathy. "It was like somebody realizing and feeling the loss—what it would be like for them to feel the loss of everything. There was just tons of support, like people in stores just openly asking questions. I felt such a strong connection, you know, the kind of connection I long for all the time and that I usually just enjoy with intimate friends and clients. I remember thinking that I hadn't had a non-heartfelt communication with anybody for two or three weeks and how wonderful that was." That sense of heartfelt communication between people, even strangers, is part of the sense of solidarity that comes from really being present with another human being.

To be present with another who is experiencing such radical change, whether from a natural or man-made disaster, is quite challenging for the sensitive human being. Earth is teaching us to be real, to live in reality as it is—a reality full of paradoxes like betrayal to trust, catabolism to anabolism, death to life, inner to outer, physical to nonphysical, and grief to joy. Earth experiences all these with complete equanimity. Betrayal of the planet is initiating us into her sacred teachings. Earth knows and demonstrates the secret of being present. Our planet is a model for us. The planet has managed to survive phenomenal changes in her four and a half billion years of history.

Instead of just responding to life like an unconscious microbe and blindly participating in the catabolic and anabolic processes of Gaia's metabolism, we are in the process of becoming Self-conscious. Personal transformation through the spiritual evolution of social consciousness is an expression of the evolution of life on Earth. Coping with life and death disasters puts us to the test, both personally and collectively. The ancients were well aware of the spiritual power of Self-consciousness and the mysteries of Earthly evolution. Once, there were secret societies that trained initiates in Gaia's mysteries of life and death, transformation and regeneration. On the temple walls at the ancient Greek pilgrimage site Eleusis it is written: "Beautiful indeed is the Mystery given us by the blessed gods: death is for mortals no longer an evil, but a blessing."[14] At Eleusis, the secret teachings of the ancients were transmitted through the reenactment of the sacred drama in which the Lord of the Underworld, Pluto-Hades, carried away Demeter's daughter, Kore-Persephone, into his realm to become his consort and queen.

Gaia and Demeter are both names for the Earth Mother. The story is an allegory. Kore, the naive, innocent child of Earth, is transformed into Persephone through her separation from Demeter and by her, albeit unwilling, marriage to the archetypal force of death. Death brings her into maturity as a sovereign being. Persephone, whose name literally means "bringer of destruction," becomes the Queen of the Underworld and takes on the office of Goddess of Spring and Renewal.

This paradox of destruction and creative renewal is the secret teaching of the Eleusinian mystery school.

Though the temples are closed and worship of the ancient deities has long been banned, the archetypes are alive and well. Today, the ancient mythic dramas are played out unconsciously by the collective. Environmental disasters remind us of our separation from Mother Nature, as we children of Earth are abducted into the underworld by death and destruction. But this is not the end of the story. It is here that the sacred initiation begins. We humans are being brought into our maturity to be transformed from bringers of destruction to agents of renewal. Just as Demeter wailed before the gods and mortals when she realized her daughter was taken from her, Earth is crying out, demanding that we reunite with Mother Nature. In her annual return to Demeter, Persephone became the Goddess of Spring. We are also being called to return to rediscover the power of working in harmony with nature's cycles of renewal.

We are taking a collective initiation into consciousness, shifting from unconsciousness to global Self-awareness. Collectively, we are at the gates of Eleusis and the archetypes themselves are our initiators. Persephone, the Bringer of Destruction, has drawn the Lord of Death out into the open long enough to abduct us all into a world of annihilation and destruction. If you listen to media reports, the mass mind is quite convinced that we are, in fact, dying, and that there is no life after death. We have forgotten to remember the universal teaching that death is the gateway to new knowledge and rebirth. Within the human community, we find each stage of the death and dying process. Denial, anger, rationalization, grief, and acceptance are being acted out by individuals and groups worldwide. For example, many of us are in denial about our participation in killing life on this planet.

Some of us respond to this denial with seething anger, looking for someone to blame. Fantastic rationalizations justify any given position. For example, Dow Chemical and ten other herbicide manufacturers fought tooth and nail against the ban of 2,4,5-T in court, arguing that the EPA's study was not scientific. Needless to say, the eight women who suffered miscarriages also felt they had a righteous gripe. Laurence Pringle, whose *Science for Survival* series of books for younger readers explains that, after the United States dropped the A-bomb on Hiroshima and Nagasaki, scientists and officials were "filled with guilt over the death and destruction they had caused. . . . This feeling of guilt, more than any other reason, led the United States government to invest billions of dollars to develop peacetime uses of nuclear energy, in a kind of crusade to show that nuclear energy could be a force for good."[15]

The rationalization that nuclear energy could be used constructively as well as destructively to justify our killing so many people in such a horrible way at the end of World War II led to the formation of the Atomic Energy Commission in 1946. The AEC's dual purpose, to promote nuclear energy and to regulate its constructive uses, led to the proliferation of nuclear electric plants in the United States. The destructive side effects, evidenced by accidents like the Three Mile Island and Chernobyl incidents, are combined with age-old religious prophecies that predict massive Earth changes and the end of the world or state that the judgment day is upon us. Both the scientific community, with their hair-raising stories of environmental pollution, and age-old religious dogmas, with their stories of tribulation, paint a bleak picture of a world beyond redemption, a world caught in hell.

All of life on this planet is subject to death, and we play a role in this process. In acceptance of the grief and pain of death, our hearts open and we rediscover our essential unity with all life. Through death we also discover our immortal roots. The essence of life, which has been evolving for twenty billion years in our universe, and for over four billion years on this planet, continues to live as myriad evolving life forms. To touch the grief of loss of an entire planet teeming with life is just too staggering to feel. For many of us, it is too painful to really fully accept that we, too, are betrayers. Some of us have fallen into deep despair and depression. Yet, some of us, like James Lovelock, John Seed, Joanna Macy, and others who are actively involved in an emerging field called deep ecology[16] are able to touch the grief and not get lost in it. At a conference called *Reaching Out,* Joanna Macy described the shift from despair to acceptance in a story she told us about a conversation she had with John Seed.

> When I was walking through the rain forests with John Seed six years ago, in one of the remaining stands of rain forest in Australia, he was telling me about the politics of the government and the lumber company, and how hard it was [to demonstrate in protest against the deforestation of the rain forests].
>
> I asked him, "In defending the rain forest, how do you escape despair?" And he said, "I don't. But when I feel despair, I try to

remember this: that it is not me, John Seed, working to defend the rain forest. Rather, the Rain Forest is defending herself through me. I am just a lifeform formed out of the rain forest."[17]

Traditional people of the world have kept these teachings and practices alive for many generations. For example, I had an opportunity to hear Dr. Anthony Kweku Andoh speak in San Francisco. A British trained botanist, Dr. Kweku Andoh was born in Ghana, West Africa, and initiated into the spirit consciousness of the animal and vegetable kingdom by his father, Joseph Emmanuel Andoh. His father was a traditional healer and custodian of the secrets of the flora and fauna of the African rain forests. Anthony followed in his father's footsteps and became the keeper of these ancient teachings. In his address, Dr. Kweku Andoh proposed the following:

> The traditional doctors [of Africa] can help Europe and America by bringing you back to recognizing your connection with the Earth, the Source, the Mother. That spark called life, which is the Divine Spirit. . . .
> The traditional doctors of Africa can connect you with the life forces by teaching you the old ways. . . . In all African cultures, from big cities to the rural back roads, the ancient traditions are practiced on a daily basis. They remember the ancestors [in ceremony and ritual] leaving offerings . . . feasting with the Gods, and searching the skies at night to find the stars which have guided their people safely for the past eleven million years. Africa has never forgotten Her Mother, the Source, the Sun and all the elements which assist the Sun in His/Her work; the moon, the river, the soil, the birds and flowers. African[s] never forgot to remember them and to offer up praise and reverence to God in all His/Her manifestations.[18]

There are individuals like Dr. Anthony Kweku Andoh, along with people like John Seed, who are speaking out and sharing what they know to be true for the sake of all peoples and for the sake of life on our planet. Betrayal of the planet brings us into a new relationship with our world.

Betrayal leads to death. But death is not the end. We have learned in our personal lives that betrayal is the gateway to new knowledge, which catapults us beyond the gates of death, beyond the fear of the unknown, to renewal and rebirth. Something continues to live. Whatever it is that is reborn expresses even greater harmony with the whole. Part of moving from death to birth is to use the tension of transition as impetus to take a creative leap into the unknown. Creative tension is a part of birth. We have tension between modern scientific technologies and ancient intuitive technologies. To heal the betrayal of the planet, we are being asked to discover a dream that resolves this tension.

Legend has it that this is not the first time we have faced this challenge. According to esoteric sources, the legendary civilization of Atlantis was well versed in advanced technology. It is told that during the Ages of Virgo and Leo, between 10,000 to 8000 B.C., our legendary ancestors came from the stars. Some of our ancient star brethren chose to mate with the daughters of Earth. Those who remained formed a star colony on Earth and called it the land of Atlantis. Stories tell of using light-, sound-, and crystal-based technologies to supply the energy needs of a highly advanced civilization. Atlanteans were also known for their aptitude in the intuitive sciences, which included using a wide range of psychic skills for diagnosis and treatment of physical and mental illness and to maintain their complex technological systems. The ancient intuitive technologies, including palmistry, astrology, numerology, geomancy, and the other intuitive sciences, folklore on crystals and gems, vibrational use of sound and color, as well as folk teachings on herbal lore, are said to be remnants from this last golden age, the age of the legendary lost civilization called Atlantis.

On a global level, we are still healing the wounds from this collective dream that says that, through our misuse of technology, we destroyed ourselves and were swallowed up by tidal waves sometime between 8000 to 6000 B.C., during the Age of Cancer. While we are dreaming the dream of our next golden age, we are recovering from the fall of the last. If we base our next golden age on traditions handed down to us from legendary Atlantis, our collective dream says that we are untrustworthy, that we will destroy ourselves again. Healing betrayal requires that we move beyond the traditions of the past and discover a deeper truth, meaning, or purpose upon which to base our dreams.

According to mythologer Robert Graves, the last golden age was a matriarchal civilization revolving around a queen bee. During the silver age, the silvery moon became the dominant symbol. By the bronze age, matriarchy gave way to patriarchal systems of government. As I said in Chapter 7, the iron age, also known as the age of Kali, the Dark Goddess, is the epitome of darkness. It is also the time that epitomizes patriarchal rule, a Father-God without the presence of Great Mother. Though Anthony Kweku Andoh said the Africans have not forgotten their Mother as the Source, many of us have. Especially when we start to believe that a force as powerful as an archetype can somehow be subdued, dominated, or suppressed. Many of us live with the misconception that patriarchy overpowered the matriarchy just as we live with the misconception that we are bound to replay the destruction of Atlantis in our own day and age. Myth and legend reflect archetypal reality. Archetypes are expressions of universal principle forces, divine characterizations of an infinite universal intelligence. Archetypal forces are not mortal and they are not human. We no more have the power to dominate and subdue the force of an archetype than we have the power to change how fast our planet will orbit around the Sun.

Classics scholar and astrologer Demetra George presents this radical notion about the shift from matriarchy to patriarchy in her book *Mysteries of the Dark Moon.* Demetra suggests that, like the moon, which has a full-moon phase and a dark-moon phase, the archetypal feminine shows us her light and then recedes into darkness. During the dark-moon phase, it looks as though the archetypal feminine has completely disappeared. The shift from matriarchy to patriarchy follows this natural cycle until, during the dark-moon phase, patriarchal social order rules as king without a queen. This is pretty much the order of our day, especially since the Dark Ages, which peaked around the year A.D. 1000 Today, the tiniest sliver of moonlight, a slender crescent of light, is breaking through the darkness as we plant the seeds for the next full-moon cycle.

Phases of darkness are times when the Dark Goddess, like the Egyptian goddess Nephthys, whom I discussed in Chapter 5, begins to work her magic. Like Nephthys who awakens us to creative possibilities that are beyond our wildest dreams, we are each being called to a new life. The dark-moon cycle has its deeper purpose, whether it is expressed through a natural or man-made disaster, as the fall of a civilization, or even on personal levels, like being dismissed from one's job or being betrayed by one's lover, mother, father, or friend. The journey from betrayal teaches us to trust the path of life. In the darkness of night, the reflected light of intuition becomes the guide. Deep within each of our individual psyches a new dream is being born—not the dream of lost Atlantis, or any other time in history, but a dream that has value, meaning, and purpose now.

We are being called upon to dream in new dream. We are creating new myths and legends for our time. In the ancient past, we knew that our Earth was part of a larger universe. We are remembering this now as well. Our Earth is a planet that revolves in circles within circles around the center of an expanding, spiraling universe. Our Earth orbits around our Sun. Our solar system revolves around our Milky Way galaxy, which happens to spiral around a central black hole.[19] Representations of Great Mother surround us as she encircles us with her universal symbols. She is asking us, individually and collectively, "What do you revolve around? What is at your center?" Let the secret center of your being, the wisdom from your many human and nonhuman incarnations, influence you as you meditate on these questions. Through your link to all knowledge, past, present, and future, discover the knowledge that heals all: that which renews and rebirths. Then allow your influence, which is born from this center, to flow out and touch others.

Imagine that you are part of a mythic quest and you are living a hero's journey through life. Let me return to Hannah to give you an example. In 1985, Hannah attended a gathering of women in Ojai, California. The group was led by a Native American medicine woman. During the weekend of ritual Hannah made a heartfelt, personal commitment to dedicate herself to the Earth and, like priestesses of old, to honor the feminine in all her powers. In addition to her private practice as a transpersonal psychotherapist, Hannah began to take women on vision quests into nature, to introduce women to the power and majesty of the Earth, and to revive participants' personal contact with Mother Nature.

When Hannah and I met for breakfast about four months after the fire in the Oakland Hills, Hannah said, "I feel transformed in my cellular knowledge of destruction. That is a mood of Earth. The notion that the Earth is angry or having her way with us is too simplistic. But the lesson of the fire has much to do with our relationship with Her—Mother Kali comes close, or Pele [the volcano goddess of Hawaii]. The power of surging fire is like 'woman power'—passion, anger, revenge—but all these are projections which miss something larger, more real, and not personal."

Before Hannah and her family packed up to leave their home in the nick of time, Hannah climbed onto the roof of the house she had lived in for sixteen years, the only home her fourteen-year-old daughter had ever known. Hannah watered the roof in hopes of saving her home from the fire, until, from those heights she saw and felt the immensity of the blaze, the wave of flames lapping over and down the hillside toward their home. Hannah said a prayer, "If it be Thy will, save my house, and if not, I give this to you." After offering her home to the divine, a sense of uncanny equanimity followed. Hannah described it as this: "I met fire. I did not conceptualize, control, fear, or categorize. I met fire—like the meeting Martin Buber speaks of [in his book *I—Thou*]—it is a different relationship than domination or stewardship. It is a meeting I had with the mountains, with the oceans, with the directions in Costa Rica. Those were all relatively safe, creative, growing meetings. This one with fire was of a different hue.

"The sense is respecting the power of destruction, of understanding the dark, deforming, annihilating yin side of Earth," Hannah continued. "We cannot come into right relationship with the planet until we see her naked, holding no secrets, no denial; until we trust that life goes on—whether in the way of creative growing or in the way of unforming, digesting, and returning; until we know it *all* as life, nothing 'outside the pale,' no 'it.'" Hannah and I talked about the fire being another of Earth's initiations, a continuation of her vows to be a "priestess of the Earth." Hannah concluded, "This whole experience just serves! It serves my work, it serves whatever understanding I'm suppose to be bringing to it, whatever it is I am to say or do." I asked Hannah if the fire served her personally as well as professionally. Without hesitation, Hannah confirmed this hypothesis. "It just cut through so much. It cut through everything that felt like a veil around me, like those places where I didn't know what my next step was."

The best example of this was in her marriage relationship with Frank. Frank and Hannah were married six years before. Frank moved into Hannah and Amy's home, a cozy, two-bedroom cottage. Both Frank and Hannah somehow also managed to work at home, coordinating client appointments in what had once been the living room. It was tight and cramped, and during the last two years of their marriage, Frank was thinking of separating and finding his own place. After the fire, with no property to divide, the separation and dissolution of the marriage would have been very easy. But what became even more apparent, was the deep bond and commitment the entire family felt toward each other. The fire moved Hannah, Frank, and Amy to their next step: a bigger house and an unambivalent commitment to live their lives together as a family. Mother Earth had initiated her priestess into the mysteries. "Beautiful indeed is the Mystery given us by the blessed gods: Death is for mortals no longer an evil, but a blessing."

The planet Earth is our guardian and guide. Our modern culture has become rather removed from the teachings of the Earth. The ancients, those who retained these teachings, are known to have built their cities and temples upon sacred sites all over the world. John Steele, an expert on sacred sites, says that sacred sites throughout the world are places that nurture healing, inspire prophecy, foster fertility and creativity, and record and measure celestial phenomena in relationship to Earth.[20] The sacred sites were built on highly energized points on Earth, like acupuncture points for Earth's energy system.[21] In the human psyche, our inner resources resonate with the outer natural resources of a place. The power of these two working in concert builds the bridge to our unknown universal or cosmic resources.

Tapping into our cosmic resources helps us expand our knowledge of the past and allows us to reach for new dreams of the future. Imagine a time in which we have collectively passed the five tests of betrayal and integrated the five teachings. Instead of experiencing resentment, which turns to seething anger and projection of the shadow, we communicate and negotiate with each other as we listen to and speak the truth with compassion. Generalizing fades away as we consciously use our intuition to perceive deeper truths to understand ourselves and each other. These truths guide each individual to use both inner and outer resources to fulfill a cosmic cause. Then, instead of feeling lost, we each find we have deeper purpose in life, and through commitment to its fulfillment, we naturally contribute to the betterment and welfare of others in our world. Finally, instead of using control and manipulation, we each are free to be who we are, to give forth our gifts to the world and to trust the flow of life as it expresses itself through us and returns us to itself over and over again.

Through inner direction and Self-awareness, we each know what needs to be done. The fire in the hills spoke to Susan and inspired her to volunteer her services to the Red Cross. The disaster at Chernobyl spoke to Joanna Macy, and she took a political stand to advocate the banning of nuclear reactors in the United States. Volcanoes speak to volcanologists, and thousands of people in the Philippines benefit from their unique relationship. Like each of these people, we work alone and with others in service of the whole. We have the potential to cooperatively use existing inner and outer resources creatively. Then we may ACT together, with all the people of our world.

Natural and man-made disasters are training us to cooperate with each other. We are learning to trust the process of life that cycles through darkness to return us to the Source of creativity and light within our being. This is the collective leap we are taking. We leap into the unknown within and touch the Creative as we reach out into our unknown future together. The journey from betrayal to trust trains us to respond to the unknown in new ways with forgiveness, compassion, cooperation, and creativity. Our unknown future then fulfills a divine dream of a golden age in which humanity is Self-conscious, acting in harmony and balance with the divine Source of all.

Everything in the physical universe is an expression of the divine. Imagine, now, what it would be like to stretch your consciousness, to expand to be as big as our universe. Just think of it, our Sun is one of billions of stars in our galaxy; and our galaxy, is one of billions of galaxies in our universe. And our universe is still expanding. So far, we've been able to send people to the Moon and we have sent probes to the outer reaches of our solar system and beyond. For the first time in recorded history, our Self-perspective is no longer earthbound.

Our relationship with life on Earth is training us to be trustworthy off-world travelers. Just as we are one with our world, so are we one with our universe. Natural and man-made disasters train us to act as one, to become humane guardians and guides for each other and for all of life on our planet. Being guardians of the Earth does not make it OK for us to send our atomic refuse into space just because we decide we can do it. We become humane guardians by following the guidance from our divine Source within, which is the same secret Source at the center of all that exists. We receive guidance and direction when we are in a state of beloved union with this Source. As Isha Schwaller de Lubicz said, this is the union of height and depth within consciousness.

Our planet is birthing us into our universe. We are making the shift from being human children of the Earth to being Gaia's humane guardians. Just because there is a black hole at the center of our galaxy, let us not project fear onto it. Those dark depths will take us on a journey into new dimensions someday. As we face the unknown universe, let us not project the shadow into the darkness of the mystery. Let us learn from the mystery teachings from our own ancient past and apply them now, moment by moment, as we stretch to meet the universe.

EXERCISE 8-A

Connect with Your Ancestors

1. Do you feel a special kinship with any particular part of nature (stars, sun, planets, plants, cats, birds, etc.)? How does this part of nature reflect a part of your own nature?

2. Is there a part of nature that frightens you? How does this part of nature reflect a part of your shadow?

3. Bring these parts of nature into your life in some way.
   • Engage in activities that integrate these parts of nature into your life, such as photography, exploring nature, or visiting a park, pet store, or zoo.
   • Study these parts of nature.
   • Use what you learn as metaphors for aspects of your nature.
   • Let these parts of nature inspire you. Write a poem, story, or meditation piece.

4. Imagine that all of nature is part of your family. You may feel closer to some parts of nature than others. Identify your "immediate family"— those animals, birds, planets, and elements with whom you feel a special bond. Name them and identify what makes them your immediate family.

EXERCISE 8-B

Reflect on the Betrayal of the Planet

1. What did you learn from this chapter?

2. How much do you TRUST? How comfortable or uncomfortable are you with being dependent on others, independent and autonomous, or interdependent?

3. If you have a prayer or wish for the Earth, what is it?

4. How would our world be a different place if your prayer were answered?

5. Is there any part of your prayer for the Earth that could be a personal prayer for you in your life? If you were a part of the "answer" to your prayer for the Earth, how would you be? What would you do differently? How would you interact with others differently?

EXERCISE 8-C

Discover Your Myth

Your myth is the dream of your soul. Tell your personal life's journey as a healing story, as an initiation of the soul. Use your personal experience as an example of initiation. Use the phases of initiation—separation, purification, symbolic death, new knowledge, and rebirth as an outline for your personal healing story and myth.

Chapter 9

Betrayal, Trust, and Forgiveness

From Retribution to Reconciliation

$\mathbf{B}$eth Savage was barely breathing when she was rushed to the hospital. She was the victim of a terrorist attack on November 28, 1992. Emergency open-heart surgery, together with abdominal surgery that removed half of her intestine brought her back from the brink of death. Even today she still has enough shrapnel left in her body to set off the alarms at airport security. Ms. Savage described her own suffering in detail, the horrors of terrorism, the surgery, recovery, and convalescence—including how this had brought about a complete psychological breakdown and had done untold damage to her family and children.

"But all in all," she continued, "What I must say is, through the trauma of it all, I honestly feel richer. I think it's been a really enriching experience for me and a growing curve, and I think it's given me the ability to relate to other people who may be going through trauma."[1]

The Truth and Reconciliation Commission in South Africa asked her if there was anything she was hoping the commission might do for her. She replied, "What I would really, really like is, I would like to meet that man that threw that grenade in an attitude of forgiveness and hope that he could forgive me too for whatever reason. But I would very much like to meet them."[2] Remarkably, her wish came true in April 1998 at the amnesty hearing of Mr. Thembelani Xundu, the former Azanian People's Liberation Army (APLA) commander responsible for her injuries. After meeting with Mr. Xundu, currently a major in the South

African National Defense Force (SANDF), she reported that her night-mares about the attack had subsided.

Truth and reconciliation: These age-old concepts are all together new when applied to masses of people. As the spiritual evolution of human consciousness becomes more obvious en masse, forgiveness and reconciliation are becoming templates for political and social justice, gradually replacing the old standards of revenge, retribution, repentance, and restitution. In South Africa, truth-telling, official acknowl-edgment, apologies, forgiveness, amnesty, and reconciliation have been described as the "miracle" that brought about peaceful transition from apartheid to democracy in 1994.

Upon his release from prison, Nelson Mandela personally chose for-giveness over revenge, hatred, and bloodshed. For Mandela and his com-rades, human dignity and respect for all South Africans in a democratic and free South Africa was the vision that inspired courage, conscience, and commitment. Treating others with dignity and respect, while requiring dignity and respect from others—even his prison guards dur-ing his twenty-seven years in prison—was the stand he took.

The key to any transition depends on how we build a bridge between our unenlightened past and our greatest dreams for the future. Healing collective betrayals means embracing collective dreams based on univer-sal and eternal truths. The vision of human dignity is the foundation for the transition into post-apartheid rule, both individually and collectively. The government in South Africa felt that to begin this process nation-wide, the first step toward the restoration of human dignity for both vic-tims and perpetrators would be to offer individuals the opportunity to testify before the Truth and Reconciliation Commission. It is recognized that not everyone is able to forgive or apologize. It is possible to have reconciliation with out forgiveness (as happens when we agree to dis-agree) or to offer acknowledgment, compensation, or restitution. Yet there are stirring stories of reconciliation and forgiveness that are a model for what is emerging in mass consciousness. Consciousness con-tinues to expand collectively as individual growth extends into social and political institutions.

South Africa, as a nation, is a demonstration of the journey from betrayal to trust—though there is still a long way to go in transforming mass consciousness. It is possible to move beyond the desire for vengeance, control, and manipulation to true freedom. The commission itself is an example of how the vision and power of deeper universal and eternal truths spread beyond the individual and small groups, to masses of people and can ultimately transform society's institutions and human consciousness worldwide. Instead of looking to the old ways, or to external standards to determine justice, we must turn inward to discover our truth. The "truth" we discover may, initially, make sense only to us—like Beth Savage, who found that even through all the trauma, her life was richer than before. Truth enriches us, inspires us, heals us. In order to receive this more universal truth, we must access deeper spiritual resources within our being. We use our inner resources to gain strength and understanding. We are inspired with a vital dream, a greater purpose, regardless of the challenges we face. We speak out, take a stand, live our truth. We each play our part in *giving-forth* our true Self to the world.

Forgiveness is much more than a social contract—a mouthing of words for the sake of another. Spiritually, forgiveness suggests that we reclaim and respect rejected or disowned aspects of ourselves—a process that ultimately requires us to return to and redeem the power of our transcendent Self. We recognize our essential unity. Unity is not only a state of harmony amidst the conflicting parts of our own nature. From a transcendent, greater perspective, one recognizes one's unity and solidarity with all of life. We rise above the paradox of seeming contradictions—of ordinary and greater selves, or of self and other. Separation ceases. We are all betrayed, and we are all betrayers. Ms. Savage and Mr. Xundu's stories help all of us recognize how betrayer and betrayed are one. Forgiveness is the result of personal liberation that comes from spiritual growth and personal awakening. From a transcendent perspective, all differences are reconciled. We recognize our solidarity in the pain of human suffering and our striving for transcendent values, such as love, safety, peace, esteem, dignity, and purpose.

In the *Truth and Reconciliation Commission's Final Report,* in the section entitled "Toward the Restoration of Human Dignity: Perpetrators," Cynthia Ngewu gives us insight into this part of the process. At the forum on Reconciliation, Reconstruction and Economic Justice in Cape Town on March 19, 1997, she described how her son was killed by the police in the "Gugulethu Seven" incident. She was also asked how she saw the notion of reconciliation, Ms. Ngewu responded as follows:

What we are hoping for when we embrace the notion of reconciliation is that we restore the humanity to those who were perpetrators. We do not want to return evil by another evil. We simply want to ensure that the perpetrators are returned to humanity. . . . We do not want to see people suffer in the same way that we did suffer, and we did not want our families to have suffered. We do not want to return the suffering that was imposed upon us. We do not want to return the evil that perpetrators committed to the nation. We want to demonstrate humaneness towards them, so that they in turn may restore their own humanity.[3]

Forgiveness is a demonstration of our true humanity. Like Nelson Mandela and Cynthia Ngewu, we join with others of like mind, those who share our values, dreams, and ideals. We are not alone. Rather than reacting, fighting back, or seeking justice through revenge, we return to our inner resources and spiritual power. We *give-forth* our humanity to others and forgive them (and ourselves) for being human—each of us on the learning curve prior to an evolutionary leap in consciousness. We extend our compassion to others, listen to their truths, and trust in the process of social responsibility and the spiritual awakening humanity.

Reconciliation can be a step in the journey of forgiveness. Ultimately, full redemption is what is called for. Self-redemption is forgiveness in action. It demonstrates a personal spiritual awakening that extends beyond oneself into our social interactions with each other. Redemption is a state of being that goes beyond confession, repentance, and compensation. Self-redemption requires personal courage and creativity as well as culpability. We do more than just right wrongs. We begin to actively engage in building a new future, here, now, moment by moment. It requires a new level of participation, a full commitment to *give-forth* all of who and what we truly are—creative beings engaged in both personal and social transformation.

I'd like to give you another example of social responsibility and the spiritual evolution of humanity. While the first edition of this book was being prepared for publication by the editors of Celestial Arts, I received an invitation from a local bookstore to read a section from the autobiography of Nesta Rovina, a South African–born friend of mine who is an active member of Friends of Yesh Gvul. Yesh Gvul is made up of "refuseniks," Israeli officers and soldiers who refuse to serve in the occupied territories in Israel.

Gvul is a Hebrew word that means both "border" and "limit." Hence, *Yesh Gvul* means "there is a border" or "there is a limit," referring to both the borders of Israel before the occupation in 1967 and to the fact that there is a limit to what Israelis and Palestinians are willing to endure as a result of occupation. Since Nesta was in Israel at the time of the event, she asked me to stand in for her at the reading. I had the privilege of sharing the podium with Igal Ezraty, founding member of Yesh Gvul. Yesh Gvul is dedicated to the negotiation of a lasting peace settlement through the elimination of oppression that stems from Israeli occupation, and to the establishment a two-state solution to the Palestinian-Israeli conflict in the Middle East.

When I arrived at Black Oak Books in Berkeley, California, people were pouring in, filling up the seats brought in for the event. By the time I began the reading, even the standing room was packed. After I delivered Nesta's piece, Igal also shared his personal story. It was a story of courage and trust. He started by telling us that before becoming a refusenik, he had once been a founding member of a kibbutz settlement in the occupied Sinai Desert prior to the Camp David Peace Accord between Egypt and Israel. (Settling the occupied territories is one of the government's traditional strategies to establish its presence and political policies in the Middle East.) At the age of twenty-six, when Igal was part of a division that invaded Lebanon, something shifted.

His unit was told that they would be in Lebanon for a day or two, just inside the border, to protect the Galilee. After a week on Lebanese soil, and after finding himself forty kilometers from Beirut, Igal asked his commanding officer if this mission was truly for defense purposes. His commander didn't have any answers and just said that they were all doing what they were told to do. Over 15,000 Palestinians and 650 Israelis were killed during the Lebanese invasion.

Igal painted a vivid picture of the grim reality of being stationed in the occupied territories since the Intifada, the Palestinian uprisings. He found himself in the untenable position of becoming a murderer and oppressor. Military protocol commands the use of force on civilian Palestinian populations. Igal was asked to restrain not soldiers on the battlefield, but civilians, people like himself, people striving for freedom and self-determination. Following the dictates of military duty required beating and imprisoning civilians, including children, without any cause other than the suspicion of insurgence. Igal's story is an example of what happens

when one is put in the position of either betraying one's duty, as determined by external sources, or betraying one's self, as dictated by a deeper
truth expressed through the still, silent, whispering voice of conscience.
Being required to defend his right to be free by oppressing others, in this
case Palestinians, was the deathblow that led him to a quest for a new way.

Like all Israelis, Igal went into the army and was trained to defend his
country in the face of the threat of war. Israeli youths serve a mandatory
three years in the military after high school. [4] Military service continues as
mandatory reserve duty, up to six weeks a year until the age of fifty-five for
men and until the age of twenty-four for women. Yesh Gvul was founded
during the Lebanon war in 1982, and Igal became part of a new tradition to
"refuse to take part in the brutal repression of an occupied civilian population."[5] In 1992, at the age of thirty-five, Igal Ezraty was one of two thousand
refuseniks. He and two hundred other soldiers have already served time in
jail for refusing to perform army duties. Igal translated the figures into
terms our American audience could understand. He told us that this is
equivalent to one hundred thousand American soldiers refusing to fight,
with ten thousand receiving jail sentences.

As I mentioned in Chapter 7, when we take a stand that is contrary to
the social order, we will undoubtedly be accused of being betrayers.
Sometimes, within the context of social justice, this means facing a prison
sentence. As Igal was talking, I began to reflect on other individuals in modern history, exemplars of new, nontraditional responses to social injustice,
including Mahatma Gandhi in India, and Dr. Martin Luther King, Jr., in the
United States, and Nelson Mandela in South Africa. I remembered what
Henry David Thoreau wrote about following the dictates of conscience
while he sat in jail after refusing to pay his poll tax. Thoreau wrote:

> . . . As I stood considering the walls of solid stone, two or three
> feet thick . . . I could not help being struck with the foolishness
> of that institution which treated me as if I were mere flesh and
> blood and bones, to be locked up. . . . I saw that, if there was a
> wall of stone between me and my townsmen, there was a still
> more difficult one to climb or break through before they could
> get to be as free as I was.[6]

Spiritual freedom is the essential teaching of the fifth emotional
ordeal of the betrayal-to-trust initiation of the soul. Being free to be true

to the dictates of conscience ultimately heals betrayal and allows us to redeem ourselves in our social relationships.

Igal had been to prison twice for refusing to serve in the occupied territories. This did not deter him from continuing to take a stand. Even when not refusing to do service, Igal speaks out for freedom from oppression. He is a teacher of acting at Tel Aviv University, and his work *The Protocols* is a thirty-five-hour marathon theater piece that reenacts the actual transcripts of military trials of soldiers accused of anti-civilian violence in the occupied territories. This drama has won him nationwide recognition as an advocate for peace and social justice in Israel. At Black Oak Books, Igal excerpted ten minutes from the transcripts and invited four volunteers from the audience to play the part of judge, prosecution, defense, and defendant for an ad hoc mini-production of the play.

We sat awestruck as we learned firsthand the "protocols for restraining resisters." This included the pitiless beatings of Palestinians of all ages and enforced imprisonment without due process. Most disturbing was the portion of the transcript that typified the hardened, compassionless mental attitude that must be cultivated in order to rationalize the inhumane actions of the military, as exemplified by the captain who was on trial. He matter-of-factly asserted that it is better and more effective to beat a human being, even if it is a child, rather than destroy his or her family home, car, or other material possessions. Igal reminded us that Israeli soldiers are no better or worse than any other soldiers. The horror of being ordered to beat human beings, which is unavoidable in order to maintain a state of occupation, injures both the oppressors and the oppressed.

Nelson Mandela echoes this wisdom in his book *Long Walk to Freedom*: "When I walked out of prison, that was my mission, to liberate the oppressed and the oppressor both. Some say that has now been achieved [in South Africa]. But I know that this is not the case, the truth is we are not yet free; we have merely achieved the freedom to be free, the right not to be oppressed. We have not taken the final step of our journey, but the first step on a longer and more difficult road."[7] This final step is up to each and every one of us. It cannot be ordered, mandated, or legislated. It requires a personal awakening to the deeper truths that in essence we are all one, we are all free, and our spiritual journey is without end. For those of us in the earlier stages of the betrayal-to-trust process, our own cynicism, paranoia, and hurt blind us from this truth.

Yet, these same hurts can lead us to a profound healing that inspires an inner spiritual awakening.

While on his tour of the United States, Igal told American audiences how one billion of the four billion dollars of U.S. aid was being spent annually on settling the occupied territories with militant Jewish settlers in addition to all the money already allotted to the military. Igal outlined how the Israeli economy is intimately tied to the United States, and that since Israel is economically dependent on the United States, Americans have the power to take an active role in stopping the United States from supporting the oppression of the Palestinian people.

One person in the audience cynically commented, "Repression of oppressed people is a tactic perfected by our government and is happening all over the United States even now. How would it be possible for us to have any impact?" Stages one, two, three, and four of betrayal are all contained in that question: righteous resentment toward the U.S. government, denying the positive aspects within the system, cynical generalization, and the abandonment of the dream of true democracy in the United States. Igal's response was simple. "It depends on if you believe in tyranny and oppression or in freedom and peace. I, for one, believe that we are moving toward peace, and that we will eventually all come to know that peace gives us more advantage and is ultimately better for everybody concerned." Igal concluded his statement with the pithy remark, "If you see oppression, speak out for freedom. Whether it is here or there, or anywhere else does not matter as much as letting your voice be heard."

Betrayal ultimately teaches us to trust in the process of evolution rather than trust in our betrayers. Who we are and the choices we make can have a far-reaching impact on all of life, like the ripple from a single pebble flung into a pond. Rosa Parks, an African American woman who in 1955 refused to follow the Montgomery bus driver's edict to empty the first row of seats designated for blacks when two white men boarded the crowded bus, is a perfect example. She was arrested and jailed for not abiding by the strict segregation laws, and her trial put the laws themselves on trial. We never know the full effect of our single, solitary action. It was this incident, and the ensuing bus boycott by Montgomery blacks that positioned Dr. Martin Luther King, Jr., as an African American civil rights leader in the United States. King said:

If anybody had asked me a year ago to head this movement, I tell you very honestly that I would have run a mile to get away from it. . . . As I became involved, and as people began to derive inspiration from their involvement, I realized that the choice leaves your own hands.[8]

One may never know the full impact of one's seemingly simple solitary action. When we speak out for a truly just cause that extends beyond self-serving expediency, something magical happens. The tides of the time swell to meet the deeper spiritual undercurrents that are driving our collective evolution.

Nonviolence and civil disobedience are alternatives to our worldwide tradition of violence, the idea that we have to "fight with military might for peace." As Gandhi said in his autobiography, "Every moment of my life I realize that God is putting me on my trial."[9] Instead of succumbing to a standard fear reaction that assumes the worst—like Thoreau's fear, "If I don't pay my taxes, then I'll go to jail," or Igal's "If I don't serve in the occupied territories, then I'll go to prison and my family will be without money," or Rosa Parks's "If I don't give up my seat, I'll get thrown in jail and not only me and my family will be in trouble, but all negroes will pay the price"—one is challenged to try something new, something nontraditional. We redeem our true Self through action that expresses wisdom, beauty, faith, or our greater spirit. We ACT rather than react with the more traditional fear responses of denial, anger, rationalization, or depression.

Spiritual freedom liberates us to act creatively rather than react to life merely from suspicion, control, and manipulation. In other words, we learn to demonstrate trust through our actions in the world. Right action is determined by an inner sense of direction that glorifies and enriches the human spirit through authentic self-expression. To act in new, nontraditional, nonbetraying ways is a continual spiritual practice. We *give-forth* our truth, and we forgive others for being wherever they may be on their own evolutionary journey. Every contribution that moves us in the direction of humanity has its impact. For example, not that long ago the thought of refusing to serve in the military was absolutely unheard of among Israeli youths. Igal reported that, while visiting the high school in which he used to teach, 17 percent of the student body were considering refusing to serve in the occupied territories. This is totally new behavior within Israeli culture.

Margaret Mead, in her book *Culture and Commitment*,[10] wrote about social change and cultural evolution based on her observation of primitive, historic, and contemporary post–World War II cultures. Mead discovered that cultural change follows a distinct pattern that continues to redefine how the future vision for society is transmitted and on whose authority this vision is made. Instead of looking to past traditions for tried-and-true answers to the meaning of life, cultures in transition seek new answers from nontraditional resources within the community. *Postfigurative, cofigurative,* and *prefigurative* cultural models describe the shift in authority as cultures evolve.

In *postfigurative* cultures, authority is derived from the past, and the older generation transmits the values of the culture to the younger members of society. The image of the future, and therefore the purpose and meaning of life, is passed down by the elders. The elders cease to be experts on living when social change accelerates. For example, in our culture, many parents, let alone grandparents, are not able to teach their children how to use computers, so children learn that their parents do not have the skills to teach them how to cope with modern life and current trends. Cultures in transition cease to look to the elders for guidance, and one's contemporaries hold the sway of authority. The act of looking to one's contemporaries for guidelines on living Mead calls *cofiguration*. The civil rights movement, women's movement, peace movement, and hippie movement of the sixties and seventies are all examples of cofiguration. During this time, cultural values were redefined worldwide. Finally, Mead identifies a third phase of cultural evolution, a *prefigurative* culture in which the value and meaning of the future is not yet formed in the minds of contemporaries or elders. It is society's youth who hold the vision of the future.

Mead hypothesizes that respect for children and looking to the culture's youth, like the Israeli high-school students previously mentioned, marks the shift to prefiguration. Other indicators may include such widespread recent trends that emphasize "healing the inner child." Value for a meaningful future is cultivated by nurturing the innovative, creative, and imaginative qualities that are inherent in childhood. Self-trust (Great Mother) and Self-direction (Divine Father) beget our emerging vision of the future. The figure or image of the future that is born from this union creatively harmonizes and balances the contrasting needs between one's self and other individuals within one's community, social

BETRAYAL, TRUST, AND FORGIVENESS

group, or society as a whole. Cultural anthropologist Angeles Arrien suggests that creative, prefigurative cultural models, in which individuals are raised to follow their creativity and to follow the authority within one's heart, will define the future vision of society.

The future is the dream child of each individual within the culture. Expressing one's dream for the future is the first step. Building one's dream, and making it reality, is the next step. This takes creativity, cooperation, communication, compassion, commitment to one's dreams, and spiritual freedom. Then personal healing extends to societal healing. For example, the people of Beit Sahur, a Palestinian town in the West Bank, refused to pay taxes to the Israeli government to, in essence, finance their own occupation. The people of Beit Sahur and members of Yesh Gvul joined forces and put out a statement to the government of Israel and to the world community demanding an end to occupation. In their joint statement they declared: "We aim toward a moment when Palestinian Arabs and Israeli Jews may at last be able to meet as citizens of neighbor nations without the excess baggage of shame, guilt, dread, and hate."[11]

The idea that Palestinians living in occupied territories and Israeli officers and soldiers would ever come together to demand that the government of Israel cease erecting settlements, end occupation, and work toward a lasting peace through the establishment of two states an entirely new vision. It is a spontaneous creative act on the part of all those involved. Citizen diplomacy between people from the United States and the former U.S.S.R., especially during the eighties, is another example of the power of spontaneous creativity to redefine the cultural values and visions of our collective future. By synergistically acting on our dreams, we each make our own mark in society and transform society as a whole. Today, our society is a global society. What each of us does in our own backyard extends to our brothers and sisters all over the world, to all of humanity.

As I said in Chapter 7, the rebirth of society and the renewal of a golden age for all of humanity requires the discovery of a unifying, meaningful vision that all peoples can embrace. Though we may forget, we are living in legendary times. The remarkable political, social, and technological miracles that have come to pass in the last century surpass all the monuments built since Antipater of Sidon recorded the Seven Wonders of the World in the second century B.C. The juxtaposition of our creation of technologies that make life easier create a contrast when compared to the continued manufacture of weapons and other products that could completely annihilate all that we have created. These are paradoxical times. The often contrasting or contradictory influences that we live under create tremendous psychic tension. This is the creative tension of birth, where we seem to vacillate between old and new approaches to social responsibility. The increasing intensity indicates that we are in the transition stage of rebirth—moving toward integration.

Birth emphasizes the feminine principle in consciousness. The emergence of the feminine as a cultural force is one of the markers of our movement toward the next golden age. The creative power of the archetypal Great Mother also represents the creative power within human consciousness to initiate bold new approaches to age-old social problems.

I had a very interesting dream that typifies this shift toward creative solutions to social injustice. My memory of the dream opens with a scene in which I am sitting on a bus listening to a conversation between a woman with a German accent and an older lady identified as "the secretary to the President." We were all on a bus going somewhere, about twenty of us. We were a group of women and one man, all connected to the government in some way, like a political entourage to this woman from behind the Iron Curtain. She was a foreign dignitary to our country. She was meeting with the president to open negotiations, and a top American aide was assigned to her. According to the "secretary to the President" he had a covert assignment—to "knock her up" to disgrace her in the eyes of her government and to discredit her reputation with our own government. The pregnant foreign dignitary was in tears. She said to us all, "There is no room in your constitution for love."

I said, "That is not true. Our constitution is founded on our 'God given rights,' and the God of the Christians is a God of love."

"That may be true in theory, Rabbi, but not in practice," she said in reply.

By this time we arrived at our destination. We disembarked from the bus and sat together in a large circle in the park. One woman in our group said, "Let's do some shadow work to clear this."

I closed my eyes and went inside to find out what my shadow material was. While I meditated, one woman gave instructions. I opened my eyes and noticed all the women had paired up. They were telling each other what they liked and didn't like about each other and how their personal preferences were really about their own particular blocks or talents that they projected out onto others.

Then I noticed that the one man in our group was sitting alone. None of the women thought to pair up with him to do this shadow work. As I observed this, he felt me looking at him. We made eye contact. I sat next to him so we could own our projections. As we got started, another woman suddenly said, "I know how to shift the energy."

And, suddenly, Gladys Knight and the Pips were coming toward us singing "Dancing in the Streets." Men and women and boys and girls from all over the park started gathering with us in our circle, and we all started to dance together in line dances and circle dances—joyously clapping, singing, and having fun.

I said, "Now what we need is media attention to publicize this event," and suddenly reporters, camcorders, and microphones swarmed toward us.

Hordes of reporters surrounded the pregnant foreign dignitary. She looked overwhelmed. I stepped in saying, "Please don't harass her, she's feeling really vulnerable right now." They said they needed a statement. I said, "I'll make a statement."

I started to talk, and as I reviewed the injustice of her pregnancy and the lack of respect for her womanhood, I started to relive it—my anger built up again—the music and the singing continued, and I realized that I was so angry I could barely speak. Then someone else started talking about how we shifted the energy, and all the reporters went over to her to get "the real story."

This dream has many layers of meaning. The most glaring is the stark recognition that there is an "iron curtain" between men and women—between the masculine and feminine in our culture. This dream symbolically identifies several social injustices in our system, not only intimating the use of political subterfuge, but also establishing our want of a government that respects the feminine, nurtures and supports spiritual realities, and governs from love rather than sensationalism. The dream indicates that owning the collective shadow is part of the process that allows us to shift. In the dream, Knight brings a new day with music, song, and dance. The real change occurs when we make a creative shift—when we sing our soul's song and dance our dreams awake.

The pregnant foreign dignitary is a rich symbol. Pregnancy is a promise of life for future generations. Being foreign, the new life may be different than our expectations, yet full of dignity, worth, and value. The dream indicates that our current institutions may not yet recognize the full worth of the creative, mysterious, feminine potential. Imagine what it would be like to have a government and institutions that respect the creative and mysterious. Imagine what kind of government and institutions we would have if our leaders nurtured our God-given rights by recognizing that we are both nonphysical, spiritual beings as well as physical, human animals, and that our constitution—that is, our makeup as human beings—bespeaks that we blend both animal and spiritual realities. What would our laws be like if they were not based simply on an animal behaviorism of reward and punishment? How would we treat ourselves and each other? Our constitution is love and it is expressed through humane, compassionate, wise action rather than control and manipulation through reward and punishment, positive and negative conditioning.

I intuit that the integration of the feminine into the political arena, including bringing women and feminine models of leadership into government, is a precognitive image. When I speak of integrating the feminine into the political arena, I am referring to a shift from our present, exclusive, "good old boys" hierarchical structure of government to something more inclusive. The dream symbolizes this shift as a circle—the governmental entourage sat together in a circle and took their cue from the most vulnerable or needy individual in the group. They all felt affected by the pain of this one person and then came together to consciously shift the group energy to better and empower everyone in the group. Once everyone, including the lone man, was connected and in contact with the group intent, the whole energy of the group shifted to a joyous state. Opposites united. Men and women, boys and girls, foreigners and Americans, whites and blacks, Christians and Jews, all joined together dancing and singing. The dream portends that the promise for future generations is a life that respects the integration of self and Self, as reflected in all the opposites within our nature and in society. This all-encompassing unification is symbolic of the renewal of a golden age for humanity.

Ten years later, I had the good fortune to see the beginnings of this dream come true. The Council for Canadian Unity, the Aboriginal Opportunities Committee of the Calgary Chamber of Commerce, and the Canada West Foundation cohosted a conference for sixty influential aboriginal and non-aboriginal women in the Calgary area. The intent: to share, learn from each other, and develop a deeper understanding of the challenges facing aboriginal youth. Aboriginal youth may be seen as a group in society that are especially vulnerable and in need of our collective support, and as youth they hold the promise for future generations. Respect for children and looking to the culture's youth may also be an indication of prefiguration, a sign that we are, at last, moving into another phase of cultural transition.

The conference offered a wide range of speakers and programs, including a panel of young women who shared their needs, concerns, and dreams with us. Canadian political leaders, elders from the Blackfoot Nations, and the president of the Metis Nation spoke. Plus, leaders from the business community, social services, and education, and cultural leaders (like the reigning World Champion Hoop Dance and bundle carriers), among others, all contributed to the sharing circle.

I had been invited to facilitate a program called "Addressing Racism" together with a Cree friend and colleague of mine, Cheryl Makokis. We created a space where we, as women, could come together to share how racism had impacted our lives. It was important to do more than just intellectually discuss the topic. Following the format of a listening circle, women created a sacred healing space for each other to share our pain, hurts, angers, shame—feelings we do not usually share with others, let alone in a conference that is decidedly political. Telling the truth to ourselves and each other about the pain of our personal histories as reflections of Canadian History (the impact of forced enrollments in Residential Schools, life in both urban settings and on reserves, along with ongoing stereotyping, discrimination, and prejudice—its impact on our own lives, on our communities, the lives of aboriginal youth, and future generations) gave us a chance to genuinely understand each other and to become allies in each other's healing.

The impact of coming together and sharing ideas, strengths, and vulnerabilities is astounding. Stories of networking, new alliances, and creativity were brought to my attention in the days following the conference. For example, one of the young women on the Youth Panel described her vision for creating a mentoring program for elementary school aboriginal youth by pairing them with college-age individuals and recent college graduates from the aboriginal community. She had been told that existing programs had priority and was diverted by reams of red tape, regulations, and rules as she tried to negotiate the politics of social services, funding, and government agencies. The vice president of the region's largest charity was also in attendance at our sharing circle. She was one of several "women of influence" in attendance at the Crossroads 2000 who offered to help make this dream a reality. Six months later, the following April, I bumped into this same young lady at a powwow and learned that Big Brothers and Big Sisters of Calgary agreed to sponsor her aboriginal youth mentorship program.

As Mead indicated, perhaps we are beginning to see the birth of a prefigurative culture in which the value and meaning of the future is dependent on valuing the youth and their contributions. By the close of the conference, participants from the Blackfoot Nations and Blood Reserve outside Lethbridge, the Cree Nation near Edmonton, and the president of the Metis Nation each made contact with the regional director of the Council for Canadian Unity to discuss organizing a similar conference in support of aboriginal youth in their communities.

The fact that this was a group of women coming together to network and brainstorm on building new alliances in order to collaborate on issues facing aboriginal youth is significant. In *You Just Don't Understand: Women and Men in Conversation*, sociolinguist Deborah Tannen, Ph.D., discusses gender differences in the conversational styles of men and women. These differences epitomize what I mean when I suggest that we integrate the feminine into government and politics. For example, Tannen says that, according to her research, a man relates to the world:

> . . . as an individual in a hierarchical social order in which he [is] . . . either one-up or one-down. In this [man's] world, conversations are negotiations in which people try to achieve and maintain the upper hand if they can, and protect themselves from others' attempts to put them down and push them around. Life, then, is a contest, a struggle to preserve independence [and status] and avoid failure. . . .
>
> [A woman is] an individual in a network of connections. In this world, conversations are negotiations for closeness in which people try to seek and give confirmation and support, and to reach consensus. They try to protect themselves from others' attempts to push them away. Life, then, is a community, a struggle to preserve intimacy and avoid isolation.[12]

Imagine what a consensus style of government would be like, one based on establishing linking networks of support to preserve our communities for future generations and eliminate social, political, and economic isolation. The dream prophetically suggests that as we integrate the power of the feminine into the circle of government, "the real story" will come out. Our world is a place of joy, laughter, dance, and song for all people.

My dream was a teaching dream. It shows us a way we can move toward a new golden age. First we recognize the anger and grief. Next, we work with the shadow. Then we get creative and construct a new golden age for humanity. Igal's theater piece *The Protocols* is but one example of the power of creative action rather than traditional betrayal reactions to counter social injustice. We are just beginning to explore our creativity as we learn to express ourselves socially and politically in ways that exemplify TRUST instead of betrayal. The arts have always reflected the social and political collective consciousness of the times. The arts also shape and direct our future vision for society.

To the Romans and Greeks, the patron goddess of culture, history, and the arts was Venus-Aphrodite, the Goddess of Love and Beauty. In this ancient mythos, Venus-Aphrodite was the only divinity who had any affection for Mars-Ares, the Lord of War. From their union, divine Harmonia (Harmony) was born into the world. Compare this offspring to Mars-Ares's other progeny, Phobus (Terror), Deimus (Trembling), and Panic. Ares "has a train of attendants on the battlefield. . . . His sister is there, Eris, which means Discord, and Strife, her son. The Goddess of War, Enyo—in Latin Bellona—walks beside him, and with her are Terror and Trembling and Panic."[13] Our battles within the psyche and our sociopolitical battles evoke strife, discord, terror, trembling, and panic. But in the presence of divine love, our aggressive or defensive Mars-like nature is transformed. Harmony is born.

The archetypal pattern suggests that we unite Mars and Venus within our being to bring harmony into our lives and into the world. Imagine the impact of political action and social responsibility if each gesture were a conscious prayer invoking love and beauty instead of the worship of Mars and his attendants. As we integrate the archetypal feminine force of our divine-love nature into politics, social action has the power to return beauty to our lives and to bring harmony, balance, and healing to our society.

To grow we must follow Venus's example and embrace and redeem the forgotten, unconscious, unforgivable, offensive, hostile, or regressed elements within ourselves and within society. The symbol of "pairs of women all sitting together and doing shadow work," in contrast to "one lone man sitting without a mate" is a very rich symbol. Like the man who was excluded from the shadow work in the circle of women, we don't see our collective shadow. The shadow hides in our blind spots. Whether personal or collective, we can work on our shadow within ourselves, as my dream ego did through the symbol of closing her eyes and meditating. But, when we open our eyes to our interactions with each other, the shadow really becomes evident. The dream teaches that we need each other to provoke this essential soul-searching. In this example, men and women are invited to do their shadow work within themselves and with each other. When men and women get together, make eye contact ("I" contact), then the energy shifts to singing, dancing, and rejoicing.

There is another teaching in this dream. The dream demonstrates over and over again the power of thought, and how energy follows thought. There are several instances of this, like in a lucid dream the need for media attention brings a flood of reporters, or when the dream ego starts retelling the story of the top American aide's covert assignment to impregnate the foreign dignitary, she starts living the indignation all over again. This reliving of anger that is supposedly already resolved is also a distinct teaching. It reminds us to distinguish between the experience of anger that is part of the process of transformation prior to owning the shadow (during the death part of the cycle of initiation), and the experience of anger that is evoked during the transition stage of the birth part of the cycle.

During transition, it is easy to get caught in all of one's same old patterns, just as my dream ego became caught in the anger. She was so angry she couldn't speak. When you are in transition, you may become caught in the anger, pain, and grief of betrayal all over again and feel like you are dying instead of being born. How we view our experience during the transition stage of birth makes all the difference in the world. If we recognize that we are in transition and just push through the feelings, then we will be delivered into the birth of a new way. If we get caught in the anger, pain, and grief of transition, then we may end up going through the entire death phase again—until we awaken to the awareness of the new knowledge that there is another way.

The dream indicates that there are those among us who will help us shift. We are not alone. It is important for us to remember that we are in a global cultural transition right now—a transition to a golden age that unites all the world's peoples. We can expect that all the old patterns that have been killing us socially, economically, politically, and historically— these old, betraying ways—will become even more intense until we push through this transition to a new way.

The new way is not yet formed. Yet, with the aid of both inner and outer resources we can intuit our way through the darkness toward the light of a new dawn. Intuition allows us to envision a future that draws from the infinite Source of wisdom within the psyche-soul. As we open to soul memory, every one of us has the power to remember a time, whether actual or legendary (as with the memory of a dream, past life, or future life), in which we, personally, made the transition. In your meditations, use your intuition to feel, see, remember, and reawaken your memories of a golden age. Let this be the voice of conscience that guides you in your interactions with others.

Daily life is the temple. Those who choose to follow the path of initiation are being trained in the sacred inner temple of their heart. Here one discovers the divinity within one's own nature. When we dedicate ourselves to being a living, breathing example of this principle, our life becomes an expression of the holy. Following the way of the inner temple does not bring an individual more status in life, it simply provides more insight into one's own nature and encourages an individual to enter into life fully, no matter what form one's outer calling may take. Gandhi said it like this:

> To see the universal and all-pervading Spirit of Truth face to face one must be able to love the meanest of creation as oneself. And a man who aspires after that cannot afford to keep out of any field of life. That is why my devotion to Truth has drawn me into the field of politics; and I can say without the slightest hesitation, and yet in all humility, that those who say that religion has nothing to do with politics do not know what religion means.[14]

All of life is sacred. Our work in the world is a prayer to the divine, regardless of our chosen profession or career. First Nations people of the Americas speak of these same principles within the context of the sacred hoop, or medicine wheel. There is a place for everyone and everything in creation. We all have a place on the sacred hoop of life. We all know in our heart of hearts what is humane and what is not. When we act from this truth, we act humanely. Humanity is the process and the goal. There is no separation. Let this union between ends and means be the guide to right action and social justice.

Reconcile Betrayer and Betrayed

Forgiveness implies the necessity to be seen, heard, and understood by ourselves, and then, having redeemed our true Self, we extend this understanding out to others in the form of forgiveness. One way to stay with the practice of forgiveness is to find a betrayal-to-trust study buddy, or gather a few friends together to form a betrayal-to-trust Self-study group, or sharing circle.

1. After reviewing all the chapters in the book with a betrayal-to-trust study buddy or group and sharing your experiences of the exercises with each other (see Appendix), reflect on the questions listed below.
   - Whom have we loved this past year?
   - Whom have we hated?
   - Whom have we caused pain?
   - Who has caused us pain?
   - What have the greatest learnings been from these experiences?
   - What steps have we taken to realize our full potential?
   - What have we done to help us become who we are at our innermost depths?
   - Do we believe we can become that?
   - What stands in our way?
   - What is the next thing we need to do to redeem ourselves?

2. Make a commitment to practice TRUST from Chapters 1 and 2. Share your experiences and insights with each other.

3. Create a safe place to be together, a sacred place where you can explore issues of betrayal, trust, and forgiveness. Perhaps start each meeting with the FORGIVE meditation on page 157. Let each meeting also be a sharing circle—a place where each individual has time to simply share, without interruption, wherever they are, whatever their experience may be.

Create a Sharing Circle

The sharing circle is a North American aboriginal concept reflective of aboriginal law throughout the Americas before the European influence. This law was based on four principles: caring, sharing, honesty, and respect.

In aboriginal culture, the facilitator of a circle is an elder who has received a transfer of rights (a bundle carrier, pipe carrier, etc.) in acknowledgment of their specific knowledge and understanding, and their ability to be an example of caring, sharing, honesty, and respect.

Since we don't have such individuals who have been qualified by tradition in our society, we can adapt the role of leadership by following the wisdom of consciousness-raising groups, such as the women's movement. In an egalitarian model, the role of facilitator is transferred to each participant—each taking a turn to facilitate a meeting. It is the responsibility of the facilitator to be authentic and true to oneself while demonstrating and facilitating the principles of caring, sharing, honesty, and respect within the circle.

Caring

The facilitator of the group opens and closes the circle. It is the facilitator's role to create an environment of safety and caring by being a model of the four principles.

1. Begin the circle with a prayer, mediation, or other acknowledgment of the sacred, and recognize the of power of coming together to learn and understand ourselves and each other by sharing our insights and experiences with each other.

2. Read the ground rules. The group may define these in your first meeting, or you may use the guidelines in the Appendix as an example.

3. Lead the sharing by being the first to speak, thus setting the example.

4. Close the circle with a prayer of gratitude, or acknowledgment of appreciation to all the participants.

Sharing

Be present. You do not need to fix, change, or alter anyone's experience. Honor each member of the circle, wherever they may be in their personal journey from betrayal to trust, by giving them the gift of listening with your heart, instead of with your critical, judging mind.

Honesty

Each person in a sharing circle must have time to be seen, heard, and understood, and to share the truth of their experience with honest expression of where they are physically, emotionally, mentally, or spiritually.

1. Each person shares whatever they wish to share, without interruption, cross-talk, or conversation. There should be no comment or judgment from others in the circle.

2. The Answering Feather, as used by the Seneca and other North American First Nations people, may be a useful tool in a circle. If the person speaking wishes to address a member of the circle directly for feedback, information, or suggestions, they pass the Answering Feather to the individual after they have asked a question. The person with the feather responds, and then return the feather to the speaker.

3. After the speaker completes their sharing, they pass the Answering Feather to the next person, clockwise. Then the next speaker begins to share.

Respect

Remember that each person's experience is a reflection of a particular phase of the journey, and their own greater Self is in charge of their healing.

EXERCISE 9-C

Consider an Apology

Is there anyone you feel you need to say "I'm sorry" to? Is there someone you might have hurt, or someone you have not talked to in a long time because you feel guilty, ashamed, or as if you owe them an apology? Perhaps you acted from vengeance or a desire to make them understand how hurt you were by wanting to make them hurt too.

1. How might you make amends or redeem yourself in the relationship? Review your own inner work by rereading or completing the exercises in Chapters 1, 2, 3, and 4.

2. Imagine what you might like to say to them.

3. Write a letter in your journal to the person you hurt to help clarify your thoughts.

4. Share your thoughts, feelings, and experiences with your betrayal-to-trust study buddy, study group, or sharing circle.

   • Perhaps choose two people from the group to role play your apology. Direct them as you imagine it might go. Note what you observe, and ask them how they felt while enacting the exchange.

   • Notice your own feelings when you do this exercise. Pay attention to the wisdom of your body, heart, mind, and spirit. Practice TRUST (see page 16) and FORGIVE (see page 157) until you are clear on what is true (objectively, personally, universally, and eternally).

   • Consult with a therapist, counselor, mentor, or healer if you need more than your group can provide. Clarify your fears, and do the deeper level of healing that would allow you to fully redeem the power of your true Self. Then act with integrity, according to your inner guidance, toward both yourself and the other person.

5. If you feel it would bring healing instead of pain or greater rewound-
ing to the other person, pick up the phone and set up a meeting. Or, if
appropriate, write and mail a letter to make amends to the person you
hurt. If the person is no longer living, do the same in meditation, by
communing with their spirit; or write the letter, and read it to them at
their graveside—perhaps bury the letter there, or in your garden, a
park, or another place of beauty.

EXERCISE 9-D

Examine Your Concept of Justice

A while back a friend and colleague of mine sent me an e-mail titled "Justice" that offers a creative alternative to our current Western law-and-order model of justice. Consider adapting this form of justice to relationships with your betrayal-to-trust Self-study group, family, coworkers, or community.

In the Babemba tribe of South Africa, when a person acts irresponsibly or unjustly, he is placed in the center of the village, alone and unfettered. All work ceases, and every man, woman and child in the village gathers in a large circle around the accused individual. Then each person in the tribe, regardless of age, begins to talk out loud to the accused, one at a time, about all the good things the person in the center of the circle has done in his lifetime. Every incident, every experience that can be recalled with any detail and accuracy is recounted. All his positive attributes, good deeds, strengths and kindnesses are recited carefully and at length. No one is permitted to fabricate, exaggerate or be facetious about his accomplishments or the positive aspects of his personality. The tribal ceremony often lasts several days and does not cease until everyone is drained of every positive comment he can muster about the person in question. At the end, the tribal circle is broken, a joyous celebration takes place, and the person is symbolically and literally welcomed back into the tribe.

EXERCISE 9-E

Build the Golden Age Now

In your meditations, use your intuition to feel, see, remember, and awaken your visions, dreams, and memories of a golden age. Let the Source from which you derive this vision be the voice of conscience that guides you in your interactions with others.

Appendix
Tips for Trainers of Betrayal-to-Trust Groups

This appendix is designed to help group facilitators, trainers, and teachers of betrayal-to-trust groups use the material in this book as a text for group psycho-educational process. Below you will find information on:

1. The Role of Facilitator
2. The Use of Intuition to Connect with Your Sacred Self and Others
3. Formats
4. Time Management
5. Group Dynamics
6. Sample Ground Rules

The Role of Facilitator

As a group facilitator, instead of being the expert, your role is more like a companion and guide on the path of initiation, a fellow traveler on the journey of spiritual awakening and an exemplar of the process. In this model, everyone is somewhere on the path, somewhere on his or her own journey from betrayal to trust and forgiveness. After you have had some personal experience moving through symbolic death to new knowledge and rebirth, it is easier to see where others are along their path, as well as identify where, in your own life, you are in different phases of growth. For example, you may find that some parts of your life are feeling more alive and free, while other parts of your life are symbolically dying or need to change.

Frequently, the process of facilitating this course, by going through the book chapter by chapter with another person or by guiding a group through each chapter, allows an even deeper layer of integration of the material for the facilitator. Depending on your previous training and experience, you will find the material in this book a valuable tool to facilitate personal growth for both yourself and others.

In addition to creating a lesson plan for each chapter, it is important to ask yourself a few questions. Take some time to focus on your reason or intent for wanting to train others in moving through the process from betrayal to trust and forgiveness. The questions below are offered as a way to help you meet your particular needs and goals.

- What brings you to this work?
- How do you plan on applying this program in your community or with your circle of friends?
- What do you want to see happen for yourself as you facilitate a betrayal-to-trust group?
- How do you see your role as the leader of the group?
- What are your specific learning goals for each chapter?
- What kind of exercises or group processes will demonstrate the material from each chapter?
- What do you want to see happen for your friends, students, group participants, or community as a result of participating in a betrayal-to-trust group?
- How do you see yourself creating an environment where that happens?

Groups have tremendous power. Each participant is usually at a different stage along the path, and thus, each participant becomes a wonderful teacher and model of the phase or stage they are experiencing. Separation, purification, symbolic death, new knowledge, and rebirth all have a chance to be discussed and even demonstrated by group members at each stage, and each person's process is honored as a worthy lesson along the way. As group facilitators or teachers, we are able to help others identify for themselves where they might be in their own process of soul-initiation, wherever they may be on their personal journey from betrayal to trust.

The Use of Intuition to Connect with Sacred Self and Others

This book is full of many ideas and exercises to help you and your group participants apply the material presented in each chapter. Part of your role as a betrayal-to-trust study group facilitator is to help group participants gain new knowledge that is received intuitively, instead of only old knowledge based exclusively on a rational analysis of past experiences believed to be the cause of the current emotional reactions.

The journey from betrayal to trust and forgiveness requires that we open our inner eyes and ears. Participants need to develop and use their intuition to practice moving from soul tests to soul teachings. The key to learning spiritual lessons is to create an environment that allows participants to experience their sacred Self. Because of this, a variety of intuitive tools and teachings from cross-cultural spiritual traditions can be effectively integrated into the group process to facilitate insight, illumination, and personal healing. Consider the methods listed below:

- Use ceremony, ritual, storytelling, silence, guided meditation or visualization, song, chanting, dancing, and creative expression to facilitate group process and to foster a personal connection to the inner Source of healing, intelligence, and power within oneself.
- Use synchronicity and various "intuitive tools" (runes, angel cards, dream cards, power cards, medicine cards, animal cards, dreams, etc.). Check the new age section of your local bookstore for ideas.
- Use the body as an intuitive tool—sensing and speaking from the body-felt experience. For ideas, see Chapters 2, 5, and 6.
- Use homework and Self-study as a form of developing personal spiritual practice to help integrate the personal teachings received in group meetings.

Formats

Betrayal-to-trust groups can follow different formats depending on the needs and interests of the groups' members. Here are some guidelines and sample formats to help you structure your meetings.

- Each group meeting best begins with a moment of meditation to help group members settle into themselves.
- Check-in and check-out periods give group participants the opportunity to share thoughts and experiences stimulated by the material in the book, and share personal learnings with group members.
- After the check-in, the group facilitator may choose to present the material for the week. Prepare a ten- to fifteen-minute presentation for your group. (Each member may present a different chapter, or a group facilitator may choose to present each

chapter.) Write a short book report or course outline for the important points you want to cover in the group and verbally review the chapter for the other group members.

- Facilitate a ten- to fifteen-minute discussion and dialogue between group members by posing questions, reviewing homework together, or inviting responses from other group members.
- Discuss what each of you considered the most important learning or issues.
- Share your experience of the exercises and practices in each chapter.
- Participate in some form of innerwork in each group to demonstrate TRUST.
- Close the group with a check-out. Each member of the group has an opportunity to summarize their experience by sharing self-observations, ah-ha's, insights, appreciations, or new learnings.
- The facilitator closes the check-out with a summary of new learning, identifies exercises or reading in the book, and suggests personal Self-study practices for members to explore between group meetings.

General Format

1. Opening prayer or meditation: Use the FORGIVE meditation in Chapter 6 or read the Wound, Truth, and Healing at the beginning of the chapter to be discussed that week, followed by several minutes of silent meditation and reflection on the chapter.
2. Check-in: Identify how or where you are on your personal journey, how the chapter speaks to you, what you are learning, or your growing edge.
3. Experiential process: Use intuition and intuitive tools as a means of connecting with sacred Self.
4. Check-out: Make sure each person has time to summarize their experience in the group. Emphasize commitment to Self-study practices between groups.

Sharing Circle Format

See Exercise 9-B for details. The principles of caring, sharing, honesty, and respect guide the process. Each person shares as much or as little as they wish. When they are finished sharing the next person continues. Check-in and check-out may comprise the entire process. Focus each group meeting on the group members' experiences of a particular chapter.

Study Group Format

Time is more structured for a two-and-a-half hour psycho-educational format. See Time Management for suggestions.

1. Check-in (30 minutes). *Sharing is limited to a couple of minutes per person.*
2. Review and discuss chapter (45 minutes).
3. Experiential process (45 minutes).
4. Check-out (30 minutes). *Sharing is limited to a couple of minutes per person.*

Time Management

To facilitate going through the material from a chosen chapter within the structured format of a group meeting, group members must take responsibility for becoming self-monitoring with regard to the amount of time that is spent on personal sharing. Because groups may have a range of members with differing needs—some who seem to take very little time sharing, and others who may seem to monopolize a lot of time—the group may choose to structure the length of time each person has to speak. One way to become more self-monitoring is to introduce the concept of a timekeeper. After a couple of meetings, as people get the hang of sharing in a group, you might find you can dispense with the timekeeper role. Let the group know that the role of timekeeper rotates among the group members in the following manner:

1. Each person has an agreed amount of time for sharing: two to three minutes is usually sufficient for check-in or check-out.
2. The person to the left of the speaker is the timekeeper. It is their responsibility to signal the speaker that their time is coming to a close.
3. If the person sharing has not come to a natural conclusion, the time-keeper to the left is instructed to give the person a thirty-second signal. Whether by raising a feather, ringing a soft bell, tapping a drum, or some other method, the person sharing has time to finish their thought and conclude their sharing.

4. The timepiece and method for signaling are passed to the next person, and the previous timekeeper now has an opportunity to share.

The amount of time spent sharing may depend on the number of people present in the group. For example, for ten people to share for two minutes each plus a thirty-second signal takes twenty-five minutes to go around the group one time. Three minutes for each with a thirty-second signal will require thirty-five minutes total.

Group Dynamics

Groups are known to go through predictable stages of development. These stages have been called *forming, storming, norming, performing,* and *mourning.*[1] From a transpersonal perspective, in addition to social-psychological challenges, there are also spiritual challenges at each stage of group development. Below is a review of the different stages of group process from a transpersonal perspective:

Forming
Group members and facilitator are all mirrors of a sacred universal Self, reflections of one greater consciousness. Each person has a unique part to play and contribute to the whole, and each group contains a deeper spiritual purpose as revealed through lessons learned by each individual and by the group as a whole. Sometimes the lesson for the facilitator is patience—to be a Johnny Appleseed and trust that the seeds planted will sprout according to the greater spiritual Source of wisdom that ultimately guides each participant's healing journey.

Storming
Some members may play the role of bringing into awareness parts of Self that are denied, disowned, or rejected; hence projecting shadow elements out onto others. Conflict is an opportunity to learn to reconnect with projected aspects of Self and to open the heart—that is, to learn to be compassionately present with oneself and others. Along with modeling compassion, nonjudgmental awareness, and presence, the facilitator teaches by example and models all the qualities as listed below in Norming and Performing.

Norming

This is a time for discovery and creation of space for each individual's unique experience and contribution. One's personal experience and style of expression becomes a teaching and an example from which other group members learn their own life lessons. Members develop a personal link to a universal Self through Self-awareness and Self-responsibility as explored through intuition development, synchronicity, Self-trust, and inner-directedness.

Performing

Members use self-exploration to delve into the value, meaning, or purpose of the group, including individual lessons learned and how they are applied outside of the group in other parts of life. They learn to act with greater personal integrity, authenticity, and Self-trust. They become models for others.

Mourning

This stage represents the symbolic death and rebirth phases of the process. With the end of group comes the opportunity to be a living example of the lessons learned. Create a closing ritual that includes the acknowledgment of learnings and appreciations. Identify what is new or coming into being in each group member's life as a result of the group. Let each member share what they have learned from the other individual group members or describe the gifts that each member *gave-forth* to the group.

Sample Ground Rules

Ground rules help create safety for group members. In the first meeting, discuss and establish ground rules along with determining the times, dates, and places where group members will meet. For a study group, a useful ground rule might be, for example, that everyone agrees to read the chapter or do a particular exercise before coming to the group. Confidentiality is one of the most important ground rules. Confidentiality means that we do not discuss personal material that members share within the group with individuals outside of the group. Self-responsibility is another important ground rule—it means taking care of ourselves by paying attention to our needs and limits. This may include anything from establishing a time and place to meet, to bathroom breaks, stretch breaks, and snacks, to how much you choose to share or not share, along with defining what sharing consists of. In addition to the unique rules of your group, here are some important rules to consider:

1. Preparation: What you put into the group will determine what you get out of it.
2. Confidentiality: What is said here, stays here.
3. Attendance: Be on time. Be present physically, mentally, and emotionally. Call if you need to be absent.
4. Self-responsibility: Take care of your own needs. Give examples, and ask the group for examples.
5. Sharing: Speak from your own experience—make "I" statements. No cross-talk or interruptions when someone is sharing.
6. Suspension of judgment: Listen with your heart. Open to the wisdom and truth contained in each person's experience, wherever they may be on their personal journey from betrayal to trust.

Endnotes

Chapter 1—Journey from Betrayal to Trust

1. Jacob Grimm and Wilhelm K. Grimm, *Grimm's Tales for Young and Old: The Complete Stories* (New York: Doubleday, 1983).

2. Ibid., 4.

3. Eric Partridge, *Origins: A Short Etymological Dictionary of Modern English* (New York: Greenwich House, 1983), 733.

4. James Hillman, *Loose Ends: Primary Papers in Archetypal Psychology* (Dallas: Spring Publications, 1989).

5. Elisabeth Kübler-Ross, *On Death and Dying* (New York: Macmillan, 1974).

6. James Hillman, "Betrayal," *Guild Lecture* no. 128 (London: The Guild of Pastoral Psychology, 1964), 23.

7. Partridge, 740.

8. "Intuition—*Tuition* is adopted from M[iddle] F[rench]—F[rench] (sense 'protection'), which derives it from L[atin] tuitiōnem, acc[usative] of tuitiō, a guarding, a protecting, from tuitūs, var[iation] of tutus, p[ast] p[articiple] of tuērī, to guard, hence to look at, observe…" (Partridge, 742).

9. Grimm and Grimm.

Chapter 2—Betrayal of the Mother

1. June G. Bletzer, *The Donning International Encyclopedic Psychic Dictionary,* edited by Richard A. Horwege (Norfolk, Va.: The Donning Company, 1986), 558.

2. Carl G. Jung, *Analytical Psychology: Its Theory and Practice* (New York: Vintage Books, 1970), 180.

3. Ehud Ben-Yehuda, editor, *Ben-Yehuda's Pocket English-Hebrew Hebrew-English Dictionary* (New York: Pocket Books, 1964), 24.

4. Florence Scovel Shinn, *The Game of Life and How to Play It* (Brooklyn, N.Y.: Gerald J. Rickard, 1941), 8–9.

5. Demetra George, *Mysteries of the Dark Moon: The Healing Power of the Dark Goddess* (New York: HarperCollins, 1992).

6. Ellen Bass and Laura Davis, *The Courage to Heal* (New York: Harper & Row, 1988).

7. D. Corydon Hammond, Dean H. Hepworth, and Veon G. Smith, *Improving Therapeutic Communication: A Guide for Developing Effective Techniques* (San Francisco: Jossey-Bass, 1977).

Chapter 3—Betrayal of the Father

1. Chaim Potok, *The Chosen* (New York: Simon and Schuster, 1967), 169–70.

2. Hillman, *Loose Ends,* 68.

3. Robert Bly, *Iron John: A Book about Men* (Reading, Mass.: Addison-Wesley, 1990), 109.

4. Kahlil Gibran, *The Prophet* (New York: Knopf, 1982), 17.

5. Bly, 112.

6. Shinn, 56–57.

Chapter 4—Betrayal of the Beloved

1. Isha Schwaller de Lubicz, *The Opening of the Way* (New York: Inner Traditions, 1981), 125–26.

2. Jean Houston, *The Search for the Beloved* (Los Angeles: Jeremy P. Tarcher, 1987), 117.

3. R. J. Stewart, *The UnderWorld Initiation* (Wellingborough, Northamptonshire, U.K.: Aquarian Press, 1985), 118–19.

4. Annette Lawson, "All about Adultery . . . Today," *Bottom Line Personal* (February 15, 1990): 14.

5. Stewart, 122.

Chapter 5—Betrayal of the Body

1. "The Papyrus of Hunefer," 19th Dynasty, 1370 B.C. The original is on display at the British Museum, London, Department of Egyptian Antiquities, no. 9901.

2. Isha Schwaller de Lubicz, *Her-Bak: Egyptian Initiate* (New York: Inner Traditions, 1978), 290.

3. Amam also goes by the name of Amemet, Ammit, or Ammut.

4. John Anthony West, *The Traveler's Key to Ancient Egypt* (New York: Knopf, 1985), 64.

5. On the canopic jars, the Four Sons of Horus have animal heads. Each protects a vital organ of the deceased. Jackal-headed Duamutef guards the stomach; Imsety, with a human head, protects the liver; baboon-headed Hapy holds the lungs; and hawk-headed Qebhsennuf watches over the intestines.

6. Schwaller de Lubicz, *Her-Bak,* 48.

7. Joan Grant, *Winged Pharaoh* (Columbus, Ohio: Ariel, 1985).

8. Jung, 22.

Chapter 6—Betrayal of Self

1. Daniel C. Matt, *The Essential Kabbalah: The Heart of Jewish Mysticism,* (Edison, N.J.: Castle Books, 1997), 4.

2. Judie Bopp and the Four Worlds Development Project, *The Sacred Tree* (Lethbridge, Alberta, Can.: Four Worlds Development Project, 1984).

3. This table is an integration of my studies in the *kabbalah,* combined with material from Ruth Turner (as presented at the Canadian Psychologists Association in June 1998); material from Seneca teacher Jamie Sands, including her book *Sacred Path Cards;* studies with Angeles Arrien, including her book *The Four Fold Way;* teachings from *The Sacred Tree,* compiled by the Four World Development Project (an intertribal aboriginal group of elders who gathered in Lethbridge, Alberta); and studies with Sun Bear, including his book *The Medicine Wheel* and video *Power.*

Chapter 7—Betrayal of Society

1. Henry David Thoreau, *Walden,* edited by Brooks Atkinson (New York: Random House, 1950), 288.

2. Viktor E. Frankl, *Man's Search for Meaning* (New York: Washington Square Press, 1985), 98.

3. The United States has the highest number of citizens behind bars compared to all other industrialized nations, with a prison population of two million, and fifteen hundred being added to their ranks every day. Robin Casarjian, *Corrections in the U.S.: The Picure Today* (Boston: Lionheart Foundation, 1999).

4. In Canada, there are over 600 recognized bands, and as of March 3, 2000, the Bureau of Indian Affairs has recognized 556 tribal entities. Plus, there are over 200 unrecognized tribes in the forty-eight contiguous United States and Alaska.

5. We tend to lump all groups of peoples together, like "Indians," "Blacks," and "Hispanics." Within each generalization are many subgroups with their own histories and unique cultural gifts. For example, blacks from the West Indies have a very different black experience than African Americans brought over as slaves to the United States. Emancipation came earlier for the West Indians than for those in the United States. Their freedom brought full rights to citizenship. At the time of the West Indian slave's emancipation, slave owners made up only 5 percent of the population and indigenous people comprised only 10 percent. The emancipated slaves, who were 85 percent of the population, quickly moved into land ownership and established their autonomous power in the culture— something that many African Americans whose ancestors were slaves in this country have yet to experience.

For more information about this group of people, as well as the fascinating history of other cultural groups that comprise the U.S. population, I'd like to recommend Janet Brice's article "West Indian Families," in *Ethnicity and Family Therapy,* edited by Monica McGoldrick, Joe Giordano, and John K. Pearce (New York: Guilford Press, 1984).

6. Derald Wing Sue, *Counseling the Culturally Different: Theory and Practice* (New York: John Wiley and Sons, 1981), 66.

7. Ibid., 68.

8. Donald R. Atkinson, George Morten, and Derald W. Sue, *Counseling American Minorities* (Boston: McGraw Hill, 1998), 35.

9. Bletzer, 259.

10. Frankl, 95.

11. Omar Y Garrison, *Tantra: The Yoga of Sex* (New York: The Julian Press, 1964), xix.

12. The Hindu system quantifies the length of a given age and qualifies it as golden, silver, bronze, or iron. "A Mahāyuga lasts 12,000 years. . . . The 12,000 years of a Mahāyuga were considered 'divine years,' each lasting 360 years, which gives a total of 4,320,000 years for a single cosmic cycle." A Mahāyuga is made up of the four mythic ages: Krta Yuga, the golden age; Tretā Yuga, the silver age; Dvāpara Yuga, the bronze age; and the Kali Yuga, the iron age. The golden Krta Yuga lasts 4,000 years with 400 years of dawn and 400 years of dusk. Next, the Tretā Yuga lasts 3,000 years, with 300 years of dawn and 300 years of dusk. The Dvāpara Yuga measures 2,000 years, with 200 years of dawn and 200 years of twilight. Finally, the Kali Yuga lasts 1,000 years, with 100 years of dawn and 100 years of dusk. Mircea Eliade, *Cosmos and History* (New York: Harper & Row, 1959).

13. Instead of using a pseudonym, I am using Alfonso Williams's real name and the real name of the United Volunteers for Homeless Persons and Families. Unlike others who have graciously contributed their stories and are protected by anonymity, Alfonso Williams and UVHP&F are protected by publicity and exposure.

14. Jerry Carroll, "Reviving a Grim Neighborhood," *San Francisco Chronicle* (January 15, 1985): 14.

15. Mihaly Csikszentmihalyi, *Flow: The Psychology of Optimal Experience* (New York: HarperPerennial, 1991), 217–18.

16. Resourceful Women, *Managing Inherited Wealth* Program Schedule (Fall 1991): 1.

Chapter 8—Betrayal of the Planet

1. "Awake after 600 Years: A deadly volcano in the Pacific 'Ring of Fire,'" *Newsweek* (June 24, 1991): 37.

2. Dr. Paul Handler, "It's Time to Talk about the Weather," *Bottom Line Personal* 12, no. 17 (September 15, 1991): 9–10.

3. Norman Myers, *The Gaia Atlas of Future Worlds: Challenge and Opportunity in an Age of Change* (New York: Anchor Books, 1991), 147.

4. Stephen J. Zipko, *Toxic Threat* (New York: Julian Messner, 1986), 92.

5. In molecular biology, catabolism and anabolism are basic metabolic processes that break down and synthesize the molecular constituents of a cell. "Much of the metabolism of even the most diverse of organisms is exceedingly similar; the

differences in many of the metabolic pathways of humans, oak trees, mushrooms, and jellyfish are very slight. . . . Catabolism serves two purposes: (1) it releases the energy for anabolism . . . and (2) it serves as a source of raw materials for anabolic processes." Helena Curtis, *Biology,* 4th edition (New York: Worth, 1983), 166.

6. Laurence Pringle, *Nuclear Energy: Troubled Past, Uncertain Future* (New York: Macmillan, 1989). Pages 66–67 contain maps that show how the winds changed from April 26 through May 1, 1986.

7. Ibid., 65.

8. Ibid., 65–67. On April 28, two days after the accident, the invisible radioactive cloud headed back to the USSR, covering Kiev for days. The winds traveled northeast, and then back around to the southwest over the next few days, making a wide circle from close to Moscow and beyond, moving south toward the Black Sea and into Turkey by May 1.

9. For more information about the effects of the Chernobyl accident on world populations, see Margaret Anstee, *World Chronicle,* no. 441 (New York: United Nations, 1990). For a free transcript of this program, send a self-addressed, stamped envelope to World Chronicle #441, United Nations, Room S-827, New York, NY 10017.

10. Hillman, "Betrayal," 23.

11. Anstee.

12. *World Chronicle* transcript, 3.

13. *Reaching Out,* hosted by Ram Das, week 9 with Joanna Macy. Audiocassette available through Choicepoint, 1543 Lakeside Drive, Oakland, CA 94612, (510) 465-1973.

14. Mircea Eliade, *From Primitives to Zen* (San Francisco: Harper & Row, 1977), 300.

15. Pringle, 3.

16. Warwick Fox, *Toward a Transpersonal Ecology* (Boston: Shambhala, 1990).

17. *Reaching Out,* week 9 with Joanna Macy.

18. Dr. Anthony Kweku Andoh, "Formation of the North American Branch of IOTMPR," *Sankofa Journal* 1, no. 1 (Summer 1991): 1–4.

19. Charles H. Townes and Reinhard Genzel, "What Is Happening at the Center of Our Galaxy?" *Scientific American* 262, no. 4 (April 1990): 46–55.

20. John Steele, *Geomancy, Consciousness, and Sacred Sites.* Videocassette available through Trigon Communications, Inc., P.O. Box 1713, Ansonia Station, New York, NY 10023.

21. Steven Post, "Intercultural Geomancy: An Introduction of Geomancy, Part 3," *Site Saver* 1, no. 3 (Summer 1991): 3.

Chapter 9—Betrayal, Trust, and Forgiveness

1. South Africa Chief Executive Officer and Chief Accounting Officer, *Truth and Reconciliation Commission Final Report,* vol. 5, chap. 9 (presented to President Nelson Mandela on October 29, 1998): "Forgiveness," paragraph 39. Available on the Internet.

2. Ibid., paragraph 40.

3. Ibid., "Toward the Restoration of Human Dignity: Perpetrators," paragraph 33.

4. Single young women serve twenty-four to thirty months. Married or pregnant women are excused from serving.

5. From an ad in *Ha'aretz,* (January 3, 1989). Reprinted in *Friends of Yesh Gvul,* no. 7 (Spring 1992). Available through Friends of Yesh Gvul, 1678 Shattuck Avenue, Box #6, Berkeley, CA 94709, (510) 848-9391.

6. Thoreau, 650.

7. Nelson Mandela, *Long Walk to Freedom* (Randburg, South Africa: Macdonald Purnell, 1994), 617.

8. Robert Jakoubek, *Martin Luther King, Jr.* (New York: Chelsea House Publishers, 1989), 57.

9. Mohandas K. Gandhi, *An Autobiography: The Story of My Experiments with Truth* (Boston: Beacon Press, 1957), 441.

10. Margaret Mead, *Culture and Commitment: A Study of the Generation Gap* (New York: Natural History Press, 1970).

11. "Yesh Gvul Renews Support for Beit Sahur," *Friends of Yesh Gvul,* no. 7 (Spring 1992): 2.

12. Deborah Tannen, Ph.D., *You Just Don't Understand: Women and Men in Conversation* (New York: William Morrow and Co., 1990), 24–25.

13. Edith Hamilton, *Mythology: Timeless Tales of Gods and Heroes* (New York: Mentor, 1969), 34.

14. Gandhi, 504.

Appendix—Tips for Trainers of Betrayal-to-Trust Groups

1. B. W. Tuckerman, "Developmental Sequence in Small Groups," *Psychological Bulletin* no. 63: 384–99.

Suggested Reading

Childhood Wounds and Family Violence

Betrayal of Innocence: Incest and Its Devastation, Susan Forward and Craig Buck (New York: Penguin, 1979).

Breaking Down the Wall of Silence: The Liberating Experience of Facing Painful Truth (revised edition), Alice Miller, translated by Simon Worrall (New York: Plume, 1997).

The Courage to Heal, Ellen Bass and Laura Davis (New York: Harper & Row, 1988).

Making Peace with Your Parents: The Key to Enriching Your Life and All Your Relationships, Leonard Felder and Harold H. Bloomfield (New York: Ballantine, 1996).

No Visible Wounds: Identifying Nonphysical Abuse of Women by Their Men, Mary Susan Miller, Ph.D. (New York: Fawcett Books, 1996).

Prisoners of Childhood: The Drama of the Gifted Child, Alice Miller, translated by Ruth Ward (New York: Basic Books, 1981).

Toxic Parents: Overcoming Their Hurtful Legacy and Reclaiming Your Life, Susan Forward (New York: Bantam, 1989).

When Violence Begins at Home: A Comprehensive Guide to Understanding and Ending Domestic Abuse, Karen Wilson (Alameda, Calif.: Hunter House, 1997).

Forgiveness

The Art of Forgiving: When You Need to Forgive and Don't Know How, Lewis Smedes (Nashville: Ballantine, 1996).

Dimensions of Forgiveness: Psychological Research & Theological Perspectives (Laws of Life Symposia Series, vol. 1), edited by Everett L. Worthington (Radnor, Penn.: Templeton Foundation Press, 2000).

Exploring Forgiveness, edited by Robert Enright and Joanna North (Madison, Wis.: University of Wisconsin Press, 1998).

Families and Forgiveness, Terry Hargrave (New York: Brunner/Mazel, 1994).

To Forgive Is Human: How to Put Your Past in the Past, Everett L. Worthington (Westmont, Ill.: InterVarsity Press, 1997).

Forgiving Yourself: A Step-by-Step Guide to Making Peace with Your Mistakes and Getting on with Your Life, Beverly Flanigan (New York: Hungry Minds, 1997).

How to Forgive When You Can't Forget, Rabbi Charles Klein (Bellmore, N.Y.: Liebling Press, 1995).

Infidelity, Sexuality, and Relationship Issues

Adultery: The Forgivable Sin, Bonnie Eaker Well, Ph.D. (New York: Birch Lane Press, 1993).

Back from Betrayal: Recovering from His Affairs, Jennifer P. Schneider (New York: Ballantine, 1990).

Ecstasy through Tantra, Jonn Mumford (St. Paul, Minn.: Llewellyn, 1988).

Getting the Love You Want, Harville Hendrix (New York: Harper & Row, 1988).

Journey of the Heart: Intimate Relationship and the Path of Love, John Welwood (New York: HarperPerennial, 1990).

Making Your Second Marriage a First Class Success, Doug and Naomi Moseley (Rocklin, Calif.: Prima Publishing, 1998).

The Monogamy Myth, Peggy Vaughan (New York: New Market Press, 1989).

Polyamory: The New Love without Limits: Secrets of Sustainable Intimate Relationships, Deborah M. Anapol (San Rafael, Calif.: Intinet Resource Center, 1997).

Private Lies: Infidelity and the Betrayal of Intimacy, Frank Pittman (New York: Norton & Co., 1989).

The Sacred Fire: The Story of Sex in Religion, B. Z. Goldberg (Garden City, N.Y.: Garden City Publishing, 1930).

The Search for the Beloved: Journeys in Sacred Psychology, Jean Houston (Los Angeles: Jeremy P. Tarcher, 1987).

Tantra: The Yoga of Sex, Omar V. Garrison (New York: The Julian Press, 1964).

You Just Don't Understand: Women and Men in Conversation, Deborah Tannen, Ph.D. (New York: William Morrow and Co., 1990).

Your Sexual Secrets: When to Keep Them, When and How to Tell, Marty Klein (New York: E. P. Dutton, 1988).

Social Consciousness

An Autobiography: The Story of My Experiments with Truth, Mohandas K. Gandhi (Boston: Beacon Press, 1957).

Counseling the Culturally Different: Theory and Practice, Derald W. Sue (New York: John Wiley & Sons, 1981).

Ethnicity and Family Therapy, edited by Monica McGoldrick, John K. Pearce, and Joseph Giordano (New York: Guilford Press, 1984).

Hiroshima in Memoriam and Today: Hiroshima as a Testimony of Peace for Mankind, Hitoshi Takayama (Hiroshima: BIC Company, 1982). To order, write to 241-3 iida, Hachihonmatu-cho, Higashi Hiroshima, Japan, 739-01.

Long Walk to Freedom, Nelson Mandela (Randburg, South Africa: Macdonald, Purnell, 1994).

Martin Luther King, Jr., Robert Jakoubek (New York: Chelsea House Publishers, 1989).

My First White Friend, Patricia Raybon (New York: Viking Press, 1996).

Nuclear Energy: Troubled Past, Uncertain Future, Laurence Pringle (New York: Macmillan, 1989).

The Things They Say Behind Your Back: Stereotypes and the Myths behind Them, William B. Helmreich (Garden City, N.Y.: Doubleday, 1982).

Walden and Other Writings of Henry David Thoreau, Henry David Thoreau, edited by Brooks Atkinson (New York: Random House, 1950).

We Gave Away a Fortune: Stories of People Who Have Devoted Themselves and Their Wealth to Peace, Justice and the Environment, Christopher Mogil, Anne Slepian, and Peter Woodrow (Philadelphia: New Society Publishers, 1992).

Transpersonal, Clinical, and Archetypal Psychology

Analytical Psychology: Its Theory and Practice, C. G. Jung (New York: Vintage, 1970).

Asteroid Goddesses: The Mythology, Psychology and Astrology of the Reemerging Feminine, Demetra George (San Diego: ACS Publications, 1986).

Cosmos and History, Mircea Eliade (New York: Harper & Row, 1959).

A Dictionary of Symbols (2nd edition), J. E. Cirlot, translated by Jack Sage (New York: Philosophical Library, 1983).

The Donning International Encyclopedic Psychic Dictionary, June G. Bletzer, edited by Richard A. Horwege (Norfolk, Va.: Donning Company, 1986).

Flow: The Psychology of Optimal Experience, Mihaly Csikszentmihalyi (New York: HarperPerennial, 1991).

From Primitives to Zen: A Thematic Sourcebook of the History of Religions, Mircea Eliade (San Francisco: Harper & Row, 1977).

Funk & Wagnalls Standard Dictionary of Folklore, Mythology, and Legend, edited by Maria Leach (New York: Funk & Wagnalls, 1972).

The Game of Life and How to Play It, Florence Scovel Shinn (Brooklyn, N.Y: Gerald J. Rickard, 1941).

The Goddess: Mythological Images of the Feminine, Christine Downing (New York: Crossroad Publishing, 1981).

The Greek Myths, Robert Graves (New York: George Braziller, 1959).

Grimm's Tales for Young and Old: The Complete Stories, Jacob Grimm and Wilhelm K. Grimm (New York: Doubleday, 1983).

The Hero with a Thousand Faces, Joseph Campbell (Princeton, N.J.: Princeton University Press, 1973).

Improving Therapeutic Communication, D. Coryden Hammond, Dean H. Hepworth, and Voen G. Smith (San Francisco: Jossey-Bass Publishers, 1978).

Iron John: A Book about Men, Robert Bly (Reading, Mass.: Addison-Wesley, 1990).

Loose Ends: Primary Papers in Archetypal Psychology, James Hillman (Dallas: Spring Publications, 1989).

Man's Search for Meaning, Viktor E. Frankl (New York: Washington Square Press, 1985).

Mysteries of the Dark Moon: The Healing Power of the Dark Goddess, Demetra George (New York: HarperCollins, 1992).

Mythology: Timeless Tales of Gods and Heroes, Edith Hamilton (New York: Mentor, 1969).

On Death and Dying, Elisabeth Kübler-Ross (New York: Macmillan, 1974).

Toward a Transpersonal Ecology: Developing New Foundations for Environmentalism, Warwick Fox (Boston: Shambhala, 1990).

The UnderWorld Initiation: A Journey towards Psychic Transformation, R. J. Stewart (Wellingborough, Northamptonshire, U.K.: Aquarian Press, 1985).

The Woman's Encyclopedia of Myths and Secrets, Barbara G. Walker (San Francisco: Harper & Row, 1983).

World as Lover, World as Self, Joanna Macy (Berkeley, Calif.: Parallax Press, 1991).

Index

Author's Note

For more information about betrayal-to-trust workshops, training programs, audio and videotapes, or other products, please send your card or letter to the address below. If you are sending a letter from the United States to Canada, please use two U.S. stamps to cover international postage costs.

Dr. Beth Hedva
P.O. Box 70141, Bowness RPO
Calgary, Alberta T3B 5K3, Canada

Visit our Web site at www.BethHedva.com.

Thank you for your interest.